DEATHING

Everyone who is born is someday going to die. Some of us will die peacefully in our sleep, some will die in accidents, and some as the result of diseases, cancer or AIDS. Because we don't usually know *when* we are going to die, most of us are frightened of death. We don't want to talk about it, don't want to face it, and we run from it as long as we can. And some of us die a lonely death—in a hospital, surrounded by strangers and white sheets, while family and loved ones are kept out of the room at the final moment.

Anya Foos-Graber believes that death, like birth, should be a shining, light-filled, conscious moment. Death is not a disease. It is the most natural passage we will make since birth. Looking at death before the time comes is like learning about natural childbirth before having a baby. Just as women are choosing to be conscious participants in the birth process, Foos-Graber feels that all of us should be conscious as well of our eventual death— that we should prepare for it the way the Tibetan Buddhists and American Indians used to do. The author calls this process of conscious preparation *deathing*.

The book presents two teaching stories, illustrating both a conscious death and an unconscious one. The second half of the book is a step-by-step manual, containing complete instruction and simple exercises—such as breathing and visualization—so you can prepare for the final moments of your life.

Other books have been written about grief, about wills, about taking care of your affairs. This is a book about taking care of yourself, and how to be helpful to someone you care for. *Deathing* has two aims: to make sure that the dying are comfortable and comforted as they die, and to help all of us prepare for the greatest adventure we will face since birth.

DEATHING

Dedicated to Sathya Sai Baba

and

the "Enlightenment Project"
in all its guises and disguises.

DEATHING

*An
Intelligent
Alternative
for
the Final
Moments
of Life*

Anya Foos-Graber

NICOLAS-HAYS, INC.
York Beach, Maine

First published in 1989 by
Nicolas-Hays, Inc.
Box 612
York Beach, ME 03910

Distributed to the trade by
Samuel Weiser, Inc.
Box 612
York Beach, ME 03910

Selections from *Life After Life* by Dr. Raymond A. Moody, Jr., are reprinted with permission of Mockingbird Books, Inc. Selections from *Leaves of Grass* by Walt Whitman are reprinted courtesy of Bantam Books. Quotations from Sathya Sai Baba, as reproduced in *My Baba and I*, by John. S. Hislop, are reprinted with permission from the author. Diagrams from *Fundamentals of Yoga* are reproduced by permission of the author, Dr. Ramamurti S. Mishra. Selection from *Pilgrim at Tinker Creek* is reproduced by permission from the author. Portions of this work were first published in 1984 by Addison-Wesley, Boston.

Library of Congress Cataloging-in-Publication Data

Foos-Graber, Anya.
　　Deathing: an intelligent alternative for the final moments of
life / Anya Foos-Graber.
　　　　p.　　cm.
　　Bibliography: p.
　　Includes index.
　　　1. Death—Psychological aspects. I. Title.
　　BF789.D4F66　1989
　　155.9'37—dc19　　　　　　　　　　　　　　　　89-30884
　　ISBN 0-89254-016-8　　　　　　　　　　　　　　CIP

Cover photography © 1989 Herbert Linn

Printed in the United States of America

◇ ◇

CONTENTS

Foreword..xi
by Kenneth Ring, Ph.D.

Preface...xvii
by Ramamurti S. Mishra, M.D.

Acknowledgments xix

Part I
Introduction 1

Part II
Tom Breacher's Departure
and The Deathing of Selma 31

Part III
The Manual of Deathing 197
Resources 359
Index...391

◇ ◇

LIST OF EXERCISES

The First Technique 317
   Vibration Exercise 317
The Second Technique 319
   Breathing 320
   Relaxation 321
The Third Technique 323
   Sensing...324
   Dynamic Meditation..325
   Meditation on Your Electrical Body 327
The Fourth Technique 329
   Visualization..329
The Fifth Technique..331
   Withdrawal of Consciousness 332
The Sixth Technique 213
The Final Exercise...337
   The Trial Run 337

"Let me tell you one thing: However you are, you are Mine. I will not give you up. Wherever you are, you are near Me; you cannot go beyond My Reach. . . Remember that with every step, you are nearing God, and, God too, when you take one step towards Him, takes ten towards you. There is no stopping place in this pilgrimage; it is one continuous journey, through day and night, through valley and desert, through tears and smiles, through death and birth, through tomb and womb. When the road ends, and the Goal is gained, the pilgrim finds that he has traveled only from himself to himself, that the way was long and lonesome, but, the God that led him unto was all the while in him, around him, with him, and beside him."

Sathya Sai Baba

I think that the dying pray at the last not "please," but "thank you," as a guest thanks his host at the door. . . . . The universe was not made in jest but in solemn incomprehensible earnest. By a power that is unfathomably secret, and holy, and fleet. There is nothing to be done about it, but ignore it, or see.

Annie Dillard
Pilgrim at Tinker Creek

"Anyone who, at the end of life, quits the body remembering Me, attains immediately to My Nature, and there is no doubt of this. In whatever condition one quits his present body, in his next life, he will attain to that state of being without fail."

The Sixth Technique
Bhavagad Gita (8:5, 6, 7)

◇ ◇

FOREWORD

The end of a millennium, like the end of an individual life, signals a time when the ordinary pursuits of human activity tend to take on a transcendent dimension. It is—or at least it can be—a period when long-dormant knowledge suddenly leaps into prominence with the force of an apodictic revelation in much the same way that a dying individual may see in the flash of a retrospective reflection the underlying pattern of his life, which somehow sanctifies it and embeds it in a divine context. That context was *always* there, of course; but it may take a special set of circumstances to illuminate it.

So it is in our own age during which time the *fact* of death has repeatedly clamored for its own proper recognition as one of the great moments of *life*. To be sure, the fact of death itself has always been acknowledged, however diverse the meanings humanity has ascribed to it. In our own era, however, death has come to have a hideous face and most of us accordingly have learned to turn reflexively away from it as a means of blunting our terror of it. It may be useful to take a moment here to outline some of the reasons why death has come to be so feared in the 20th century.

Hardly any reflection is required to realize that we have grown up in an era in which technology is inseparable from death, and often determines the forms that it takes. There was a time, after all, when many of us died quickly of an infectious disease, amid the familiar surroundings of home and family. Now we die, usually of cardiovascular disease or of cancer, in the alien world of the modern medical hospital, or among strangers in a nursing home. Respirators and CPR may prolong our lives, but they do not make dying any easier. Indeed, they may merely enhance the feeling of technological impersonality that now so frequently pervades our final moments on earth. And here, of course, I am limiting myself to the "routine ways of death" in our culture. Having lived through this most bloody of all centuries, how can we ever free ourselves of those fearful images of mass-death that have scarred our collective psyche: the millions upon millions killed in our global wars; the names that come to mind so readily to symbolize the horror of mass-death in our time: Auschwitz, Dresden, Babi Yar, Gulag, Guernica, Hiroshima, Vietnam. Beyond all these deaths that are past imagining, none of us needs to be reminded of the planetary peril we all face in the midst of our escalating nuclear crisis, where not merely are our own personal lives or our country's fate at stake, but the very continuance of life on earth. Everywhere, then, technology dominates the mindscape of death and under these circumstances, is it any wonder that we recoil more than ever at the bare thought of it?

How paradoxical, then, that in the very heart of these spectres of technological death there has risen, like a collective angel of mercy, a *new* view of death which, when seen with clarity, holds the power to strip death of its terror and to humanize our ways of dying as the end of our millennium approaches. Indeed, the *death awareness movement,* as it has been called, is now already more than a quarter of a century old and, if anything, is *gaining* momentum. If it continues to do so, it promises to restore, by the end of this century, humanity's traditional *holistic* practices of conscious dying—a way of dying that fully honors and abets the transcendental process that is itself inherent in the moment of death. I say "restore" because humanity has long had this knowledge, and for centuries in many cultures this ancient wisdom was drawn upon in helping dying individuals to effect the transition into death. With the rise and eventual triumph of technologically based medicine, these practices fell into disrepute and neglect and were, for a time, almost completely lost sight of. It is one of the ironies of the death awareness movement that it was also medical technology that eventually served to disclose the relevance of these practices once again to us.

In the past decade, many thousands of persons in the United States alone have begun to describe a remarkable phenomenon that they claim occurred to them while they were on the threshold of death. The experience that many such persons related, which was called a *near-death experience* (NDE) by one of its earliest researchers, Dr. Raymond A. Moody, is astonishingly similar in its main features which usually include a sense of quitting the physical body and rising above it, as well as a tremendous feeling of peace, expansion, liberation, and love. The cardinal aspect of these NDEs, for many of the individuals who reported them, was an experience of what is almost always described as "the Light." Though it really is indescribable, this experience involves a sense of complete perfection, absolute peace, total acceptance, and unconditional love. Almost everyone who experiences "the Light" and then returns to physical life declares with the greatest emphasis that it is no longer possible to fear death. Far from being "the grim reaper," death, for these individuals, is the encounter with the Beloved.

Of course, it is modern resuscitation technology which has created, as it were, this pool of near-death survivors. Without CPR, for example, many, indeed the vast majority, of these persons would have died and, obviously, their experiences would have died with them. Without CPR, NDEs might never have been discovered and publicized and their implications, likewise, would have been lost. But precisely because of modern medical technology and the opportunity it afforded for near-death research, we have learned during the past ten years that the NDE is an authentic and widespread phenomenon. There now have been many scientific books and professional articles written that have amply documented the NDE and its aftereffects and that it is often associated with a near-death crisis, however that condition may come about.

According to the prestigious Gallup Poll, it may be that as many as eight million adult Americans have undergone an NDE. Anya Foos-Graber, the author of this book, is one of these eight million. Like many of the near-death survivors whom I have met in the course of my own work, she has been given an understanding of death that she felt compelled to share with a wider audience. I may be going out on a limb to say this, but from my personal contact with hundreds of near-death survivors over the past ten years, I have become increasingly convinced that their NDEs have been, in many cases, a catalyst for their own spiritual development and that, *collectively*, they may be thought of as "teachers for the New Age" who, because they understand the mysteries and meaning of death from the perspective of their own unforgettable personal encounters with death, are especially equipped to instruct us concerning how we may better prepare for the moment of death itself. And, indeed, quite a few near-death survivors have already been active in sharing their insights through articles, books, television programs, lectures, and in their direct work with dying persons, through which many have been led to their own NDEs.

Yet Anya is not merely one of eight million near-death survivors; in fact, her own NDE is only barely alluded to in this book. Anya is also a deep and knowledgeable student of the ancient wisdom, especially yoga, and, as such, she has been able to see and to articulate the connection between modern NDE research and the ancient teachings regarding the moment of death. As Dr. Moody (who is a psychiatrist *and* philosopher) himself pointed out, there is undoubtedly a connection to be made here, but he was able to do no more than to trace briefly a few possible parallels. Anya, however, has done much more than this, and just what she has accomplished is vitally significant: She has *integrated* this knowledge with NDE research and thereby fashioned a fully modern practical *manual* for the dying person. Specifically, Anya has shown us how to increase the likelihood that by dying a *prepared* death we, too, will enter into the effulgence of the Light with total awareness of the transcendental nature of our being.

For this way of dying, Anya has seen fit to introduce a new and somewhat strange-sounding word in our vocabulary: *deathing*. Deathing is conscious dying: it is dying that is not left to chance or contingency. As a concept, deathing is, of course, analogous to birthing—the process of giving birth. Deathing, too, is like giving birth—only to yourself. It demands conscious participation and full awareness if it is to be done correctly and beautifully, as the ancient wisdom tells us.

But how are we moderns to learn the act of deathing? To provide this instruction, Anya has relied upon a twofold method, ingenious in its simplicity but absolutely effective in its aim. She first offers us "a teaching tale"—a narrative in which we are introduced to two case studies, Tom and Selma, who present to us contrasting portraits in death: Tom dies, but we are shown Selma's *deathing*. The differences are clear and the lessons self-evident. In her story, incidentally, Anya describes the death experiences of Tom and Selma with rare art; her accounts here do much to bring home the power and wonder of these experiences in a way only a master novelist could convey. In depicting Selma's deathing, some of the techniques involved in conscious dying are briefly sketched. In the section that follows, Anya has written a manual of deathing in which the various techniques and exercises are fully but simply described. This manual is designed both for the individual who desires to practice deathing as well as for the friend who wishes to assist the process. Of course, as Anya makes plain, these exercises are meant to be *practiced* and mastered *before* one is in any immediate or obvious danger of dying, so that the moment of death, whenever is does come, is one of conditioned deathing, not adventitious dying.

Just one word about these exercises: The reader may well wonder on what they are based, and even more pointedly, how we can possibly gauge their effectiveness. The techniques themselves are adapted largely from yogic teachings and those of Tibetan Buddhism, but they are free of esoteric language and are phrased in a thoroughly modern idiom. As such, they are stripped of their original religious context and may be used by persons of any contemporary religious persuasion, including the absence of one. They are also, as I have already suggested, broadly consistent with the phenomenology of the near-death experience insofar as they relate to the experience of the Light. Neither tradition nor modern research, however, can guarantee that these exercises will necessarily bring about the desired effects in all instances. At this point, we have only anecdotal data and historical vignettes to suggest that they can indeed be useful in promoting deathing; we have no proof. My hope, nevertheless, is that the methods Anya's book commends to us will not only be tried but subjected to the close scrutiny they require; and that at least some of the individuals who are persuaded by this book to use them will write to Anya concerning their experiences with them so that we might begin to form an empirical evaluation of them (send letters to Ariel Foundation, listed under Organizations).

In any case, I regard Anya's book as providing an extremely valuable and necessary impetus to the death awareness movement through her reintroduction of the art of deathing into modern life. I hope you will find it a source not only of guidance but of inspiration for your life—and deathing. Life on this planet may be fraught with uncertainty, but books like Anya's are helping us all to understand that at death the universe discloses itself to us as Radiant Love and Eternal Life and welcomes us home.

Kenneth Ring, Ph.D.

◇ ◇

PREFACE

The advent of this book into modern thought introduces a humane and dignified method or approach to dying which provides believer and skeptic alike with an alternative to what too often is a distressing, clumsy affair. For all that is born must die, and creation is always coming and going . . . to be experienced as process.

Deathing: An Intelligent Alternative for the Final Moments of Life is a book that needs to be read and then put into practice. Simply to read it, however, releases a powerful detergent for the laundry of modern consciousness, for Western consciousness has been polluted by a misconception of what it is to be human— especially in regard to misidentifying the psyche with the body. Quite rightly, Anya Foos-Graber has shown that "right dying" or deathing, and "right living" interpenetrate as life process. The process of life cannot be understood without knowing the process of death and vice versa.

Since all events of life, good and bad, are stored like seeds which can sprout effects either in this life or the next, and the moment of transition (called death) is such an event—an especially powerful event—it is well to keep an environment of good thoughts and good cheer at the time. It is best of all to keep an unclouded awareness represented by blue sky, sun, or a guru. By practicing the release of limitations, as described by the exercises in this book, the spiritual substratum of life can be penetrated, tasted, and known, however long or briefly. You then realize you are a part of this greater reality, just as a gold ring will always be gold—even when it is melted and reformed, even as the infant you once were is now an adult—not by chance but because of life process. This transcendent awareness can be practiced so that it stays by you at transition, even in accidental death or coma.

When you begin to work with the network of systems in your body, it is like sending electrical impulses through wires. When you are able to work without a body (whether you are dead or alive), the experience is like that of being an electronic impulse—the current of "I-am" consciousness itself—you are no longer defined by the lamp you light. But, either with a body or without one, when the personal "I-am" has transpersonalized to the cosmic and universal "I-am" consciousness, the nonvolitional aspect of death and rebirth ceases, and death has not the former meaning for you. It is liberation.

Perhaps the most commendable suggestion in this book of *good news*, is that you can use the transitional moment itself as a tool for the liberation of consciousness. Practice for this transitional moment becomes as well the liberator of your life, with benefits streaming into job, family, and interpersonal relationships in both inner and outer environments. Let experience be your guide. This is a book about *life*, not death, as it is commonly misunderstood, and it's a potent life insurance policy.

Ramamurti S. Mishra, M.D.
(Brahmananda Sarasvati)

◇ ◇

ACKNOWLEDGMENTS

At a time in humanity's history when psychotherapy, modern physics, and spiritual practice of the perennial philosophy are joining forces, I thank and ask the blessings of all Enlightened Ones of diverse traditions, past and present, who teach the strategies of liberation from which this book modestly partakes. I ask that the inevitable errors of commission and omission be compensated for by their grace.

Specifically, I thank Pythagoras, no longer a "forgotten man," as one archeologist friend called him on location in Samos, Greece, in 1972. I also thank the Kabir-connected world teacher, Sathya Sai Baba, for his inspiration for this venture, as well as Brahmananda Sarasvati, Ramamurti S. Mishra, M.D., the director of the Ananda Ashram in Monroe, NY.

I thank and ask the blessings of Khempo Kathar Rinpoche, the Abbot of the KTD Monastery in Woodstock, NY, and his peers and disciples of the Kagyu lineage of Milarepa, which in turn spring from the Buddha. This lineage has given the "go" to releasing much formerly classified death education material. With the advent of the lineage holder, the 17th Karmapa, the coming years will see a new relationship between Buddhism and the transpersonal psychotherapies of the West. This contributes toward a universal religion, into which all variants and predecessors will fit like spokes in a wheel. The existing catalyst, the avatar Sathya Sai Baba, is already forty-five years into that endeavor. His Sai logo represents all world religions under one banner.

I thank my beloved first teacher, Paul Twitchell, who planted in me the idea of a liberation such as *Deathing* is part of. I thank his successor, Harold Klemp, for carrying on his tradition. I thank Da Free John, whose example of our evolutionary potential has ripened in modern times. I thank Lady Yeshe Tsogyel/Kata Dakai for her presence and blessings, as well as all others who participated in the Enlightenment Project—our goal and our original nature alike.

With deep affection and gratitude, I thank my parents Harriet Nelson and Paul Graber, sons Jerod and Ben Paul, Eleanor Szanto, Nancy Stetson and Garth Branahey, for the grants of love and support which helped me see this work and many others into manifestation. I thank my friends Louis Acker, Debbie Bengston, and the Atcherson family, Linda Jones, and Hope Linz for assistance. I thank the Hartley Film Foundation for its commitment to making the film *Deathing: An Introduction to Conscious Dying,* and Elda Hartley for her belief, her assistance, and for her example of tireless, selfless service to humanity, which has inspired me past my limits. I thank Doris Chase and Jim Ferguson for their interest in the Selma character, as well as Lucie Arnaz Luckinbill for sharing publicly how she used *deathing* to assist her father's transition. I thank as well, all those who must go unnamed, but who have helped in this venture. Blessings on us all.

There have been others over the years—those who helped me with the first edition of *Deathing.* First, thanks go to Edward Baxter and Brad Calrowe, Kenneth Ring for his friendship and understanding, and to all those that helped—Chris Kuppig, Mary Ann Jeszeck, Pixie Rogers, Rex and Janet Doane, Marcus Fischer, John Whitty, David Zajac, Dorothy Harrington, Kathryn Salerno-Griffin, Tom and Betty LaPointe, Demetrios Fanis,

Cecilia Manthay, Ken Smith, and Betty and Mike Gold, Deirdre Pepin, Taryn Pool, Vilhjalmur Bjarnar, the Comey family, June Lowrey, Christopher Terry, Kathleen McLaughlin, Carolyn Winters, Jessie Foos, Metka and Stefka Krašovec, Marij Pregelj, Jud Gould, Marty Refkin, John Sullivan, Reid Daitzman, M.D., Karen Ranung, Joesph Neal, Michael La Flamma, Martin Brofman, Lionel Cornwell, Sally Gouverneur, Robin Manna, Richard Adams, Bob Hays, and Vyas. I also want to thank all the "Selmas" and "Toms" from whom I have learned so much and who urged me to share. Thank you, everyone.

PART I

INTRODUCTION

I celebrate myself, and sing myself,
And what I assume you shall assume,
For every atom belonging to me as good belongs to
  you . . .
I pass death with the dying, and birth with the
  new-wash'd babe and am not contain'd between my
  hat and boots, . . .

Walt Whitman
Leaves of Grass, "Song of Myself"

◇ ◇

INTRODUCTION

The death moment has been forgotten by our society. Rather than accepting death as the culmination of physical life, and seeing it as a beginning of a new chapter of consciousness, most people view its inevitability as tragic. Death is a curse that comes to each of us, whether or not we want it. So we mourn it as an end to the good life, a void that capriciously claims us at a moment's notice. This final abyss is spoken of in hushed, regretful tones, and usually in connection with grief, crisis, and mourning. Nothing makes us so uncomfortable as having to think ahead to the final days of our parents or spouse or closest friends, or having to consider the deaths of our children. This deep cultural bias against death has cleaved it from life. As a result, we deny ourselves a valid part of our birthright and neglect the vital connection between life and death—the moment of death.

We rarely are taught to accept the reality of our final moments or that those moments even have effects. Most people never learn how to die, nor are they given the opportunity to prepare for their departure. The actual process of dying is resisted and forgotten as much as possible; it is hidden, shunned. As a result, dying people are relegated to invisible corners of our society. During their final hours they often are excluded from the rest of life, and subsumed in the technical and impersonal world of medicine.

Modern medicine has developed in a way that emphasizes the pursuit of life-saving measures at all costs. Therefore, instead of taking responsibility for the dying process, we turn to technology to delay it. Medals are given to doctors for the patients they save, not for those whose deaths they make easier. In fact, in our active, life-oriented society, death represents the ultimate failure of modern achievements; it means that the life-prolonging measures in which we have so much invested have fallen short. Because of the emphasis on technical solutions, little value is given to learning to accept and confront death. The very power that has lengthened our lives also has separated us from our biological roots. We have paid for the rapid technological advance with an alienation from ourselves, our bodies, and the world we live in. At the death moment, when our biological frailty becomes most apparent, we find ourselves helpless and unprepared, unconnected to what we are leaving, or where we are going.

Trying to avoid the act of dying has only made us more afraid of it. Because we won't confront it, we can't control it; we are unable to shape it into the type of death we would want, as we have tried to shape our lives. At the moment of death people often are under sedation, unable to consciously participate in the singular process of dying. The attitude prevails that death should be allowed to take care of itself because, after all, it is living that is hard. This platitude, unfortunately, is just a placebo; most of us fear death greatly. By pretending that dying will readily proceed on its own, we create needless tensions. Energy that could better be put into living is diverted into fears of mortality that rarely can be expressed and remain unresolved. We can salvage this waste, however.

The anxiety which besets us individually can be seen in the society at large as well. Not only are the social and emotional contexts around each of us devoid of the power that comes from facing and accepting death, but our institutions are not able to respond to its insistent presence. Understandably, people feel profoundly alone. There are no rites of passage to ease the inevitable. At a time when people most need attention, they are placed inside impersonal institutions. With the last parts of their selfhood stripped away, the sick become another cog in a system that is supposed to be oriented toward patient care, but which often functions more like an assembly line. Best efforts usually are made to provide a good environment for dying, but too often the institutions are inept at this important moment. Rather than allowing people to die with kindness, dignity, and consciousness, they compel many people to die alone and unaware.

My intent is to place the death moment back in its rightful place, as our birthright, and to encourage its fullest expression whenever possible. I believe that it is possible to establish in our society an attitude of respect toward a vacating body and the dying person's right to depart in peace, thus establishing an after-life consciousness. By rejoining death with the rest of life, all of us will experience a joy and a release of the energy that is currently locked up in our fear and evasions. We can also prepare for the tomorrows of the soul.

Death has not always been treated as it is today. Long before the triumph of modern medicine, there was a craft of dying. In medieval times, people in the Western world approached death in a more natural way than we do now. In those days, the parameter of death defined life; even the main theme of literature was "momento mori—remember death," which, far from being morbid, meant that life was to be recalled as a spiritual continuity. Within the Catholic church, last rites were performed to ease the transition from life to death. These traditions were based on a distinct psychology of consciousness that is no longer acknowledged today. These rites may still be performed, but their true function is rarely understood today.

With the advent of technology, Westerners became separated from the fundamentals of their biological existence. Repressions about sex, birth, and death became increasingly meshed in social styles of behavior. Victorian prudery extended to a vocabulary of symbolic cover-up in which even the legs of a chair were called limbs. Death was equally obscured.

While Western traditions for dying declined, Eastern practices continued, although they were deliberately kept secret until recently. The Egyptian and Tibetan Books of the Dead reveal life to be a series of changes starting at birth and continuing through the moment of death into afterlife and rebirth. These precise and detailed guidebooks recognize different levels of consciousness involved in living and in dying—states that are experienced in meditation and in the practice of disciplines such as yoga that integrate physical, psychological, and spiritual concerns. Some Tibetan Buddhist lore has been conveyed to the West through translations of its Book of the Dead and by the rash of Eastern teachers who have emigrated to the West. Nevertheless, the significance of the act of dying by and large has been lost in our society and it needs to be regained as a conscious act.

Although, by convention, the death process has been shunned, it is starting to reappear as a topic of conversation and a matter of interest. Death can't be ignored for long; it won't stay quietly out of sight, democratic as it is. Many people are thinking about it, often because of unusual or seemingly inexplicable events they have heard about or experienced themselves. For instance, some people report having been visited by a loved one who has just died—a parent, child, husband or wife, or close friend. Still surprised, they try to tell what the visit was like, perhaps attempt to figure out what it meant. Others talk of experiencing altered levels of consciousness when they are in conditions of clinical death. The states of consciousness that they describe are called the "near-death experience," or NDE, and are similar to those attained by people who have meditated conscientiously over a number of years, or who have spontaneously experienced altered consciousness.

Many people who have experienced NDE, ironically, have been pushed to question the process of dying and its relationship to living a fulfilled life because of the very medical technology that has helped keep death in the closet for so long. Because of modern medicine, people who have clinically died often can be resuscitated and brought back to life again on an unprecedented scale. Resuscitation techniques usually are applied in hospitals when people "die"—which, according to the clinical definition, means that a heart stops beating, breathing ceases, and the EEG fails to record the presence of brain waves. But modern medical technologies can revive the biological body so that patients who were declared "dead" can live once more. Most usually, these people return with an expanded view of life. This near-death experience is shared by so many people that it has become somewhat of a cultural phenomenon. A recent Gallup Poll reports that about eight million people have survived a near-death experience. Because their numbers are so large, their experiences are bound to effect societal change. They are not people who claim to have psychic powers or who have experimented with trying to reach different levels of consciousness. On the contrary, they are everyday people who probably had little interest in death until they died—or nearly died.

Some people who once were declared clinically dead cannot remember anything that elapsed from the moment they lost consciousness until they regained it, just as dreams are often forgotten upon waking. Their near-death experience in subtle realms remains forgotten time for them. Many others can remember the experience, but find it difficult to describe, and they are afraid of other people's reactions. However, an astonishing number of survivors can retell the event with complete clarity and detail. Some recall seeing the operating room from the vantage point of the ceiling. Although these reports vary greatly, they also overlap and share many similarities.

In the late 1970s, Dr. Raymond Moody, a physician, documented the story of the near-death experience in *Life After Life.* He introduced such terms as the "tunnel," "out-of-body state," the "light," and the "figure of light," which have since become common parlance about the almost-dying process. Drawing on accounts of hundreds of people whom he interviewed from all over the world, Moody compiled a model of the near-death experience. The following scenario closely resembles many of the stories that he heard, although not all of the case histories share all of the model's features.

· · ·

A man is dying and, as he reaches the point of greatest physical distress, he hears himself pronounced dead by his doctor. He begins to hear an uncomfortable noise, a loud ringing or buzzing, and at the same time feels himself moving very rapidly through a long tunnel. After this, he suddenly finds himself outside his own physical body, still in the same immediate physical environment, and sees his own body from a distance, as though he is a spectator. He watches the resuscitation attempt from this vantage point and is in a state of emotional upheaval.

After a while, he collects himself and becomes more accustomed to his odd condition. He notices that he still has a "body," but one of a very different nature and with very different powers from the physical body he has left behind. Soon other things begin to happen. Others come to meet him and help him. He glimpses the spirits of relatives and friends who have already died, and a loving, warm spirit of a kind he has never encountered before—a being of light—appears before him. This being asks him a question, nonverbally, to make him evaluate his life and helps him along by showing him a panoramic, instantaneous playback of the major events of his life. At some point, he finds himself approaching some sort of a barrier or border, apparently representing the limit between earthly life and the next life. Yet, he finds that he must go back to the earth, that the time for his death has not yet come. At this point he resists, for by now he is taken up with his experiences in the afterlife and does not want to return. He is overwhelmed by intense feelings of joy, love, and peace. Despite his attitude, though, he somehow reunites with his physical body and lives.

Later he tries to tell others, but he has trouble doing so. In the first place, he can find no words to describe these unearthly episodes. He also finds that others scoff, so he stops telling other people. Still, the experience affects his life profoundly, especially his views about death and its relationship to life.[1]

• • •

Most people who can describe their near-death experience mention a tunnel, tube, or pipe through which they travel after having left their bodies, usually moving toward a bright light. They often experience a life review, and sometimes glimpses of the future; ordinarily they report back undescribable experiences of ecstasy and the feeling of being one with all life. Because these recollections seem to imply that "near-death" involves a unique mental state, they suggest that consciousness exists in a wider context than that usually described by contemporary, body-based psychology.

I view the tunnel in Moody's model as a change in the level of a person's consciousness. It may be that during a near-death experience, consciousness shifts its locus away from the physical body. Someone who had never experienced this radical a shift in consciousness might call it "leaving the body." Those a little more practiced or accustomed to the event might refer to it as simply being someplace else. In this state, people feel freed of

---

[1]Raymond Moody, *Life After Life* (New York: Mockingbird Books, 1976), pp. 21–23. Used by permission. Now available in paperback from Bantam.

the three-dimensional limits of a time-bound world that usually surrounds us. Their entire existence seems simultaneous, although they describe having felt the sensation of a past, present, and future. The place they mention having moved to is sometimes called "the astral plane." It seems to be an actual dimension of existence. The "body" used for expression of consciousness on the astral plane is sometimes called "the secondary body," or "light body." The ancient Egyptians called it the "ka," while Eastern lore has many names for the different "bodies" or sheaths that are utilized in these various realms of consciousness. People also frequently report having perceived an additional "etheric body." This is the electromagnetic biofield which Samkyha yoga calls the "pranamaya kosha" that surrounds the physical body until death.

Nor is clinical death to be equated with "real death," which is the departure of the Consciousness Principle in utter abandonment of the body. The "when" of this complete departure has to be left, unfortunately, to the future findings of consciousness research. That clinical death and the departure of total consciousness from the body are not synonymous is sufficiently significant in and of itself.

It is the etheric body that *Deathing* seeks to harness in "conscious dying," for its disengagement from the physical is our means of "lift-off," our propellant for the departing Consciousness Principle. Properly focused in the conscious dying process, it runs its course, its purpose served—not unlike the placenta in the birth process, which is dispensed with after the baby is born. Yet, it is this unutilized etheric body which can cause "breech" deaths, for it can tangle or otherwise obsure a clean exit.

My observation is that when the etheric or biofield body becomes incoherent—through shock, trauma, or just the death process experienced in ignorance—it tends to clot around the subtle bodies, muffling higher perceptions. This creates an environment the Greeks called Hades, and what I call the Gray Place. Robert Monroe, in *Far Journeys,* chronicles precisely the "rings" or levels of the Gray Place, into which shock deaths, suicides, or mass deaths can precipitate one, which further substantiates a public need for information about deathing's preventative role. All these different sheaths or bodies are the expression of states of consciousness operating in actual "geographies" of inner space. The infinite, vibrating field of the universe is organized according to mathematical, harmonically resonating intervals. That is what is meant by the so-called planes and subplanes, the bardos and lokas of esoteric literature in many religious traditions. The various bodies, by whatever name they are called, correspond to (and operate on) various levels, ranging from the dense physical to the most subtle.

The sensation of being out-of-the-body[2] is one of the most distinctive features of near-death as well as death, and is included in the literature of every main religion of the world, although it was usually hidden. Judaism contained it in the secret teaching of Kabbala, the Greeks and Egyptians in their mystery schools and initiations, and the Moslem tradition in the Dervish orders, while St. Paul, who practiced this ancient art, called it "dying daily." It is also a faculty that tends to emerge in an individual who has experienced a partial or complete kundalini awakening into higher consciousness.

Today this temporary withdrawal of consciousness from the body is often referred to in the West as astral or soul travel, or OOBE (out-of-body-experience), depending on which subtle body is being used by the Consciousness Principle. The Tibetan Buddhists, on the other hand, term permanent withdrawal *Pho-Wa,* or consciousness transference, which is used only at the

---

[2]Truly, we do not project out-of-body, but actually transfer consciousness to a body other than the physical one.

moment of death by someone trained to practice it. (It can also be done for a dying person by an accomplished lama.) Pho-Wa is not to be confused with NDE or OOBE (which is also known to the Tibetans), since it is a technique to be used strictly at death. It is a method of plucking the Consciousness Principle of the dying person by means of harmonic resonance with higher forces and depositing it in the liberated zone of inner space dimensions corresponding to the Clear Light.

It is important to consider OOBE when thinking of conscious dying, or deathing: death, after all, is an extended out-of-body transference to another state of being. Robert Monroe, a well-known modern practitioner of OOBE, has written two books, *Journeys Out of the Body* (1971), and *Far Journeys* (1985). His contribution is monumental, one of the most comprehensive practical sources about the experience and practice of OOBE (outside of the Tibetan) that I have found. His material is presented in a non-religious and non-belief structured context. Paul Twitchell's *Eckankar: Key to Secret Worlds* and *The Tiger's Fang,* on the other hand, introduce readers to soul travel— distinct from astral travel—as it manifested in major religious traditions as a secret science. Both men hold that OOBE is a natural expression of our original nature that needs to be addressed by each of us.

I am indebted to a third person, Itzhak Bentov, for information about both the practice and "how to" of OOBE as a means to expand the consciousness and establish a working relationship with the universe and beyond. Bentov's book on the mechanics of consciousness, *Stalking the Wild Pendulum,* and his *The Cosmic Book: On the Mechanics of Creation,* completed by his wife, Mirtala, after his death in 1979, contain lucid descriptions of the how and why of the meditative journey into SELF/GODhood.

The power of OOBE or NDE is unmistakable. It can bring a reformulation of what people once thought was true in their world of five senses and three dimensions. They say that travel is broadening, and so it is! Therefore, people often come back from near-death with a whole new view of what it means to be human. The experience introduces them to a world in which death is not final, but merely a change of state—only another experience, after all. Many people who survived a near-death report having been overwhelmed by intense feelings of joy, love, and peace. Instead of finding the lonely void they might have expected, they discovered something beautiful. Some people even mention having had the desire, as they moved into the tunnel toward the light, of not wanting to return to earth, because of their experience of unconditional love.

Although many people may prefer not to talk about their experience because friends react with disbelief, scorn, or are similarly unreceptive, the experience often affects their lives profoundly. Many exhibit an absolute and undeniable spiritual radiance afterward, along with a new set of values. This spiritual awakening is so awesome and overwhelming that they are at once and forever thrust into a new mode of being.

Not surprisingly, the public is anxious to learn about near-death experiences. They have received continuing exposure in newspapers and magazines, on television specials, and on talk shows. This has given people a common ground for trying to understand near-death in terms of on-going consciousness past clinical death. It encourages them to think about their own deaths.

Many people now feel that they know what it is like to die and what will happen to them afterward. Like those who underwent a near-death experience directly, they may have an entirely altered view of death and its relationship to life. This understanding has helped to soften the subject of death and make it more acceptable. It also has reduced the fear of death that has gripped our society for so long, and has led the way to new thoughts and questions about the function of death. That alone has done us a great service as well as produced a climate of awareness which will more readily welcome a new and open approach toward death itself.

Still, dying remains an impersonal, often ignored act. Dying people rarely are surrounded by an uplifting environment suitable to the death moment's seriousness and potential. The time is ripe for an at-death psychology and philosophy to accompany the current predeath concerns. As much attention needs to be paid to the act of dying as has been paid to near-death experiences. Most important, however, a new method of dying itself is long overdue. Now more than ever we need to be able to unkink the terrors and anxieties that beset us in an age shadowed by the potential destruction of the entire globe. In doing this, we will unleash our energy for affirmative living.

What we need is a new way to think about dying that can ease our concerns about the questionable future and help us in our more mundane musings of what our own lives—and deaths—are all about. We need a method and an approach that will place the death moment back into the life chain that we've gotten separated from to help us see dying as a part of a natural process. We need to learn about the interplay of consciousness in all life forms. Modern rites of passage need be established to address the body, mind, and spirit of every individual, rites that respect the right of each dying person to depart in peace. Such traditions then could ease our own feelings about death and help unite sick people and their loved ones who so often are alienated from one another now.

I propose a modern craft of dying—a right and conscious way of dying—which I call deathing. Right dying, as opposed to happenstance, is a method, an attitude, a collection of certain concepts. It is a technique acquired through concentrated preparation and practice before the death moment, and conversely, it is almost effortless. Ordinarily when people die, they are unprepared and uninformed; probably they are bewildered or frightened, especially if they are alone. *Deathing* offers a way to free up dying people so they can utilize the highest potential of the transition called death and experience it as a peak moment, a culmination of life. This deliberate, practical, yet spontaneous approach toward the death moment can enable people to attain higher levels of consciousness, by whatever routings, so they can reach out to meet the Light even as it approaches them, just as we accelerate before shifting gears in a car to achieve a smooth transition.

Within this book we will learn a method of deathing to help people learn how to die which is a healing technique as well! This method provides a way for us to have dignity, attention, and control of consciousness at the death moment. It teaches a simple technique of energy perception and release which we can work on ahead of time so that more energy will flow into our lives and certainly our deaths. Those who follow these exercises for several months will recondition themselves for an expanded life and death, and discover what to expect from the final moment. This method details how to practice sensory perception and relaxation, teaches breathing and chanting techniques, as well as outlining other ways we can calm and focus ourselves. Finally, the manual explains how to facilitate the withdrawal of consciousness at the death moment so the transition from life to death can be aware, awake, responsible, and joyous. Instructions are also included so that a support person can either help you if you are conscious, or monitor you in the event of coma or unconsciousness. At the moment of death there is no time for the usual delays and hemmings and hawings of the critical mind; we must be prepared beforehand with conditioned responses that will activate automatically. Right deathing can ensure that we will be ready—rather than unaware and helpless—at the final, definitive moment of consciousness.

This book is like a tool box which someone carries to avoid being caught unprepared on the road. It can be used at any time and under any circumstances, including the physiological breakdown of old age, lingering cancer, AIDS or other devastating disease, or a sudden accident. Anyone can learn deathing, no matter what age, ability, or state of body and mind.

There is historical precedent for a method of deathing based on an expanded vision of what it is to be human. Yet, the death moment will not be the first vital action to be first hidden, then recognized, and finally embraced as part of life. The process of childbirth once was shunned as is death today. Mothers labored and gave birth under the influence of painkillers and anesthetic, as removed from the birth of their children as anesthetized patients are from their surgery.

Approximately thirty years ago, a method approach to birth was developed which returned a semblance of naturalness and joy to childbirth. Using exercises and breathing techniques, the Lamaze method of prepared natural childbirth introduced a way for women to control the physically overwhelming process of giving birth. By doing so, it took a natural event that many women feared and integrated it as a beautiful part of their lives. Now women can choose how they will bring their children into the world. They can opt for traditional medical intervention or, with their partners, they can prepare for that time and undertake a conscious and aware childbirth.

The Lamaze method is effective because it teaches women to be both aware of their bodies and to recondition certain pain reflexes using conscious control. Preparing women for labor and birth, and informing them of what will occur at each stage, helps them bring to childbirth an enlightened understanding of what is happening to them. It also involves their partners, who can offer support, guidance, and comfort during the more difficult moments, as well as enabling them to participate actively in this very important process.

Just as birth was changed by the Lamaze method, so must the death moment be addressed and redefined as a conscious act. Deathing bears the same relationship to mere death as prepared childbirth bears to conventional birth. As with its counterpart, dying does not have to be steeped in pain and difficulty. Both events are short, but they mark our consciousness and lives and can be improved by simple, thoughtful preparations. Furthermore, while only half the world's population can give birth, all humanity must die one day and therefore could benefit from learning right dying via deathing.

Deathing is still new and generally unknown to our cultural consciousness. Defining and naming the death moment and the process of right deathing will help society separate them from the stages leading up to the death moment. This distinction is the first step in creating a new awareness. These predeath stages have already been addressed by the field of death and dying. And while the stages preceding the death moment may be painful, frustrating, and terrifying, the death moment itself is beautiful when prepared for and not resisted. When people recognize the difference between the two, they will be more open to the notion of deathing. This understanding will help pave the way toward a new cultural myth and model about death and dying—a myth whose potential impact on our society should not be underestimated.

Historically, introducing new features into a society has often changed the ways its people thought, altering basic assumptions and views that might never before have been questioned. These new views were then integrated into a new perspective or vision. This process of change, which can happen within small groups of people or throughout an entire society, can be called a paradigm shift, a shift of operative assumptions about what is real in our lives. Some paradigm shifts are relatively minor, reflecting different clothing styles, speech patterns, or new vocabularies in the arts or sciences. But if many of them happen to coincide, as during the Renaissance, they can create a major change in human consciousness.

Looking backward, it is easy to discern such shifts and identify how certain features altered institutions and lifestyles.

During such a time, inventions and ideas often proliferate, art forms are created, and concepts about people and their limitations change. The changes were sometimes violent, but always fertile. New models of the universe appear; old models disappear as the new views become the norm. Today, for example, it is difficult to believe that people once neglected the care of the aged, the right of blacks or women to be able to vote and work, or the need for an integrated society. Young children who have been brought up with these innovations, however, simply see them as fundamental to what is real in their world, although this is subject to change even more in the next century.

Our society is in the midst of a spiritual awakening that will change our values and outlooks. The positive aspects of the shift often are difficult to see, for changes in cultural dimensions usually are invisible until they belong to history. In my lifetime, however, I have noticed a new commitment to holistic living that includes an interest in death. Once again death is considered to be a part of the life flow of individual and collective consciousness. People are still uncomfortable about death, yet we are able to recognize our fears and start addressing—if not releasing—them. For instance, it is easier to read about dying and the death moment than it might have been five or ten years ago, when death was still the responsibility of doctors and hospitals rather than the responsibility of each of us. The method of deathing itself may still be a novel idea, but in time it will be a commonplace concept. Just thinking about the death moment as separate from the predeath concerns currently dealt with in thanatology will start to change people and make them more receptive to the principle of deathing. This is part of the value and mission of at-death psychology.

Although the study of death was legitimized about twenty-five years ago by the introduction of thanatology into the field of psychology, it has gained acceptance only during the past decade. In the early '70s, the subject of death became permissible again. In large part this was due to the efforts of Dr. Elisabeth

Kübler-Ross, the psychiatrist primarily responsible for bringing death out of the closet. To begin with, she noted that there was a forgotten sector of humanity in our midst—the dying. Visiting the wards and private homes of the terminally ill, she went in search of this lost segment of society, to find out who they were, to learn about the final stages of life. One by one, she asked them to be her teachers. From them she learned about the stages of anxieties and fears, the unfulfilled ambitions, the hopes and expectations that dying people experienced as they tried to understand what was happening to them.

In her landmark *On Death and Dying*, which was published in 1969, Kübler-Ross proposed a model for a predeath psychology. In this model of life at the edge of death, she chronicles five stages of dying that most people experience. These stages, which constitute the normal response to death, can take place in any order. When people first learn of their impending death, they often deny it. They then may become angry, and question why they have been singled out, why they should have to die. Later on they may try to bargain, hoping to gain additional time. This may be followed by depression and finally by acceptance, either rueful and fatalistic or optimistic. By naming these stages, Kübler-Ross legitimized these reactions and gave people a way to think about their inevitable death and the deaths of others. Her ceaseless efforts to reintegrate the dying person into the ranks of the living added kindness and dignity to the last months and days of many individuals.

In the '70s, Kübler-Ross also helped publicize another aspect of death—near-death—thereby becoming this country's most controversial thanatologist, as well as its most renowned. By talking with terminally ill patients, who come and go across the edge of death more frequently than the rest of us, she heard the near-death stories of hundreds of people. Somewhere along the way, she herself went to the edge and experienced near-death, as well as a major OOBE and light experience. By publicly acknowledging her own experiences and the experiences of others, she almost singlehandedly produced the climate of awareness in our culture about the near-death phenomenon and issues of survival. Then Dr. Raymond Moody joined Kübler-Ross to help popularize the near-death phenomenon. His best-seller, *Life After Life*, offers a prototype of the near-death experience, composited from the features represented by many case histories. This vivid and useful model has given people who have not experienced near-death a concrete way to think about it. In his sequel, *Reflections on Life After Death*, Moody's scenario of the near-death experience, with its aspects of the tunnel, out-of-body projection, the light, and what appears to be the border between life and death, has several new features. Included are flashforwards of knowledge or higher wisdom which people have described as being symbolized by the image of a school or library. An additional feature, the realm of bewildered spirits, has bearing on the understanding of Tom Breacher's dilemma you will read about later in this book.

The study of near-death was taken a step further by Dr. Kenneth Ring, a psychologist interested in altered states of consciousness and familiar with them from his own encounters with those who had a near-death experience. He was further inspired to pursue this work by Moody's first book. Determined that the implications suggested by the near-death experience not be obscured by lack of formal data and published research, Ring conducted the first major scientific study of the phenomenon. Like Kübler-Ross and Moody, he talked with hundreds of people who had survived near-deaths. From this carefully documented material he conducted a rigorous examination of the near-death experience. The results of his work appeared in *Life at Death*, which was published in 1980.[3]

Ring argues that the range of experiences in the core model NDE (from the tunnel to the border) is an extended out-of-body

---

[3]Kenneth Ring, *Life at Death: A Scientific Investigation of the Near-Death Experience* (New York: McCann & Goghegan, 1980).

experience representing actual shifts between states of consciousness. By challenging people's understanding of NDE in the context of his parapsychological-holographic explanation, psychology expands to include a new view of on-going consciousness.
This new understanding, in light of these developments in neuro-
science and quantum reality, ushers in an expanded model of
the relationship between body, mind and spirit. Ring's work
helps legitimize the NDE phenomenon and the expansion of
predeath psychology to include at-death psychology. Ring's research also led him to new, more complex explanations of the
meaning of near-death experiences for our era, described in his
book, *Heading Toward Omega*.[4]

In this landmark pioneering work, Ring establishes—
through a series of startling case histories—that what happens
during an NDE has nothing inherently to do with death or the
process of dying. That is to say, NDE should be regarded as a
member of a family of related transcendent and mystical experiences that historically have always been with us, not the "new"
discovery of modern researchers. Furthermore, he postulates the
probable connection between NDE and kundalini, the evolutionary energy which can be released by nearly dying, but which
has been awakened for generations by means of the meditative
psychotherapies of yoga and other spiritual disciplines. He con-
cludes that NDE is a tool for human evolution with huge planetary implications. For a clue as to how, he turns to the means
of an exponential consciousness raising, which the findings of
research biologist Rupert Sheldrake suggest in *A New Science of
Life: The Hypothesis of Causation*.[5] This "satsang effect" he
sees as the effect of the interaction of invisible organizing fields,

---

[4]Kenneth Ring, *Heading Toward Omega: In Search of the Meaning of Near-
Death Experience* (New York: William Morrow, 1984).
[5]Rupert Sheldrake, *A New Science of Life: The Hypothesis of Causation* (Los
Angeles: Jeremy Tarcher, 1983).

which Sheldrake calls morphogenetic fields. The NDEers may well provide the critical mass to turn the tide for higher evolution, as suggested by the popular idea of the hundredth monkey effect. Since death is one avenue to higher consciousness, as well as NDE and other forms of kundalini awakening, an at-death psychology is imperative for Western culture at this time in history.[6]

An at-death psychology necessarily ushers in a re-definition of "what is a human being?" This age old consideration is already underway in consciousness research, but it must go farther as science merges with what was once the province of religion. At the practical level, at-death psychology would ward off "breech" deaths and would inspire "good" deaths with subsequent good after effects (the word "good" being better understood as "balanced," for it is not a value judgment). Moreover, at-death psychology would give the average person an inkling and some training for using the death moment as a tool for enlightenment! Nothing less! The introduction of a support person, therefore, is the modern replacement of the supportive lama in Tibetan spiritual intervention in the dying process, who becomes a therapeutic presence, a monitor, and a coach to keep the dying "on course" during the deathing experience. Why, indeed, should we leave such a huge investment as our lives to a chance encounter with death when any one of us can experience deathing? And the introduction of guru yoga, or using the name-of-God at death is an additional failsafe technique that you can learn.

• • •

My concerns with the relationship between life, death, and consciousness developed early, since clairvoyance and OOBE were common occurrences during childhood and early adolescence,

---

[6]Also see John White's *Kundalini, Evolution and Enlightenment* (New York: Anchor Books/Doubleday, 1979).

and there were also two NDEs at age 7 and 14, respectively. At 14, I fell through the ice and drifted away from the hole. The experience showed me how myriad is the nature of consciousness. In that instance, one "I" determined how to save the physical body from a vantage point above my body, and another vaster "I" was seeing alternate planetary futures that ranged from the time of Pythagoras, Buddha and Lao Tzu some three thousand years ago, into the 21st century.[7] Adulthood, however, closed the once open door until 1968 when I met my first teacher, Paul Twitchell. Studying both classical yoga and his "far-out" yoga of OOBE and consciousness unfoldment, I experienced several changes of consciousness similar to those I remembered from childhood.

In the years since then, I have witnessed the deaths of various friends and strangers, including the controlled and final moments of Paul Twitchell, who showed me that deathing was possible. This renowned and skillful adept gave me my first example of conscious and voluntary withdrawal from an impaired physical body in his final out-of-body experience. I have never forgotten the courage and control he displayed while in acute pain from a massive coronary. I tried to comfort him and act as what I would now call a support person, but at the time I was clumsy in my ignorance and inexperience. Although obviously in pain, he showed courtesy and good humor at my awkwardness. Even while dying, he was able to teach me as our consciousness shared. I chanted and breathed with him to keep his attention focused and to ease his transition. This practice, which quieted me as well, is now a fundamental part of the method for conscious deathing.

As Paul died, he labored with his breath in long-held exhalations, as I recall having done during childbirth's labor. While I

---

[7] See Ring's *Heading Toward Omega*, chapter 8, "Planetary Visions of Near-Death Experiences," pp. 217–218.

had concentrated on my breathing to help the birth, Paul breathed carefully to ease himself out of life. Slowly he performed what I now call consciousness withdrawal; as he did so, the personal connection I had always felt with him winked out. Gone—it was like the ceasing of a song—and its absence made clear what his presence had meant. But in its place was a radiant harmony that permeated the room in a much vaster presence which has never left me.

Although I had witnessed a master practice the rite of deathing—the withdrawal of consciousness—I was not able then to understand what I had seen. In fact, it took over fifteen years for the experience to germinate into the method of deathing. In large part I was motivated by many people who were open enough to share their thoughts about dying with me. One woman, Selma, talked to me at length about her impending death, and asked me to write her a set of notes she could study and try to implement for herself. I did, and those notes became the first prototype of the deathing manual.

I began to realize that many people, because of how they have lived, don't have the insight and strength Selma Rieseseg and Paul Twitchell did. Several people that I knew died completely unprepared deaths, showing me the needlessness and waste of that type of death. And then in 1978, I had a final, catalytic experience that pushed me to begin this book.

Late one night I experienced a shift of consciousness of a sort that I had frequently had as a child. I was receiving information in spurts, in the form of news clips of thousands of people dying in various ways—fire, flood, mudslides, war, starvation, disease, old age—and I realized there was a need for a structure which could serve symbolically as a bridge or road people could travel to the crossover at death. Such a construct would reduce the fear that often occurs at the final moment. This fear can obstruct the journey into other states of consciousness. I was struck by the realization that people didn't have to die in order to know how to die. We could learn how to die in advance, rehearse death and release both the fear of life and the fear of death. I understood, then, that I could write about a useful method of dying that could be accessible to anyone, anywhere, any-when, and under any conditions.

Because the material in this book sprang from other people's lives, I have turned to them again in order to instruct others. I tell the two teaching tales, the deaths of Tom and Selma, in order to contrast two forms of death available in our times: unconscious death and consciously focused death. This story-telling technique has precedent in many teaching orders, where allegorical tales are more effective than straight history. The tales are composed of a number of case histories that are condensed, using the device of fiction, to gain the moral end. In the case of these two characters, I created Tom from two separate biographies, and Selma from four.

The German and Swiss literary traditions strongly influenced the form these stories have assumed. I relied on a type of teaching story called the *Bildungsroman,* or character-development literature, which was brought to its fullest expression by Johann Wolfgang von Goethe in *Wilhelm Meister.* This type of pedagogical story was also used by the Swiss realist writers of the 19th century. Their use of the *Rahmenerzählung,* or story-within-a-frame, has been adapted here to set off much of the material as well as hold it within a fixed context.

Although the tales per se are fictional, they are far from fiction because I created them from biography. Like Moody's idealized model of near-death, which was drawn from numerous experiences, these tales should be considered to be prototypes of the features of two styles of death. However, two different styles of living contributed to these contrasting deaths. As such, the examples offer a distinct lesson about how a certain type of lifestyle can culminate in similar kinds of matching death experiences.

Tom Breacher lived a rather unconscious, unaware, unexamined life. He was a young, modern gentleman of the material-
ist vintage—skeptical, with expediency his by-word. Because of
the absence of any values aside from materialism, which tends
to omit consideration of anything but physical reality, he lacked
a framework for any kind of afterlife expectation. To complicate
matters, he died in a sudden accident, and he died in shock. It
is important to note that while his physical death itself was not
complicated or painful since it happened instantly, he died poorly
because he was not prepared for death internally. Thus there
were psychological results, including amnesia about the Light
experience which occurs for all people, according to degree of
preparation and expectation of the inner self. If he had known
anything about relaxing, prayer, or meditation, he would have
had an easier time. As it was, he died with his mind and body
greatly contracted with fear. He died without spiritual concepts
or expectations, still possessing the materialistic, ironic view
which he had held his whole life. In short, Tom died with trivial
images on his mind at the death moment and in fear rather than
serenity. He had what I call a breech death—a death that does
not go smoothly, for whatever reason.

In the contrasting teaching tale, I present Selma Rieseseg,
who died a controlled, elegant death even under pressing circumstances. Her ex-lover and alter ego is Josip Vidmar, a brilliant
consciousness researcher who challenges her prematurely about
the enlightenment potential of human nature—in life and death.
She sends him away, but later faces the same issue in a new
guise—that of death—and his teacher as well. A psychologist
of middle years, Selma seems at first as ill-suited for higher
consciousness as was Tom Breacher. But after a particularly long
day, her night ends in the Light in an out-of-body experience
that changes her life—and death. In the resultant re-examination
of her life, and after discovering her terminal cancer, she painstakingly rehearses her death in order to make it easier for herself

and for those she will leave behind. Her husband acts as her support person to provide her with a failsafe backup system as she becomes one with the Light of pure Consciousness—Reality.

Selma's character was created from four different people whom I have known. The first and original Selma, although over 70 when I met her, was full of spunk and energy. She knew of out-of-body experiences and practiced relaxation and yoga concentration and tried to live well in spite of her cantankerous nature. Nevertheless, she developed terminal cancer, which for a long time she hid from me. Now I realize why she prodded me for information.

Selma and I talked repeatedly about death and dying. She was mortally afraid, not of death, but of being drugged at the crucial moment, and would sound off about "the view from the hearse" in American life and what a commercial affair death was. She insistently cross-examined me about everything I knew or had ever read on the subject of death. The thought of a method of deathing particularly pleased her, because it could provide something solid and workable when there was nothing else left to do.

By now this Selma has been blended with a number of other people. Together they serve as an example of how deathing can be done well, offering a model toward which we all can aim.

In the manual I present a step-by-step explanation of the deathing method. This section is straightforward and easy to use, much like a how-to book or a repair manual. I have focused on instructions for the person who is deathing, and guidelines for the support person who will be acting as coach during the transition. The manual is presented in such a way that at the time of deathing it can be used as a guidebook or reference, whether the dying person is alone or has a support person.

The instructions for the person who is deathing detail a set of exercises that are derived in part from yoga. I have presented these exercises in Part III of this book, "The Manual of Deathing," and I call them the Six Techniques. Each of the techniques describes a series of exercises for the person who is preparing to die. I constantly refer to the *Sixth Technique* throughout the story of Selma and Tom in Part II, and throughout the deathing manual itself. The Sixth Technique is crucial because it enables the average person to focus on an enlightened being at the death moment and therefore free the soul. Refer to the List of Exercises at the front of this book if you want to read about these exercises first. The exercises should be practiced in advance, ideally for as long as six weeks to six months, so that you can train yourself to respond with control and serenity at the death moment, rather than constricting with fear. These exercises will help prepare your body, mind and spirit for the final transition. Other relaxation techniques include chants and deliberate, even breathing. You will also learn how to concentrate on a guru—or a loved personification of God—such as Christ, Rama, Krishna, Buddha, or saint. The focus on an enlightened being "entrains" you to the level of resonance of this figure. Spirituality is caught—not taught—ultimately. Finally, I offer a technique for the withdrawal of consciousness. This process can—and should—be rehearsed in order to ensure that the death moment brings as few surprises as possible.

The suggestions offered to the support person are to enable that individual to share the very intimate act of dying. Ideally, the support person should be a friend whom the dying person trusts, so they can practice the exercises together until each step becomes natural and automatic. It is important that the support person be clearheaded, with as little guilt or sorrow as possible, and therefore able to offer strength and an encouraging, loving presence. Because a dying person can be so easily swayed, it is crucial that anyone around be positive and helpful. Later there is space for grief as well as homage to one's friend—but not during the death moment, when a loving heart and steady, instructing mind best help the transiting person depart in peace and meet the great experience that waits to welcome each of us.

I trust that the information contained in this book will help offset the conditions that produce awkward deaths, yet not make people afraid of the very normal and natural business of death. Because there is such an obvious need for this approach, I hope it will become commonplace over the next few years. It would ease my mind to know that deathing will one day soon become as usual as preventing blood loss by pressing pressure points or applying a tourniquet, as natural as a good birth, or as mundane as smacking someone who is coughing on the back.

Let me assure you: the benefits of prepared, voluntary actions at the death moment exceed the claims of the best savings plan or life-insurance policy. By allowing yourself to think about the unthinkable, you can make it less forbidding. By facing up to your mortality, you will be able to fulfill your life in deeper, richer ways. By taking responsibility for your death, you will be doing the most practical thing you could do for yourself, and the most selfless, giving thing you could do for your loved ones.

PART II

TOM BREACHER'S DEPARTURE
&
THE DEATHING OF SELMA

Rise after rise bow the phantoms behind me,
Afar down I see the Huge first Nothing, the vapor from the
*   nostrils of death,*
I know I was even there . . . I waited unseen and always,
And slept while God carried me through the lethargic mist,

Old age superbly rising! Ineffable grace of dying days!

As to you life, I reckon you are the leavings of many deaths,
No doubt I have died myself ten thousand times before.

Walt Whitman
Leaves of Grass, "Song of Myself"

◇ ◇

TOM BREACHER'S DEPARTURE

It is not how to start, but where, in a story like this.

If you were a bird flying far above the setting of this story, you could see how the winding shaft of the Connecticut River appears like poured silver between its banks. The banks, through which the river threads like a road, range from tender chartreuse in spring, to dark green in summer, blanching from the russet of fall to a tarnished silver in winter. But today the storm obscures the river and the roads that trace it, Interstate 91 and Route 9. A side road cuts off the highway and leads to Seaward Point, a long beach and cliffline that extends into the always uneasy mix of the salt and freshwater of the estuaries. It starts on the sunrise side of the river and its tip touches the edge of the sea, where Selma's retreat house sits.

It is now winter.

January 6, 4:15 P.M. The powerful jet angled steeply into its landing pattern at Bradley Field, the last airport on the eastern seaboard not inundated by snow. Buffeted from Chicago to Hartford through the violent airspace of Storm Casper, the plane carried a full load of returning holiday seekers. It shuddered in deceleration, dropping fast. Passenger Tom Breacher abruptly leaned across his seatmate who was a tanned, leggy, young fellow, and stared for a long minute into the opaque white blankness, gnawing on a cuticle. He always had a chill sensation about landing, even under decent conditions.

Tom Breacher, executive and computer specialist for Midas Corporation, one of the largest corporations in a field that was expanding daily into aerospace operations, international communications networks, satellite receivers, television, and the like, had a great future. Standing just scant of six feet tall, with an elegant, somewhat ease-softened appearance, Tom Breacher prided himself on his self-control and ability to weather things through. Both qualities had contributed to his rapid advancement in the corporate structure. At Midas Corporation he was known as an amiable man who got things done while maintaining an air of humorous nonchalance among co-workers and strangers alike. He avoided uncomfortable situations; confrontations were kept as impersonal as possible, whether with colleagues or businesses.

Today, however, Tom Breacher's usually pleasant face scowled with distaste for the conditions in which he found himself. First there had been a foul-up in his first-class reservations. They had been paid for, but not delivered. Now this miserable trip, which even under decent conditions would not have been his choice.

Despite the turbulence, no real damage had been done to any of the passengers, although two had tripped when they ignored the captain's request to stay seated. There had been a tense moment when the plane veered sharply during the movie which ended prematurely when the projector bulb blew out. Everyone gasped, seatbelt signs flashing wildly as the plane dropped abruptly to avoid even worse weather. Afterwards there was that sense of oppression that waiting breeds on long trips or during forcible detention.

Most of the passengers, including Tom Breacher, had not eaten lunch; instead, the majority sedated themselves with too many cocktails. One baby began to cry. The harried-looking steward, who sporadically occupied the aisle seat beside Tom for a few moments' rest during the trip, sprang up to assist the mother with her child. As the plane lurched again, he struggled to catch his balance and moved toward the galley. Tom Breacher stretched out his cramped legs, easing them into the steward's now unoccupied space.

Tom Breacher's seatmate, Dr. Joseph Tuchman, did not take similar advantage of the situation. He remained motionless, gazing out the window at the swirling snow. His alert gray eyes were canny and patient, oddly ingenuous. Dr. Joseph Tuchman was 28, although he looked much younger, and was finishing his medical residency. He had been drawn to medicine as a calling, as well as a profession. That day he was returning from a holiday visit at his parents' Arizona ranch.

As the travel-worn stewardess started down the aisle routinely reminding everyone to keep their seatbelts fastened, the two men caught each other's eyes. They laughed curtly at the notion that anyone would need a reminder after the upheaval they all had been through. The plane was on the approach to Bradley Field when this short moment of laughter joined the two men in as intimate a dialogue as they would ever have. For a brief moment, Tom Breacher was most attractive, with lively dark eyes and a boyish face that his beard didn't quite dignify. He then lapsed back into his habitual sulky repose.

Tom Breacher diverted himself from the impending landing with an infusion of things past. He pondered how it had proved advantageous to leave both his profession and his fifteen-year marriage at about the same time, how an almost-Ph.D. who once considered psychology as a calling in the exciting days of the 1960s instead had trained for linguistics as a profession, only to switch over into computer science as a vocation. When he joined Midas, he became upwardly mobile and met the vice-president's daughter, Angela, to whom he now was engaged. His body warmed at the thought of dinner tonight with Angela.

All in all, the former-professor-turned-executive was happy in his life choices, although sometimes he missed the friends he'd shared, who somehow typically do not regroup when such spinoffs from job and family occur in divorce. Out of character with his new executive self, but in a kind of discontent that he rarely admitted, Tom had gone to an art show opening at the university the week before New Year's. There he'd met several old friends and even his former department chairman's wife, Dr. Selma Rieseseg, whom he hadn't seen in six years. She'd remarried after her husband's death, earned a Ph.D. in psychology, and now was a psychotherapist in the Essex area. It was odd, Tom thought idly, that in the same week he would both meet her and then read that she was connected with a conference at which Elisabeth Kübler-Ross was to be guest lecturer. He guessed Selma must have changed a great deal. Meeting her again after so long had stirred up old memories . . . old dreams and aspirations he had forgotten, ones which were not all in keeping with the sleekly contoured world he now occupied.

Tom's disquieting reverie was broken off by the wrenching sound of the landing gear setting down. The captain's voice announced that is was raining in Hartford and that they would be able to land at Bradley Field after all; they wouldn't have to reroute to wait out the storm. Despite the passengers' flightlong inconveniences, they would arrive on time due to Storm Casper's favorable tail winds. Nearly the entire cabin cheered then, and a healing chatter started up like locusts in early spring, rising to midsummer's volume.

It was just 4:24 P.M. when, despite delays and the vagaries of nature, the big jet managed to set down an entire six minutes earlier than the expected arrival time. This fact would change the destinies of at least three people. The plane was still taxiing toward the ramp. A rainy twilight was visible through the windows when the two men stood up to gather their belongings, taking an indifferent leave of one another with a casual nod as they put on their coats. They swiftly became part of the holiday crowd that streamed down the ramp into the tunnel-shaped carpeted corridor that stretched to where eager, relieved friends and relatives waited. However, no one in the surging, exultant crowd of hugging and kissing people was there to meet Tom Breacher; but, then, he did not expect anyone.

Tom prepared to dash to the parking lot where he'd left his red Mazda RX7 three days before, while Joseph went into the main lobby to call the hospital to let them know that he was on his way; he had night duty in Emergency. The young physician would now arrive at Hartford Hospital in time to breech deliver Mrs. Grant's boy, Christopher, without serious delay or discomfort for either mother or child. The extra few minutes may have assured young Christopher's survival, since the cord had been snugged around his neck.

• • •

Meanwhile, a blue Volvo drove up to the main terminal at Bradley International Airport. Two of the three occupants would be boarding that day to go west. The driver, Dr. Selma Rieseseg, was no longer young, but she was striking, with her almost-white hair and her blue eyes which seemed to smolder in some banked fire. She was reasonably well known in Hartford, despite her passion for privacy. Her distinguished looks and acid delivery, as well as the fact that she was not too pleased with institutional medicine, were common gossip among the staff of the Hartford Hospital.

Just then the sliding doors opened and Tom Breacher burst from the terminal. He winced as a gust of cold rain hit his face when he dashed onto the sidewalk and ducked into the slanting rain. Dr. Selma Rieseseg lifted her head sharply in recognition as Tom hurried by and almost collided with one of Selma's passengers—a diminutive but formidable woman in a European-styled suit—without so much as a muttered apology. Selma started to call him, but thought better of the impulse. Both women stared after him as he sprinted across the parking lot, raincoat flapping around his knees.

Selma snorted outright, more in consternation than amusement; there could have been an accident. But the woman and gentleman whom she assisted both shrugged and Selma thought she noticed the woman's wise, tolerant brown eyes behind rimless glasses, laughing. Tom Breacher never knew with whom he had almost collided, nor that he had passed Selma Rieseseg for the third time this week, in one fashion or another, after not having had contact for so long. Selma wondered briefly how Tom came to be at the airport and found it peculiar that she, too, kept running into Tom, almost literally, after a hiatus of six years. His parking lot sprint seemed somewhat out of character with the rather stuffy fellow she'd met at the art show opening.

Selma's party approached the departure gate. The flight attendant was polite, but anxious to see the pair on board. With affection, Selma watched the two figures disappear down the tube-corridor that led to the plane. She started the drive back to Seaward Point which was a little over an hour's trip under good conditions. She knew the roads well, so she wasn't nervous despite the oncoming snow; but she was tired and wanted to get this day over with. She guessed she'd spend Sunday resting and reading alone at the house on the shore, then go back to Middletown on Monday and have breakfast with Arne. She had appointments with patients all that day and her son, Erik, was due in from college that evening. She missed having the house full of kids; it would be fun to have Erik home for awhile. But for now, she was overdue for a long weekend alone at Seaward Point. Tuesday was already booked with patients, and on

Wednesday she had to go to the hospital to get the reports on a routine exam.

There was a cyst; she'd gone at Arne's insistence to a specialist he knew. In vain she'd tried to tell him that she'd had lumps come and go for years . . . just benign cysts. Granted, this one was a bit bigger than some, but there was nothing to it. However, as he had pressured her to have it checked, she humored him. Since they'd only been married six years, he didn't know about her habit of ignoring them. Selma was a firm believer in creating her own reality, which included the enjoyment of stalwart good health, stringent exercise, and immoderate overwork.

• • •

Tom Breacher had no difficulty finding his car. He was puffing a bit from the swift sprint in this unnameable stuff that came down like snow, looked like rain on the pavement, but skidded underfoot like ice. He slid into the bucket seat, comforted to be even this close to home after a grim day. His face still bore the expression of minor irritation and some determination that he'd worn all this long day.

Loath to start out, he slouched his almost six-foot frame comfortably into the black leather seat. Tiny, furry flakes had coated the windshield already. When he turned the ignition the car started immediately and a classical music station resounded throughout the car with the achingly sweet Brahm's Third Symphony. It was just 4:30 P.M., the plane's scheduled arrival time. Tom didn't feel elated to have the few extra minutes which just might help him whip through the narrow stretch of four-lane highway before the traffic from Springfield merged with commuters leaving Hartford. There was one spot where everything bottlenecked; however, he'd give it a try, he thought wearily, as he drove out of the parking lot.

The intersection where airport traffic into Hartford fed into I-91 was almost bare. The last place for total congestion was coming up. He sometimes wondered why more people weren't killed at that place. He sailed past the spot that had worried him without mishap. Strange, thought Tom—the road certainly was not filled with 5:00 P.M. traffic; they must have given a storm warning for the entire area. He flipped the radio station and scanned the dial for a weather report, finding a DJ frenetically announcing the "bad company of six inches of snow by midnight." Bull, thought Tom Breacher; they'd be lucky to get away with twice that. At any rate, he'd be home before it hit. He smiled slightly as he thought of Angie's welcome, and leaned forward to peer through the beat of the windshield wipers at the oncoming traffic.

The light was fading fast, moving from blue dusk to twilight. This afternoon's storm warnings all over the East Coast edged anxiety into the drivers' thoughts, coloring their dreams and expectations, even as they drove securely within their isolated capsules down I-91 South.

Tom already was struggling to keep awake as fatigue washed over him. Jet lag usually didn't affect him so quickly; it probably was the wine he drank on the plane that was wearing off, and he was hungry. But it was only 25 minutes more until he reached home. He briefly considered stopping for a snack since they weren't going to dinner until 7:30, but decided against it. At the rate the weather was changing, it would only be much worse; even five minutes had made a difference. The snow was clouding now and spinning its hypnotic dance in the headlights. The thrump, thrump of the windshield wipers kept time with the pounding in his head. It was 5:05 P.M. Actually, Tom had many reasons for a headache.

Although Tom's too-studied air of success repelled some people such as his former seatmate, Dr. Joseph Tuchman, in many ways Thomas Breacher III was an interesting man in his predictable pursuit of the American dream. He was said to have been born to St. Louis money. Although it wasn't true, it might as well have been since everyone he knew now believed it. Actually, there were no dukedoms or second-string nobilities; he was just plain and simple American.

Tom Breacher found himself thinking about his grand-mother. From the time he remembered her, all of her joy was gone and she was a shapeless, drab woman of whom Tom Breacher was ashamed. He recalled his grandfather as a fearsome old man sitting on a bench outside the general store or in a rocking chair in the living room.

Then Tom suddenly thought that he ought to call his mother. Strange, he had never liked either of his parents. His mother was a rather blowsy, blonde woman whom he always suspected wasn't very bright, in contrast with his dark, saturnine father. He could almost believe the story about the Indian parentage that had circulated like smoke, unable to be pinned down. By the time the old man died, he'd looked like a weathered, carved tree. Sometimes Tom looked anxiously in the mirror to see if that face were coming upon him, but all he saw were the eyes . . . black, shrewd, sparkling.

Tom, overwhelmed by these thoughts, banished them from his mind, fatigue making that fairly simple. But another memory persisted. Meeting Dr. Selma Rieseseg at the art show opening a few days before his Chicago trip.

Damn, all these ghosts. Perhaps you couldn't get rid of the past after all. His mind ran ahead of the monotonous drive through the graying twilight, the road already sleeted over with a thin film; the snow was becoming increasingly thicker. The speedometer still read 60; Tom dropped it to the 55 mile-per-hour speed limit. It was dark enough now to have oncoming traffic headlights be troublesome, especially since many of the other cars were trying to get home on high beam. Didn't they know that visibility in snow was even poorer on high beam than on low? Damn.

At 5:12 P.M. Tom Breacher was just passing the last point of congestion, his headache throbbed, and he wanted to be home.

Nobody was going out to supper tonight. He had saved a lovely bottle of wine and even if they had TV dinners, home is where they would stay.

Sometimes he wondered if he'd done the right thing for himself by leaving the university; but, then, he had always known it was a stopover for him. Selma had sensed that, although her husband hadn't. And, since her husband was department chairman, he always wondered how much she had to do with the decision not to give Tom tenure.

Normally he repressed thoughts about "what ifs" with dispatch; but at 28, things had been different. He and his world had been young and idealistic; he hadn't learned yet about the real world and how to deal with it. Sometimes you had to do things that you wished you didn't have to do.

Tom Breacher's headache worsened. He was irked that these thoughts persisted. It would be enough to get home, stretch out. Tonight, dammit, he was out of character with all these rememberings.

Also it had been hard to meet Selma again—and she, with a Ph.D., too, although he'd known about that from reading about her in the papers occasionally. Meeting her had stirred up memories, lots of memories. She must be 60 now, he supposed, but still handsome, with that profile and carriage like a drill sergeant. While she still had that incredible skin that you wanted to reach out to touch, and those terrible clothes that somehow looked good on her. The wild, twisted-up hair was still falling down, but the auburn of twelve years ago now contained swatches of white. He wondered if she still went west each summer, and if she still had the house on the Sound that her old man had bought her, where she went off to be private, separate from family, her children, and probably now from her new husband as well.

At the art show opening Selma had given Tom her business card. He'd looked at it again on the plane and noticed that there was a pencil-scrawled number on it. He wondered why she'd given him her home number. Wait—come to think of it, she'd just pulled it out of her purse, so it must already been written there. Oh, well, he'd never use it anyway.

It was now 5:20 P.M., almost an hour since Tom Breacher had landed six minutes ahead of schedule. His thoughts were layered in their strata according to depth and frequency, not unlike an ocean, and moved from the light to the darkness of the deep. Thoughts played upon each other like billiard balls. Angie's face and a fire in the grate next to his reading chair came to mind. The night before he left for Chicago he'd been reading a great mystery novel. He wondered what it meant that he spent his life reading whodunits instead of doing it?

He was approaching an uncomfortable edge. A part of him wanted to pursue this dialogue, while another part shrank from the difficulty. Oh, the difficulty of deep waters. Was he too tired to partake of this fare, was it too rich a diet, too deep a dive?

With relish he imagined his reception from Angie tonight. He envisioned her face and smiled as he peered into the oncoming night, the movement and thrump of the windshield wipers unnoticed as he savored aforehand the eagerness he knew would be spilling happily across her piquant features. Angela was ten years younger than he. They both had learned from prior mates to be kinder with each other. Tonight they would drink the bottle of Bordeaux he'd saved. Tomorrow he'd call the kids and take them to Mystic Seaport or maybe the planetarium. He'd clear it with Helen. Often he wondered about her, whether she still had the dog, Trixie, and the yellow cat, Ashley. Funny how you forget to ask. He thought of Clarissa, 12 now, his daddy's girl, but withdrawn and a little somber since he'd left, even though he saw her almost as much as before. Maybe he should take her on a special trek—she'd been shortchanged from birth on. She was almost premature so they had kept her in the nursery instead of with Helen. She had a lousy birth, or are all births lousy? Yeah, he'd take her on a special trek to the ocean.

5:24 P.M. A top ten song with an insistent rhythm and a lyric of the words, "befreebebebe" switched to "learn how to live before the last day . . ."

Who among us may know his or her time of death and arrange the contents of their consciousness for that crucial transition, as natural as waking, as dramatic as birth, as attendant with snares for the unwary as any jungle—yet as fertile with potential?

5:29 P.M. The constituents of Tom Breacher's individual consciousness were distracted pieces of himself, the flotsam and jetsam of his personality, as he narrowed his eyes in sudden shock at the glaring light that spread and spread across his vision. He froze, as did time. For a long moment he watched incredulously as the truck jackknifed out of nowhere and plowed in slow motion across the center grid as if it were butter, coming right at him. The truck with his name on it. Headlights blared soundlessly.

Time slowed, then almost stopped, as he went into an endless slide, an endless glide. The moment went on and on as he stared upward into the cab at the blanched face of the driver silhouetted high above him, with no place to hide. Tom Breacher realized that he was about to die. The prayer of his childhood crossed his mind: "Pray for us sinners."

The refrain of the hauntingly accurate hit song, "Get away butterfly, get away, way, way," played as two things happened inside him at the same instant, while the truck continued to come at him in slow motion.

At first, time didn't seem to exist in the moment of impact which was still coming and coming, and into which he twisted and turned, looking for every avenue of escape as his first duty.

Finally, he knew there was no exit. Both vehicles were out of control and on a collision course. All of this happened in a matter of seconds.

In the same moment that time seemed to be put on hold, he also experienced time as being speeded up, precipitating access to the stockpile of the subconscious. Details flung out of his mental computer . . . scents, tastes of childhood, little shames and big ones, exultant stages and those less than worth commenting on. All of these memories were recorded precisely, in perfect detail.

The moment of impact was still coming. Tom sensed himself as an enduring ribbon of consciousness stretched backward from present to past and past to present in a sinuous silky circuitry past nerve and blood. He knew himself yelling forward into birth from dark uterine seas, even as he now yelled himself into death, which he dimly perceived to be a darkness in which he would drown and be lost. Tom Breacher did not stop for philosophy, although it would have been better if he had reexamined his "no exit" notion of death and redefined it as an entry. But how could he know he was headed into a world whose properties are closer to the dream state than the waking state he was about to depart so precipitously? And who would imagine that his expectations would influence his departure the same way a heavy meal eaten before bedtime sometimes influences a person's dreams?

Tom plunged into total recall of sensations and tasted his mother's milk, his own toddling steps, grabbing for a cookie, baseball, collecting for the paper route, his brother beating him at ice hockey, girls, high school, cars, drugs, alcohol, cigarettes, college, war, women . . . "What is it all about?" he heard himself asking thinly . . . and plunged back into college courses in psychology, languages, teaching . . . discontent, marriage, discontent, career change to computer science, more discontent but more money, divorce, career success . . . finis. Is that all there is . . . no answer. No answer.

He now saw very clearly in a nakedness of mind and heart all his life events, including deeds for which he could make no justification. A sense of pressure, almost of suffering, built up in him until he admitted, "It could have been better, but all is well." He was released by accepting this realization. It just is; he is. With the release, life resumed again for him—a different kind of life.

"Die," he thought in this timeless yet ongoing moment, "that's it," but somehow he was being born as well. Curiosity came upon him as he watched himself now from a vantage point high above the oncoming crash of the two vehicles. At the same time he was expelled from his body, he was also part of the body behind the wheel whose terror had clotted and whose every cell screamed into the oncoming night. "No, no, no" he heard himself yell at the oncoming headlights of the truck that bore down on him relentlessly.

At 5:30 his perception of two sets of time came back together when, with a last reflex of his physical body, he spun the steering wheel which pushed him sideways into the impact, the Mazda sliding on the icy pavement.

The headlights bore on soundlessly, although from a long way off. He felt an explosion and a moment of intense impact, past pain, as his body was blown to atoms and into a widening blossom of light.

5:31 P.M. The radio still sang "Get away butterfly, get away, way, way," but Tom Breacher was beyond hearing. The car's wheels continued spinning after the impact that tossed it like a crumpled can onto its side in a pasture off Interstate I-91. Tom Breacher snapped off like an icicle from an eave in winter, plucked like a flower in spring. Broken circuit. Finis, then . . .

He was above himself looking down at the carnage and broken metal carcass spilled in the snow. The light continued to dawn even under the acrid conditions of accidental death. And all was holy as he knew all things; except that he kept forgetting.

Tom Breacher's next experience would have special effects that were not all pleasant. For his was, so to speak, a breech death, with the residue of his former self obscuring his new vision. He was one of the thousands who doesn't present the right aspect for a normal death. For Tom, the equivalent of a midwife or doctor would have to orient him in the birth canal toward the light before all would proceed properly, and the world would go on. He would forget, land in his "nightmare," and finally wake up in the afterlife dream, rescued.

As it was, he forgot the dawning of the clear light, even as he forgot the light and himself gone supernova in the light. He forgot the refraction of the light into myriad forms of deity. He forgot, as well, his struggling muscular engagement with all fears and loves engendered in this lifetime, territory all recorded in the unconscious. He forgot, as most people do at this state, that all this panorama was himself in manifestation. He had only to recognize that to be free, but he did not.

But for now Tom ineffectually struggled with old notions about himself that were no longer useful. He tried to pick up where he had left off in the world which, of course, was not possible, since he was without a physical body. For Tom Breacher this was no test. There would be no going back to the body, to wake up as a near-death experiencer who speaks authoritatively of light and joy and has the insight to live well ever after. Nor could he discuss how he had seen his body thrown out of the car, or the way his life had flashed in front of him, or that he'd found it sorry and would have made some changes if he could have, even though he forgave himself.

All of these things he could not say. He had entered into the territory of the heart, mind, and soul without a map. He had no rules of conduct besides a fossilized religious belief and a mechanistic, reductionist view of life, call it unabashed materialism. With such a view there was no easy way for him to recognize death as a part of the life process. Nor could he describe the way he had become the universe, to partake of all that was within it. "What is life?" he cried, even as Tom Breacher saw that birth and death were the reversed ends of the same life continuum.

$\bullet \quad \bullet \quad \bullet$

Light bore down on him with immense speed, a whirling dance of blue-white dazzling light from a long tunnel. Images kept reshuffling—Angie's smile, the driver's screaming face, the impact caught in a silent amphitheater. The light was receding and Tom Breacher wanted to understand; he ached to understand the rhythm and chatter of bandwaves of realities cresting unknown patterns. The tunnel diminished in intensity as he was rerouted and suctioned out a side corridor.

Dazed, he found himself in a pasture near an overturned truck, miraculously thrown clear. His mind kept drifting and returning to look at the truck; in fascination he noted the little figures scurrying around, tugging something out of the cab. A Mazda was plowed underneath, broadsided. Oddly, his attention sometimes found itself focusing above the wreck.

He suddenly found himself by the smashed Mazda as if he'd been jerked through the air on wires. His name was being called over and over again, tonelessly. Then something strange happened. Everything was gone. Faded out. Lights and images gone. Pasture gone. Grayness only.

Now again he was in the ditch by the car. This is queer, he thought. He tested to see if he could move, if he was really himself, or if everything would go away again and he would be drowned in grayness. He peered in cautiously and saw some carcass lying half in and half out of the door, unrecognizable. Then the watery energy grabbed him down into the grey no-man's land between dimensions, then snapped him back again to the wreck where he'd placed his attention. He found himself looking at the hand which was intact, noting the signet ring. It looked familiar. Tom Breacher began to scream.

"No, no no . . . it can't be . . . no, no." He was again tossed into the air, weightless, directionless into the visceral membrane of sky, water, air, muted gray light, and grieving.

This time Tom Breacher jerked back to a woman standing in his apartment, frowning at her watch. In relief he rushed up to her. "My God, Angie, thank God you're here. I've had the most awful dream." He put out his arms to touch her and one hand went through her cheek. Tom Breacher was shocked; she never even looked up from her watch. The wall clock read 7:30, and he was supposed to be home at 7:30. Wildly he looked around the apartment, staring at the mirror behind her which reflected nothing. He stared into it and had no face. Yet Tom Breacher did not grasp the fact that he was most assuredly dead.

Next he found himself in a fleeing ambulance bearing a white-sheeted form with a widening stain of red. Fascinated, he stared at one exposed hand that escaped the shroud, the signet ring glinting. He felt numb, stupefied. Doggedly, he kept his attention on the ring, trying to remember something. Then he remembered. It was his ring, and he was dead. He felt overwhelmed by the realization, but also inspired, for Tom had some determination. He resolved that he wasn't going to be parted from himself and be put into that damned Gray Place again. He'd fight to stick by that ring. He tried to grab onto the physical dead hand that his own now went through, and stay by it.

He billowed behind the fleeing ambulance like the ghost he now was. He couldn't quite remember what had happened to him. He wouldn't admit it, at any rate. Why didn't Angie see him? Why? The siren screamed down the rainy highway back into the city from which he'd come. Grimly he clung to the signet-ringed hand as he found himself drifting among memories that were as real as when they had first occurred. It was more than confusing.

The ambulance tore through the slippery darkness in the nightmare he lived, even though he knew himself to be high above the events. The deaths he'd seen in Vietnam mixed with his own; Clarissa's birth mixed with his own, both his entry into this life and his shattering glorious entry into the Light were wound one around another. He kept coming back to the screaming face in the cab, which became Helen's anguish when she was giving birth to Clarissa, and then became his own.

He wanted to set things right. He wanted to balance the score. He wanted to go back and do it over, except he didn't know how. All he could do was cling to the signet ring. They were loading the body into the hospital now. He hunkered down by the body, grimly clutching his own hand, resisting the drifting gray waves that lapped at him, then became a tidal wave to tear him from his ring . . . NO, no, no. He cried out for his father.

Then it stopped. Other waves replaced the gray waters. Waves of calm and peacefulness melted into him and around him. But he was cautious, somewhat crazed. Furtively he opened his eyes, crouched in a fetal ball by the signet ring in the morgue cooler, numbly holding his own hand.

11:31 P.M.   Time was restructured and again Tom Breacher found himself looking down at the carnage and broken metal that spilled into the snow. But now the light continued pouring over him at immense speed down a gray, membranous tunnel into the whirling dance of blue-white dazzling light that came to meet him.

At first for Tom Breacher it was like snowflakes, this dying business. Fragments of himself flung into what still seemed to be the truck's headlights; then they were gone. The bright, achingly pure light inside and outside of him widened, whitened to a thundering roar and avalanche of white that met his newborn wail. He was being born, borne into a pinpoint, then into a tunnel. While the atom of himself dispersed, light was pouring at him, sweeping him up at immense speed into the whirling, incandescent dance of light. He experienced great floods and earthquakes, fiery molten magma, wild rushing winds, and the roar of thunder bellows vibrating at immense speed through universes and light years.

Tom Breacher passed the place of no return. He had no choice but to be welcomed through the gate into yet more light. In celebration he passed beyond the speed of light into yet more light—diamond, pearl, gold, ruby, emerald—for days.

Gone was separateness. Gone was any tunnel. Gone was any person or limit. Sacred joy flooded his being in a perfect knowledge for which there is no expression, a perfect love that surpasses understanding.

He sang while letting go into the nothingness that blazed in every cell, every membrane, and all of the circuitry of his body. He sang silently into the blazing firmament and the ground of all being. He sang in joy of this awful unity. He sang in the darkness of the light, of voidness of totality gone supernova. He sang as he shrank in bliss and agony at the light that burned through his veins to link him cell by cell with the universe.

January 9.   Tom Breacher heard someone call his name firmly and lovingly, as if that person knew him. His bad dream had now ended. The morgue and signet ring were replaced by the warmth of many suns and Tom found himself stretching, standing young and trim beside a tall, gentle stranger. After so many experiences that masqueraded as real, Tom Breacher knew this one was true. The man smiled, and then Tom ran into his father's arms for the first time in his adult life. Through tears, he heard his father say what Tom Breacher had waited all of his life to hear; "I love you, son." But of course, this came not in exact words, but in sensation, image, and love. Tom Breacher was no longer lost in the crossing.

Midnight, January 6; Seaward Point. Selma wakened to
the shrill intrusion of the telephone by her bed and sat up too
quickly, still half in a dream. Picking up the phone she heard
Tom Breacher say, "Dr. Selma Rieseseg, please help me! Help
me."

"Yes," she said slowly. She was about to ask where he was,
wondering why he didn't just call her Selma, when a completely
different but faintly familiar voice continued. She was bewildered
but listened intently. The strained young voice asked if she had
a patient or friend named Tom Breacher. "What is this all
about?" she wondered, even as she answered yes.

"Doctor, an accident case was brought in earlier tonight,
dead on arrival, clinically speaking. We brought him around
twice, but we just lost him. Identification gave us his name but
no next of kin. He had a card from your office with a handwritten
number on it. I left messages with your answering service and
tried this number . . ." he trailed off.

Selma recalled having seen Tom for the first time in years
at the art show. She'd given him her card but she was at a loss
to explain the private number. Peculiar; she was very cautious
about her unlisted number for Seaward Point.

The doctor's voice apologized for the interruption and quietly asked her if she'd come to the hospital and identify the body.
She knew that it would be simpler to get this part over with
tonight—especially if the expected foot or more of snow shut
everything down. "Yes, of course. I'll be there in an hour and a
half." Selma answered. "Whom do I ask for?" "Dr. Tuchman,"
replied the grateful voice. Selma knew him then—the young
resident. She quietly dismissed him after he'd responded with a
hearty "Good morning." She wondered what was so good about
it. Lying back on her pillow for a moment, she asked herself
toughly, "What in heaven's name happened?" The call from
Tuchman must have come shortly after Tom died. He said that
they had just lost Tom. She must check on the time of death.

She tried to recall if she'd heard Tom's voice coming from the telephone or simply from the air. How could this be? If death was cut and dried, how could Tom be in trouble? Selma felt that she was on thin ice tonight.

12:35 A.M. Six inches of new snow had already fallen when Selma edged the Volvo onto the deserted highway. She passed swiftly inland on a lonely moonlit ride through a landscape as eerie as the mountains of the moon and under snow as white as bone. Her thoughts as she drove were just as alien.

How does anybody prove his or her existence? Selma wondered. Can you ever identify someone with any certainty? Her impression of Tom at the art show was that he had changed a great deal. When he told her about his job, trouble-shooting for the Midas Corporation, and that he was anticipating a tough week in Chicago, he looked like he was going through the wars. Yet when she saw him sprinting to his car at the airport, she thought that he looked fine, except that his color was too high.

2:00 A.M. Inside the Emergency Room there were no amenities—this was business. The atmosphere was charged with tension. Selma took off her coat and strode briskly toward Dr. Tuchman, hoping to get this over with quickly.

The dead man lay resting on a steel table in a small side room off the corridor. The body was covered to the chin by a sheet, with only one hand exposed. Selma recognized the ring glinting under the overhead light, then looked at the face. The brows knit into two black folds at the base of the nose as if the light were too bright, even with his eyes closed. There were no signs of the struggle that Selma knew had ensued in the attempts to save Tom Breacher. She saw there was blood on Dr. Tuchman's trouser leg, but every trace had been erased from the calm, sheeted body. He lay as the dead always lie, heavy and unnaturally white. She wondered if he'd bled to death; she noticed that a towel had been wedged under the jaw to hold it shut. Her eyes searched Dr. Tuchman's kindly face with its blend of old wisdom and youth, as he told her that Tom had been hit broadside by a truck. The car was crumpled like a beer can. They'd had to cut him out with torches and load him from the top of the car into the ambulance. CPR started immediately and continued all the way in. He'd come around once in the ambulance, but then they had to resume CPR. "We called it at 11:30. No pulse, or respiration, due to the loss of blood because of the delay in cutting him out of the car." It remained unsaid that everything medically possible had been done for Tom Breacher.

Selma reluctantly wondered if Tom had experienced any of the changes in consciousness that were allegedly going on in near-death experiences. The question of consciousness and its relationship to the body was so important. Good God, what was an avowed behaviorist like herself doing in the middle of all of this? She felt a wail build up inside her. She still had to deal with the fact that she heard Tom's voice over the phone when his lips had been stilled. Things like this weren't supposed to happen. She wondered if the Kübler-Ross Life, Death, and Transition conference had opened her up.

This night was going on too long. She looked at her watch—3:30 A.M.—just two hours more and she'd be done with tonight. Wearily she shook her head as if to clear it of all she had seen recently. She felt herself crowding away from thinking about anything, most of all death.

The snow had begun once again as, with an energy that she didn't have, she walked to her car in the predawn. Selma slid behind the wheel and drove out of the parking lot, threading swiftly through the empty city and shooting onto the highway south of Hartford. Her snow tires bit into rimes of frozen slush. Snow hissed against the speeding tires spitting like gravel behind her. Gaining the coast road an embattled hour later, she plowed on in an ever-increasing, smothering snow. Selma, navigating by feel and good fortune, dared not slow the car, but somehow held to the almost unmarked road. Fatigue consumed her as she refused to see any more faces or let any of tonight's events take hold of her attention until she got home. With relief Selma finally smelled the ocean, passing over the bridge that stretched across an arm of the sea. Each minute cost Selma anguish as she fought sleep and a perplexed grief about Tom Breacher.

She took the turnoff more from habit than sight and pulled into the driveway. A faint depression marked the spot she'd left hours ago. Lights from the back entrance spilled out onto the snow. Selma slumped for a moment, then stumbled out of the car into another world than the one she'd left. Her heart was thumping wildly and her hands and legs were shaky with fatigue. Gratefully, although painfully, she breathed the sea air. A hard pressure had settled in her chest lately, and now it felt uncaged and about to fly out. She pressed her hands fiercely against her heart, as if to hold it in, and started toward the house that had become her secret solace over the years.

Selma often felt it had been fated for her, this house like a monolith that ruled the province of the strange estuary land between river and sea, a changeling world of salt and fresh water. There in the maritime forest of salt-dwarfed oak and pine, juneberry, sassafras and holly, by bog, swale, and dune—she knew herself home, in whatever season.

Selma knew, too, that she had pushed herself far too far tonight. Her exhausted body would not be stilled by anything less than sleep. Slowly Selma dragged herself through the soft piled snow, her heart banging wildly against her ribs. Finally she was inside and on the other side of tonight. Dawn was a smudgy blue as Selma sagged against the door, her spine feeling dissolved and empty, nervous tingling, exhaustion, and the drumbeat of her heart dominating a body long running on automatic and breaking down.

Frequently Selma stopped on the stairs to catch her breath. At last she entered her room, groped for the light switch, then halted in the dark, resting, her heart still thudding from the climb. The discomforting tingling increased, spreading from her abdomen toward her head which felt as if it might burst. Faint and sobbing for breath, she grabbed the wicker chair just inside the doorway, her only thought to get to bed before sleep claimed her with no more warning.

Then suddenly for Selma Rieseseg, the room disappeared. In its place was light. With eyes open or shut, she saw neither chair, nor bed—just the light, nothing but brilliant light. Nor could she see her hands, although she still felt their grip, through which a warm, vibrating energy moved, connecting them to the chair. Selma tried to use her analytic skills to observe and understand this new experience, but her panic was thinly veiled, juxtaposed as it was against such exceptional happiness.

Carefully she tested this new reality, still reining in panic. At first she wondered if she had gone suddenly blind, or even if she were dead. Her eyes saw nothing but an increasing torrent of brilliant seething *light* from which she felt herself both spilled and begotten. Disoriented, she directed her gaze to where her invisible fingers gripped the invisible chair, and although she could still see only light, she sensed that there were different depths that composed it. Shocked, she directed her attention to where the mirror was supposed to be, and "saw" herself as a sphere of light, a small darkened area where her eyes and heart might be—as *unity* burst inside her. Joy rose to ecstasy as light roared on in celebration, inside and outside, personal and sublimely impersonal, timely and timeless. Simultaneous to her joy, she knew that the *light* was sentient, expressing as rhythmic, cosmic surge and sound of Godsea itself at high and low tide, various musical currents and leitmotifs coming and going on their own heartbeats. A feeling, intimate as a kiss, ravaged her into invisible frequencies where she was then embraced. Every atom danced, every molecule partook, every subspecies of creature inside her body spawned, even as she was begotten of some yet higher consciousness in whose body she dwelled, as *all* was *light.* *All* celebrated joy past joy, peace past peace, knowingness of "the way it is" past celebration—even as all rests in the Void. Selma laughed out loud as this celebration of unity expressed Itself through her, orchestrated in light currents of hammered dulcimer and chimes, of flutes and drums, of violins with drone strings like some vast motor tuned to intervals unknown, all played across the sough and sound of electricities past the hearts of stars. The secret so simple was revealed; the jest—it had never been hidden. Everything is alive, aware and connected, *no separation.* She was the world and the universe and beyond, knowing all simultaneously. She laughed as her body walked slowly across the room, glory bound and glorified, heading for the bed she could not see.

As she moved, she felt the sanctity of cathedrals and the holiness of new birth. The now tingling burn in her body fanned into an interior fire moving up and outward from her abdomen, even as it raced down from her brain in fiery loops at the same moment. Selma died in splendor, dissolved in light, recognized herself as light which knew her well, like a lover playing on, igniting secret chambers of the heart, wrapping her in its secret fire, lapping at the corners of her brain. Incandescent in this interior and exterior fire, she knew herself holy and fit in the scheme of things. Nevermore could she feel alone, even were she to forget.

At just this moment of immortal recognition in a mortal frame, Selma's body toppled toward the bed she could not see, but which sustained her. Her body felled, face down, as Selma soared, centrifuged as light out the top of her head through the Secret Door—all before her body hit the bed one second later. It was 5:30 A.M. on January 6.

Selma was now out-of-body, wide-awake in that new state, marveling that reality had taken yet another turn! *Kjaere Gud,* she thought, reverting to the Norwegian of her childhood, spoken like a charm in the face of insurmountable mysteries as some use profanity, fervently. For now she could again see objects in her bedroom, which before had blazed in pre-vision light recognitions. Although stepped down from the frequency of primordial light, "objects" still hummed and seethed with strange energies on a different channel than physical reality. In this alternate way of seeing, and being, she found herself hung off the ceiling like a butterfly far above the "other" Selma body that lay in a muddled heap on the bed. She wondered which one of these selves she was, but she guessed it depended on her point of view. She laughed in joy of recognition as she knew she was five in One and the One is the real which is also light in which the five "perspectives" are tucked like a stack of Russian dolls played with by one!

Now she dropped down into what appeared to be a copy of the body on the bed, that is to say, she had a secondary light body that looked just like her physical body. A property of this strange new world was that she could see from any position she could think or expand herself into, thus making her secondary body move, disappear, or reappear. Instantly. Which presented problems, for she found herself batting all over the place, anywhere her attention dribbled, drifted, or wrenched. *Kjaere Gud,* anyhow.

Then, Dr. Selma Rieseseg's disciplined intelligence came into place just as she started to sail feet first out the window. Stilling her thoughts, she slowly, ever so gently, placed her attention back inside her bedroom. And lo, she was there where she had docked her thoughts, safe and sound in a secondary body near the physical one sprawled on the bed. "This being out of body is a bit like death!" Selma thought exultantly. Triumphant at being able to control her emotional and mental environment, which was the key to creating the "objective" events, seemingly, in this new world, she noted that after making the mental postulate to stay put, she could see events that had occurred previously in the room, superimposed like thin ghosts. Even as collaged against the "now," she could see herself a month before, as well as contrasted against earlier this weekend. She also saw herself in the future, in October. Something tried to tell her something about the future, but she didn't want to look. Like a happy child, she wanted to go play with the experience of right now, juggling in and out of these five perspectives she'd just discovered.

The thought came—but what would she do if she were actually dead? With that, Selma found herself being stuffed back into her body. An instant later, feeling vertigo and almost nausea, her body numb, Selma tried to move her head on the bed. She was stunned and the breath knocked out of her, but she was assuredly alive.

◇ ◇

THE DEATHING OF SELMA

It was still the weekend of January 6 when Selma lay listening to the sea sounds. Outside her window morning stirred, the silence of winter and night broken by uncertain twitterings as call after call was answered by first one bird, then another, in a hesitant but mounting exchange across the salt marsh. Selma lay still, weariness and happiness claiming her. She vowed to ever remember the great joy she had experienced in which knowing and participation in the universal lifeplan was revealed as her birthright. Joy alternated with a sense of loss and the yearning for a freedom to be regained, as caught in the body on the bed, she snugged the comforter about her. But for now, she would rest, absorbing this incredible experience. Selma smiled as she slipped into sleep at sunrise, January 7.

At almost noon the same day, Selma woke briefly, totally refreshed, but saddened by a dream of Tom Breacher not being able to quite reach something she attempted to hand him. He would eventually find it, she knew, but her way was easier. Dipping back into sleep, in and out of waking consciousness on an inner tide, she recalled other aspects of the dream. It had to do with something she yet must do with her life. And her death. She saw many people with hands outstretched; it was the eleventh hour. She saw herself putting something into their hands before twelve o'clock struck. Then, in the dream, it was no longer her hand that offered, but that of an unknown, loving, immensely powerful being. The known, but as yet unknown, deeply loved face and form was her last thought as she drifted off into sleep once more.

Selma woke briefly to go to the bathroom and then made herself a cup of hot milk. She drank it slowly, standing at the window, looking out, mulling events, the dream fading. It was again night, the storm was over and the moon shone clear on the fields of new snow framing the sea. It was almost as bright as day, but a shadow version, a kind of Hades, she imagined, in blues and grays with diamond glistening snow. White banked fields ranged out to merge with the beach where dunes of ice crystals lined the dark, open water. The rhythmic sweep of the lighthouse beacon was reassurance that all was as it ought to be this time of night. Resolutely, Selma pushed away the mysteries, and this time slept through until morning, January 8.

The Light Casts Shadows

When she woke she felt wonderful, a welcome change after dragging herself around for the last few months. She closed her eyes as everything that had happened since the telephone call from Dr. Tuchman came back in full detail. There was so much she couldn't explain, yet she was filled with a feeling of good will for all life. Swinging her feet out of bed, she wondered where the spartan part of her that demanded sacrifice and discipline had gone? Laughing, Selma resolved to live a more abundant life, no matter what its duration. She felt so gay that she greeted the houseplants. Even the alien presence she'd sensed in her body lately receded somewhat from this lessening of tension that the light bequeathed.

The question of whether she was enlightened did not occur to Selma. She knew only that she had been pierced by something, solar-dusted to a new way of seeing and being. There would likely be fallout and aftermath, but for now, she enjoyed breakfast on the sunporch, the future rippling from the Light Experience like the sea's reflections on the porch's stucco ceiling. Yet, she knew a part of her—the old, conservative self—wanted her to go back to sleep, to vigorously embrace her former life like a feather comforter, and bury her head in it.

Wriggling her toes inside worn leather slippers, she poured another cup of tea into the porcelain mug which had accompanied her thirty years at Seaward Point, enjoying a feast of milktea, scrambled eggs, toast and raspberry jam.

Selma's profile was especially handsome in a face where delicacy and strength no longer vied with young womanhood's prettiness, but composited with age and experience into distinction and often beauty. The aristocrat, commoner, and peasant's ways were all part of the arsenal of selves at her disposal, tuned now by this weekend's experience to conjure yet another Self from the Original Essence from which she was cast. The Self, now activated and infused in Selma, joined her to another order of human beings from which priestesses and saints, prophets and poets are often drawn. But this Selma did not yet realize, nor did she understand that this new stage of herself might need training even to maintain itself securely. Nor that this new stage would cause changes in the way the old garment of her life fit, changes she had almost taken on before, at least vicariously, but had let go when Josip had gone.

Selma, wrapped in her old blue robe, a survivor of three major relationships, felt her heart and mind melt. Something else broke as well. A peculiar feeling, she thought, and what an odd way to put it, but that was it. She was a survivor of experiences playing through her, mostly in a half-awake state, scarcely the conscious experiencer of the examined life, and she a psychologist!

For the first time, she realized how much her past had held her in a predictable progression of events she called her "life."

The self-insight opened to her last night would take time to sort, even to face. But she knew, inexorably, it would lead her to the examined life, of which the past had to be cleared, aired, and shared, at least with herself as she would try to keep herself awake to life, now. Although it would be painful since the half-life is easier. At first. She sensed, however, that the same events which had gripped her, marching her along from father to husbands and sons, herself somewhere in route, also had clues she and her generation had completely overlooked. How can theory and practice get so separated out from each other and life, she wondered. What a mystery to human life, yet so much is unquestioned as we wander our days, half-asleep.

She recalled the series of five selves or perspectives she experienced in the light-of-herself. Like a stack of Russian dolls, she'd thought at the time, each operated on its own frequency, but somehow the selves were all One as well. She had observed only the one physical body, however, and a similarly shaped, secondary body that she'd later call the "astral." There were "attachments" or perspectives operating through these two bodies, which gave access to memory of all lifeforms lived individually and collectively, as well as archetypes of proto-thought and universal lifeforms. She recalled then, how she had fainted into the bliss of being *light/sound* Itself, in an essence inside her that knew It existed, had always existed, would always exist. This It, she sensed, was the consciousness that first took shape when one woke, or was born—one's sense of existence. It persists consistently whether at 12 or 40 or 60-odd years, no matter how different the body becomes and conditions are. Such as age, she jeered mentally.

Now—as for the human being, Selma rued. Layers of mind and impulses and temperament make us resemble an onion. Peel off one layer, then another, and another, but then where is the onion? The human being, as she had experienced herself, seemed an aggregate of these different layers, rolled up like a snowball of the foods one ate, which went into the flesh of the body, as well as a collection of mental and emotional impressions which lodged in both mind and the secondary body. Some of these impressions were genetically transferred, some came from past lives, some were acquired this life, but all so very many of them were absorbed unconsciously, somewhen, somewhere, not really chosen at all. And then, Selma recalled, she had tasted this exultant other Self, who seemed to run the show, or at least knew what seemed to be going on. Letting that otherself connect with the human self changed a ten watt "normal" person into a hundred watt enlightened person—with more levels to go, she knew.

Suddenly the meld of mind and heart brought a long repressed memory up close, in technicolor, into bright light. Anguish dwelled there, and remorse. For she now saw very clearly the man named Josip whom she had loved and still loved, whom she'd sent away. The toast and jam went dry and tasteless in her mouth as she remembered a breakfast in this room with him a long time ago.

All right, she told herself toughly, living the examined life is going to be hard; there will be diamonds and rust—the light casts shadows, first. So, I will go back and unwind myself—examine me as if I were a new patient. And then the new self may graft on better. She thought of the well-earned rest she was supposed to be taking after New Year's, which so far had been bizarrely strenuous, as she ran the gamut of life and death. She'd call Arne at home and let him know she was all right. He would understand both her silence and her delay. She didn't want to—no couldn't—talk now about what had happened the weekend Tom Breacher died.

• • •

In her past, Selma had revealed most of herself to Arne Thorson—her second husband, amiable, kind, an able lawyer, and a dear friend. Some of herself had been revealed to her first husband, Dr. Rolf Asgaard, twenty years her senior and once her professor of Old Norse at her Lutheran church college. She had two children with him, pursuing a life of quiet desperation at a time it was unfashionable to be both married and a professional; so she had stayed home for years. She had thought she loved Rolf during the course of what can be called a stately and dignified marriage, despite the confusion that resulted from inheriting a life, not choosing it. Although, of course, she thought she had chosen. She had been greatly relieved to move to Connecticut, away from the associations and limits of the past. The elderly Dr. Asgaard, sensing his wife's desolation and need for privacy, procured the house on Seaward Point, as well as their home on the Connecticut River. His sister, Ingrid, came to live with them, assisting during the child-rearing years, so Selma could start a vigorous round of volunteer social work.

Selma had unique opportunities, for when undeclared issues of her inner self became too insistent, she could retreat to Seaward Point. Occasionally she took the children, but most often she went alone. After spending time in the house on the sea, with her books, music, and painting, she returned refreshed, altogether ordinary, Seaward Point being her main eccentricity.

The inaccessibility of Dr. Asgaard's beautiful young wife to any intimacy other than family had been often remarked on in the course of thirty-odd years of marriage, during relationships with three university communities. Outside of this one not uncommendable characteristic, Selma proved obliging or outspoken when it suited her, and along with Dr. Asgaard, enjoyed a conventional university social and cultural life.

The decision to turn Selma's volunteer work into a profession by earning her Ph.D. in psychology marked no real change in their lives. Mark and Erik were grown, Dr. Asgaard had retreated even more into his studies, leaving Selma free to work as a therapist. She was seen less often socially, and rarely entertained any more due to Dr. Asgaard's advancing age and scholarly isolation. Solitude actually suited them both. She spent long hours with patients, as well as maintaining an active interest in the hard-won development of the pioneer hospice program patterned after St. Christopher's in London. Inevitably, she was drawn to address the "death and dying field," as work with the dying came to be known.

Her interest in counseling those with the gravest loss, that of their own lives, Selma attributed to both a need to constantly test herself for eventual handling of like circumstances someday—for all who live, die, biologically speaking—and to her Scandinavian Lutheran upbringing. Her immigrant parents had lost country, family, and perhaps the most devastating loss of all—their language—by immigrating to America. Although the small Norwegian communities maintained a semblance of old country ways, including language, it was not the same, of course. Nor could her father, Pastor Rieseseg, who read and spoke fluent English, but with such a heavy accent as to be unacceptable to second and third generation immigrants, continue preaching in Norwegian in urban areas. So the family moved to a farm community, where he could still be a pastor in his native language, thereby losing touch with friends, music, theater and even the one electric light they'd had in town.

Selma recalled her parents equanimity amid losses, even through her father's liver cancer from which he died at 50. It had been induced, it was thought, by an overdose of X-rays in the days when dosage was unknown. For them there was always in loss something to be regained. Theirs was an attitude of not so much having to get something returned in life, as of finding the means to deal with the situation you were in, as well as always giving. You were to remedy whatever had gone awry, for self or others, if you could, and if you could not, you accepted what occurred with that equanimity again. Even death.

Imbued with this mixture of stoic and charitable as a child, Selma had the stamina to work effectively and compassionately with those who were about to die. It was only now that she realized she missed the inner core of knowledge that supported her parental environment. She'd only copied the outer nordic reserve.

Selma took her graduate degree in psychology before interest developed in the spiritual parameter that connected the death and dying field with consciousness research. She also missed Easlen, Alan Watts, Krishnamurti and the whole era of the 60's and early 70's as if she'd lived in a bubble. This omission in herself was echoed in the case stories of most of her patients. For the longest time she denied, then had to acknowledge, that it was the element of faith, whether structured inside the Norwegian Lutheran form, or not, that her immigrant family had as a resource, and which she and most of her patients did not.

For Selma, one of the most far-reaching repercussions of her unconscious conditioning concerned the way her childhood had been surrounded and infused with active hints about the transcendental side of life, which she either simply did not grasp, or else internalized as "old country" ideas to be left behind in America the beautiful, as second generation immigrants tend to do. Or perhaps, if she did once accept the hints of the esoteric and transcendental world inside the conventional and religious format of her life, she misinterpreted them as "Lutheran," not seeing the transcendental as irrespective of religious form, thus throwing the baby out with the bath water, as it were.

Selma's generation was one of an optimistic scientism, where body and mind were separate, the mind was limited to brain activity, and behaviorism was in vogue as the consensus consciousness of the times. People were clever trainable animals that could be educated to reason without any superstitious nonsense such as religion making them guilty enough to be good. The religious experience of an awake, enlightened being was indiscriminately weighed together in the same basket with cultural religionists of every sort.

During Selma's childhood, she absorbed conflicting information from her parents as most children do. She was resistant to any orthodox religious structure, and although exposed since childhood to her father's mystical bent, she was vastly ignorant of its implications, as well as its difference from the conventional religion which she despised. Her confused response was due partly to her parents' dependency on the congregation's grace for her father's meagre salary. Also, she sensed resentfully, her father had been forced to live a double life, one that was acceptable only if renamed in terms of conventional Christianity. So when Papa did yoga, he was simply doing exercises for his bad back. And if Papa walked barefoot on the grass mornings to obtain the *prana*, or life force, directly, it was called getting inspiration for his sermons. When he meditated, he was praying, and so it went; Buddha was hidden in the bottom drawer, with only Christ making a public appearance. The God her father worshipped who loved Muslims, Jews, Catholics, Blacks, Indians, and even Germans, Selma early understood was not the God of the parish where not even a Swede, not to speak of a traveling Gypsy, was tolerated. But, the peculiar truth was, Mrs. Rieseseg had been too good a salesperson. For Selma really thought her father was doing exercises for a bad back, getting inspiration for his sermons and praying. She never knew there was another scope to his spiritual activities, while he, thinking no doubt that she knew, never thought to correct the situation.

Like most parents, he assumed that when something was discussed in front of a child, especially at the dinner table—which was the cultural exchange center of the day's events about books read, people assisted, letters received—that the child heard and understood, as he did. But that is rarely so across generation lines between parent and child. Even as immigrant parents and first generation children attempt to live in both worlds, where much is cast off in the survival process by the child struggling to adapt, to "fit in" this new world. Thus, many ideas of value to Selma later were lost or misplaced in this immigrant process, until crisis or stimulus re-oriented and surfaced childhood's unconsciously learned information about how the world is. Unraveling this process revealed to Selma most graphically how numerous false, socially compensating personalities get formed early in life in each of us, which deny our original essence.

The Light Experience was such a crisis and stimulus to Selma's awaking, much like the experience associated with a deep, core level near-death has been the stimulus for millions to re-examine their lives during the last decade. Both Selma and the NDEers have had to integrate the Light Experience into their lives, thus shifting toward their original essence and its values of love, wisdom, compassion, rather than the goals and values of the false personalities built to function in a society that maintains what Charles Tart calls "consensus trance."

Pastor Rieseseg no doubt felt his children were getting a liberal education. After all he had told Selma and her brothers about the great spirituality inherent in Persian mystical literature. Some nights he read the *qhazals* of Hafiz and Rumi, some in Emerson's translations along with the psalms of David. He thought he shared his excitement about the ancient tradition of yoga, an atheistic as well as monotheistic system, addressing the nature of being itself. To him yoga was more a psychotherapy than religion in its approach to the subconscious, unconscious, and superconscious potential in humankind.

At dinner Pastor Rieseseg read letters to the family while Selma waited impatiently for him to finish so she could get up, do the dishes, and go off and read. Frankly, she normally blocked out most of this dinner conversation, or secretly nursed a novel in her lap, a fact her mother and brothers well knew. However, Selma did have some memory of the day Papa had almost been silenced. Normally, when he held forth he was uncontested by wife and four children and a Norwegian guest or two. It had been a German from Rome who bested Papa.

The guest was a Catholic Cardinal, a friend Pastor Rieseseg made in his Paris student days. They used German, interspersed with French, to converse, which is another reason Selma did not remember very much of that night except the passion of the exchange and the major topic, although Papa had done a précis afterward for the family in high seriousness.

The topic was reincarnation, an Eastern teaching which had permeated Christian doctrine for five hundred years after Christ until an important church council had it disowned by the Church in A.D. 553, which of course didn't make the teaching untrue. But what a pity the Church had moved against it! Some of the best minds in history believed in reincarnation, Pastor Rieseseg had said, highly excited. His Cardinal friend agreed on that point, but contested him passionately about the church council's act. A disclosure of recent Vatican evidence, he said vehemently, not only admitted the illegality of the supposed church council, but that the issue of the pre-existence of the soul in Origin's teachings had never even been addressed at that council, much less contested! Reincarnation therefore, *never had been anethmatized* in the Catholic Church as had been believed and acted upon by clergy and laity alike for fourteen centuries! Furthermore, he was of the mind, having read in the 1913 edition, Volume IV, of the *Catholic Encyclopedia* on the subject, as well as other reports, that there are simply no technical grounds to bar Catholics from belief in reincarnation. Pastor Rieseseg had been staggered by this news which shifted the whole grounds of Christendom. True, Emperor Justinian was assumed to have taken imperial control of the Church, dictating theological doctrines as well as secular, with serious consequences for 1400 years, but that didn't hold theological water, both men agreed. The rest of the evening was spent imagining what American Protestantism would make of reincarnation. This dreadful mistake, perpetuated by the Vatican, still persists in orthodox Christianity. Christianity, in all its myriad divisions, still mistakenly lumbers on without recourse to the compassionate teaching imbued in reincarnation—which holds that there is more than one life in which to achieve a Christ-like state.

Later, Selma would learn that the Church of England did not feel bound to any policies of the medieval Church councils. Selma wished she could have talked with her father about the impetus toward world unity that Christianity's theoretical acknowledgment of reincarnation would inspire. Religious nationalism would look pretty silly if people realized they might be born a Catholic in one life, a Protestant, Jew, Moslem, Hindu or Buddhist in others!

One other childhood impression had contributed to Selma's resistance to anything of the metaphysical unknown. One day her father had caught her playing with an ouija board she'd ordered through a magazine. "That is no plaything!" he'd thundered, warning her of possession by mischievous sprites and "earth-bound" spirits of people who had died poorly, for whatever reason. Such beings can haunt the scene where the traumatic event that had killed them occurred, mindlessly caught in their fears which produce the hells in which they burn. Or else, he continued, these earth-bound ones were people who did not know they were dead; they haunted the living trying to experience sensations vicariously through them, getting attention by any means possible. Others, knowing they were dead, lied, showed off, or made themselves feel important by impersonating celebrities, thus misleading little girls like her. Selma asked timidly, weren't there any *nice* dead people like Grams? In somewhat softer tones, Pastor Rieseseg told her that usually the nice ones moved higher than earth, and didn't gossip with little girls on a ouija board—he'd tell her more when she was older. She later never asked, and he never volunteered. Her fear of the metaphysical unknown was marked from that day, although repressed and disassociated from her memory. She never realized that this fear was a contributing influence to her compensating, belligerent, behavioristic stance that she identified with until the Light Experience.

A last formidable if unclassifiable event hovered in Selma's memory and then surfaced. Selma was 19 when her father died. Her mother was with him. Afterward, her mother's face was on fire with a joy Selma and her brothers found unseemly, under the circumstances. She'd declared that she had experienced the Christ-light at her husband's death. Nor could she be swayed from her story. At the time, Selma ascribed it to hysteria. Never for one moment did she give her mother's story credence, nor conceive that she herself could ever be wrong in her interpretation of events surrounding Papa's departure. There was an arrogance to the 30's generation, as well as Hepburn-like valor.

Years later, Selma's mother shared with Selma that Pastor Rieseseg had told her he would be with her at her crossing over, or "translation" as he had called death, which he saw as a change-of-state not unlike the melting of ice into water. Furthermore, he told her that human beings had several bodies which survived the death experience, with varying states of consciousness playing through them for use in various worlds and dimensions. These dimensions fulfilled Christ's promise of there being many mansions in the afterlife. After physical death, one occupied one of these bodies, the secondary body, for a time, long or short as the case might be. Then later one died again to that inner astral world, to continue with one's spiritual education, taking yet new forms, either angelic, or back to earth in another physical body. What did Selma think of that? Selma was nonplussed and didn't know what to think, except that it sounded crazy. But she didn't want to tell her mother that. Already she was conscious that belief structures had bearing on the style of one's life and death, whether the beliefs were true or not. There was the point, true or not.

As a psychologist, she later sifted through many levels of being for the truth of herself and others. But the search was elusive and contradictory, until her immersion in pure Essence that was the Light Experience. Having the contrast drawn radically between normal waking life and pure Essence, even if conceptualized afterwards, threw her whole life into a new perspective. Had she not walked out of Plato's cave and seen the shadows of herself for what they were?

Later, Selma, like Sir James Jeans, would come to think the universe was simply a huge thought after all, susceptible to smaller thoughts such as her own. But then, forty years earlier, she asked herself, where on earth had her father learned this sort of thing? It surely hadn't been the seminary! Later, she found out that Pastor Rieseseg had studied with a Hindu holy man turned Christian during his Paris days. This holy man had been called the St. Paul of India—miraculous healings were attributed to him. Several books about this holy man, and yoga, were found in Pastor Rieseseg's library after his death. Needless to say, none of this was discussed in the pulpit, nor was anything more radical than Papa's walking barefoot ever on display to the congregation.

In October

The year Dr. Asgaard died, Selma was pitilessly revealed to herself in an encounter next to terrifying, even as it appeared destined. Almost faithful, domestically speaking, until the end, Selma had stayed through Dr. Asgaard's fatal heart attack. But that year her truest and most faceted self had been shown to her—ignited by a man named Josip who had been at Yale as visiting professor. Extremely provocative as an author and lecturer in consciousness research, especially its relationship to mysticism and the new physics, Josip Vidmar was as personable as he was brilliant. He was the only person other than family to have shared Seaward Point. Arne Thorson, who knew of him, wisely deferred to the past. After all, he had married her, Josip had not.

It was in October, on a sunny day of bright leaves under foot and brisk clear air, that Selma entered the brilliant world from which there was no escape and from which she wanted no escape. At first. She encountered destiny in someone she never dared admit she was waiting for, a person crucial to the emergence of her long camouflaged identity, a key to her awakening, even as he summoned her soul, the soul she disavowed in youth and didn't acknowledge in adulthood, which, without him, she seemed to lose once more. Selma did not ask until too late if it was after all necessary to defend ideas and self-definitions that were, perhaps, no more than unconsciously learned behaviors and reactions—the habitual stances societies and the people in them use to bar the darkness? Easier to let in the light and open the door, but not for some.

They met on the stairs of old North Hall where she was hurrying uncharacteristically late, to a reception in Dr. Asgaard's stead. The reception was to honor the internationally known, if somewhat outrageous, academically and theologically speaking, author of *The Paradigm Shifters*—Josip Vidmar. Many found it astonishing that the divinity school had sponsored him in the first place. But, the man had impeccable connections.

Late quite habitually to his own receptions, the author of the controversy was racing behind her two steps at a time. Hearing the bound of feet and feeling someone's scrutiny, Selma turned at the door to look down at the man racing toward her. She'd flung back the hood of the Mexican sweater belted over outworn trousers that somehow became a style with the gesture. One swatch of hair had come loose, and her square, capable hands absently skewered it into place as their eyes locked, grey-blue and black. Selma felt the shock of the engagement, an impact of fencer's blades, and had an eerie, but swiftly banished thought that she was addressing a holy man, a prophet, but moreover, oh God, that she *knew him*. While Josip had the sudden, disastrous urge to tuck the lock of hair back into place and touch the flawless chamois skin, rosy and so creased and kneaded by time that it appeared as blooming as a child's. Once before, he knew, he had touched her cheek a long time ago.

For ten years he had known that he would somehow meet her again, in the flesh, on this earth and not just in the waking lucid dream and "out-of-body" state where things are closer to a wave frequency, although, like here, they appear solid enough. Shaken and exalted, he saw Selma, with her expression of formidable reserve suddenly changing to that of a startled child, in recognition, as her gaze dropped away under his like a scabbard sword. She almost ran into the hall.

He allowed her to move ahead of him, watching the long stride, and thought of the brief glimpse of her he'd had—brows drawn, lips turned up in the Apollo smile, beautiful in a decidedly archaic way, he thought, with an uncanny innocence, a schoolgirl transported into middle age, out of synchronization somehow.

Josip was on target, for while Selma was known for her bite on public issues, privately she was mild, even old-fashioned and always alone except for old Dr. Asgaard, now the boys were gone—which drove the university gossips to distraction. Meanwhile, Josip thought in an uncharacteristic panic, "Now what? I can't go up to her and say, where have you been all my life?" I don't even know her. Or, he mulled, maybe she is hopelessly pedestrian in her human personality; probably she was married, with luck she was divorced.

Josip scowled at the boy from Action News who waved a microphone in his face, his photographer side-kick grinding away: "Have you found any PSI babies, yet? Any psychic kids from the NDE studies, Professor Vidmar?" Josip answered softly in his accented, polite precise English that masked his rue, that there hadn't been time. The study was just started and would take at least five years for results. The boy looked disappointed, as if he'd hoped for a flying baby, or at least a spoon-bender like Uri Geller in pint size. Josip took the microphone then and made a statement, "The PSI human will mark a contrast as significant and as superior to modern man as did modern man to the Neanderthal, but with considerably more charity!" handing the microphone back, abruptly.

Josip reflected, death is always a means to higher consciousness, whether of a species, in ego-death, or physically, when in the act of dying one is suddenly flung outside the normal space-time constraints into superconsciousness—the clear light. To hold that inner space is the thing, through the buffeting of a series of interfacings and encounters with varying levels of consciousness, as the released kundalini tears you loose from all moorings of ordinary reality.

Moving down the hall, Josip laughed shortly at the thought that, living or dead, the species was moving toward *homo spiritus,* the liberated state in which Soul, the Consciousness Principle, is seen as the substratum and common denominator of all the selves. And there is strong evidence to support that a kind of radical consciousness transformation to that realization is going on at an unprecedented pace, he mulled. Humanity is on the threshold of an evolutionary quantum leap, a Velikovskian shift such as occurs once in a billion years, as the whole Creation moves from low C to high C—a hundredth monkey business to be sure! With millions of NDEers resonating their personal transformation collectively into Mother Earth's biofield in a morphic resonance intent on activating even the sleepyheads! The method must be resonance, he thought, from higher to lower, and the means must be kundalini energy, recorded in every ancient tradition and now being rediscovered by the West! And we're all going to get there, soon or late, he thought. He brushed away the microphone the youngster shoved at him, these thoughts unsaid, and hurried after Selma, as if to intercept her.

Selma slowed her stride after first break-necking down the hall to get away from Josip, partly so she could eavesdrop, partly for dignity's sake, since many of Rolf Asgaard's colleagues disapproved of her enough as it was, not that she cared, but for his sake. She felt Josip coming and speeded up. Just as he was about to overtake her, she slipped through the door and moved swiftly toward familiar faces, away from this presence she could feel as palpable behind her as if he had touched her. A faint tremor went through her as she tried to dislike him. Why the cheek of the man to dispose of humankind in one fell swoop as if, she thought angrily, we were brutes, Neanderthals indeed! She tried to disapprove, for this was, of course, Josip Vidmar, whom she recognized from recent news articles featuring his already controversial arrival in the United States last week.

But, she admitted grudgingly, pictures had not prepared her for the tangible shock such power, innocence, and beauty evoked, charged by the man's sheer presence, making him larger than life. His eyes remained to haunt her. Now she understood the reaction of the media, groupies and cultists on one hand, sober academics on the other, as he was claimed and disclaimed, even as several celebrities had taken him up. It was in the news, as well as in the supermarket tabloids, that Princess Xenia had thrown herself at him, calling him a natural prince, indeed *homo noeticus,* itself, inviting him on the royal yacht. She wondered if Vidmar had gone?

In addition to his arresting appearance, Vidmar had a combined academic background of physics, endocrinology, and anthropology. He had studied with Joseph Campbell, was a friend of the historian, Matthew Gottlieb, and studied with Krishnamurti and the physician sage, Ramamurti Mishra, in the 70's. While David Bohm, the English post-quantum physicist whose work Vidmar posited as being very close to explicitly dealing with consciousness, with his implicate and explicate order perhaps providing the beginning of a physics of consciousness, along with young Rupert Sheldrake, had also influenced Vidmar's ideas. The integration of transpersonal psychologies and spirituality, yet another angle to human transcendence, Vidmar had explored in his own right, with the exception of Ken Wilber's work, but more at a "do it yourself," nuts and bolts level—like his friend Bentov.

In the 70's, Vidmar had been fascinated by Itzhak Bentov's thinking, and had been one of the many to urge Ben to present his insights concerning a mechanics of consciousness as well as a mechanics of creation. Bentov had gone on to write *Stalking the Wild Pendulum* and *The Cosmic Book*. The latter would have been an interrupted journey if his wife, Mirtala, hadn't finished it from his notes after his death. Vidmar had then interspersed his quest for PSI human exemplars in a field trip with Mircea Eliade, that grand old man one of the few in the field he hadn't actively studied with.

What Vidmar had, however, in array of degrees and experience, as well as the probing, unorthodox "frontier" activity of his mind, was formidable, if not downright Leonardian, Selma readily recognized. Now that he surfaced from his relative obscurity so suddenly, and with such charisma and stir—as if he were a natural phenomenon, like a volcano's eruption or a tidal wave—he would surely run his course, at least socially, Selma reasoned. But she shivered as she knew this was not an end but just the beginning.

Vidmar had his back to her. He was being twittered over possessively by the wives of the chairmen of various departments, who were also surreptitiously trying to be seen whenever the Action News team ran the cameras. Selma snorted appreciatively in amusement and Josip turned around and caught her eyes, his own dancing. The laughter died out of of both of them, as for a faltered moment he reached out his hand, then thought differently, for he was on camera.

Persistently, the lanky youngster from Action News held the microphone toward Josip. The ploy worked and he took it as he settled his large, well-built body in the gray baggy corduroys on a low table. He wore his clothes as if he had nothing on, un-self-consciously, actually indifferently, Selma noted, his movements contrasting against her husband's formal precision.

Selma knew from reviews of Vidmar's work that Rolf had read to her, that Vidmar based his case for the existence of an already extant *homo spiritus* on extended field studies during the 70's of mystics, yogis, saints, and even an avatar, whatever that was. He called the avatar, and those like him through history, "white crows" which he said were not just white-washed black ones, like so many gurus and swamis in the West! He had tossed that off at a news conference, which was aired on the 11:00 o'clock news no less. On a talk show the following morning, Vidmar claimed a particular white crow as both his teacher and the highest exemplar of his thesis. And quipped that the PSI human, or *homo spiritus/homo noeticus* was being born and bred in every corner of the world, even Brooklyn! In fact, this evolutionary shift was happening planet wide, either induced by an already awakened teacher, or spontaneously in NDE, through meditation, religious and yogic disciplines, transpersonal techniques, and in other ways too numerous to mention at this time—"But, read my book!" he'd urged engagingly, the brilliant smile penetrating every living room across the nation. This white crow of his, and indeed, any fully realized being, he maintained, was several cuts above the PSI human which was his usual interest, as well as being instrumental in "hatching" the PSI human, big time. When asked if the pun was intended as a play on the avatar's name, Josip had just chuckled, as if to say—"Wouldn't you like to know?" And didn't comment.

"William James summed it up," Vidmar had told the newsman, "If you wish to upset the universal proposition that all crows are black, it's enough if you prove one single crow to be white! And Sathya Sai Baba is my big white crow!" he chuckled. Selma had shivered then, her anger draining out. She was starting to feel suffocated, surrounded by "all this," which she couldn't even escape at home. Before the broadcast, her husband told her over dinner that he'd received a letter from a friend of his, about this white crow of Vidmar's. His friend, the parapsychologist Erlendur Haraldsson, was doing a study on modern miracles associated with this same teacher. *Kjaere Gud,* would life never go back to the way it had been? Selma shivered again.

Now here was the man right in front of her—staring at her intensely, unavoidable. And looking like a grownup cherub, with a sweetness, yes, a lovableness, she had to say, such as a child often has. A beautiful child. Yet, noting Josip's muscular physique, she didn't find it hard to imagine him traveling alone into forbidden mountains, or the heated oven of the Indian interior to meet with little known sages; moreover, being met by some as an equal. She wondered what secrets lay behind his black eyes with their slavic inscrutableness and almond shape; brows thickly grown, a dark blue shadow under his close shave, the earlobes showing from beneath the untidy curls?

His black eyes had a sheen when he began to talk that scared Selma. "Why, he's a fanatic," she thought, "or maybe he's mad." But she knew he was all too sane for comfort, while he conveyed such conviction when he spoke, he made his preposterous statements sound reasonable, everyone nodding with agreement, even his enemies. She detected irony in the glance he sent her as he continued.

"These PSI humans have been here all the time," he said, as if there had been no break, "but in such few numbers that the normal evolutionary patterns of *homo sapiens* were not interfered with by what *could* be seen as an alternate race of people in whom the fabled kundalini energy was fully awakened." He paused for effect, looking around at the various faces, bored, interested, celebrity seekers, skeptical, and then back to

Selma who nodded in spite of herself. "These few were usually designated as priests, or holy men. Some were made via various forms of consciousness transformation embodied in the esoteric techniques of the enormously sophisticated psychotherapies that Eastern traditions actually are. Their aim is always the state of liberation, or free-flowing consciousness, unobstructed by the linear time-space we acknowledge here as real. My book goes into that in great detail. While some of this new race of people are born—such as the new evolutionary step on the ladder I call the PSI human—there are others even more advanced who, having already climbed the ladder of consciousness, are descended to specifically help younger brothers and sisters into the PSI human state, thus stopping the endless rounds of incarnation. These are high level masters and avatars, of which there are many degrees.

"A true avatar, however, is what's called a *prevesa* incarnation, like Rama, Christ, Krishna—which occurs without physical assistance from the father. The virgin birth, according to the Hindu sages, is a true phenomenon in which the Omniwill imprints Itself in human form. Such a being, resonating as it is to the vibrating field of the universe and/or cosmos, is not genetically programmed in the usual way, hence its designation as a total Advent, or sinless incarnation. The avatars, although they are rare birds indeed —" Selma winced again at the phrase—"have been historically visible, such as Rama, and the various Christs, or Vishnus, including Jesus, around whom the New Testament was written. While Krishna is one of the most spectacular avatars, immortalized by the Bhagavad Gita. The point is, the entire cosmic buddy failsafe system is planned evolutionarily and individually, although no major avatar until now has had the advantage of a planetwide media network. If this white crow wants to go public, the conditions are available." Josip was amused by the look on the boy reporter's face. "Yes, some of the things you learned in Sunday School are actually true! Not just fairy tales. But not all, to be sure." Selma's face was noncommittal.

"At any rate, sporadically through history, there have been these beings studded like constellations in the generally night sky of earth. Or else some of their students would surface as leaders—such as Plato, Alexander the Great, or Leonardo, and others too numerous to mention. Perhaps the best of the human race has always been these few—beings beyond our normal self-imposed limits of what is real—initiates of a higher order. But now, in this great birthpang of evolution, many such beings are being born in various ways and of varying levels of higher consciousness, all adding to the critical mass sufficient to lead to a chain reaction in which everyone makes the transition.

"Just one of the ways evolution is furthering itself is by this rash of near-death-experienced people, which amounts to millions of people on every continent. These people have been exposed to death's liberating libation before death—and are ever after changed. The NDE is, as you know, why I am here today. Yet, nearly dying in order to enter into some degree of exposure to altered states is a very rough entry! Meditation, especially under the guidance of a true teacher, although less dramatic, will get you there if you persist. Most people don't want to. They'd rather take a pill. Then sometimes the cosmos decides that it's time for them, and bango! spontaneous kundalini arises, by whatever means, or a truck, a heart attack, or whatever ushers them into the Light through near-death or even real death, which, after all, is just a change of state. But it is all the same Light, or universal ground of being the founders experienced—whatever the prismatic play through the spectrum of culture."

Vidmar's high-handed use of history, especially concerning his theory of the avatars' role through time—although supported by the historian, Matthew Gottlieb, and to some extent, Joseph Campbell—offended many people, as did his casual banter, cajoling and forceful by turns about grave matters. He reveled in it. While, for others, his peculiar use of language was fascinating, interspersed as it was with scientific jargon, slang, or abstruse literary references, all charged with a persuasive charm. Partly it was due to his accent, but most of all it was that nothing and everything seemed sacred to him, his handsome face lyric or ironic, by turns.

Silent for a long moment, he stared at everyone speculatively, until they dropped their eyes at his intensity. The beauty of his face, its now angelic, seraphic look, the black eyes shining, gave aesthetic credibility to what in a homelier man might not be heard, Selma knew. Although she doubted very many understood him. She certainly didn't, nor did she want to. He sounded plain crazy with all this. But the media was eating it up and ready to fly a CBS team to India to interview the white crow in question.

Vidmar quipped, the intonation and accent, although not the meaning, going straight to her heart, looking straight at Selma: "By the way, nothing would please me more than if some bright boy would take the Tibetan teachings of the Great Liberation by hearing—the oral instructions of how to regulate personal consciousness into universal consciousness during the dying process, as well as the afterlife and rebirth—and do a Reader's Digest version for ordinary people! Since death is *so* democratic on this planet, physically speaking, one might as well use it to take a crack at liberation, or becoming *homo noeticus*. One might not become liberated, but a better rebirth is surely assured by so doing. Or," he tossed off casually, "since it all has to do with resonating to the higher harmonics of the Divine, you can hitchhike on the vibe of a realized teacher at death—in safe passage as far as you want to go! At any rate, it is the near death and the annual NDE conference, as well as my book, that has brought me here today, my friends." He shrugged with a rueful look, as if to say he'd gone too far with these people. He had seemingly re-routed, but never changed course, Selma recognized, almost with amusement, pulling everyone along with him, as usual.

"We have to ask several questions. First, what is happening with NDE, which my esteemed colleague Ken Ring calls, in *Heading Toward Omega*, a generic member of what ordinarily is classified as spiritual experience. But, moreover, how does this advertent or inadvertent widescale awakening process operate in the evolutionary scheme of things? Then ask yourself what does it mean that eight million people by Gallup Poll have experienced NDE and been plunged willy-nilly with no warning into altered states, some permanently? Now ask yourself—suppose it's true that we are still evolving? Wouldn't this raise the questions of a target?" Josip shook his head and smiled his dazzling smile that seemed to pierce straight through to the heart of everyone there. Someone inhaled sharply; he had the group's undivided attention now.

"One question we are also posing, since we are dealing with millions of NDE-awakened people worldwide, which my book addresses, is—does this newly imprinted, encoded, entrained nervous system register itself genetically? Will it reproduce? In some cases, NDE people revert to former world views with vengeance—as if desperately trying to go home again to what they once knew—but their genes may still carry the encodement to higher consciousness. Or it might be that morphic resonance alone will be the triggering device for a humanity whose nervous system is already fully equipped for higher consciousness. I suspect we'll find *homo noeticus* being both born and bred—since organizing fields precede manifestation.

"There are some spectacular NDE survivors on record—some of them going from ordinary, mediocre life performance to almost genius level, intellectually and psychically—one naturally hopes they can transmit genetically. Their gifts range from the highest yogic psychic powers on down to more modest capabilities. These powers are normally attained only after years of immersion in the esoteric disciplines designed to arouse the nervous system, or kundalini, as some traditions call it, so that it can process higher reality. And normally, very few people attain these states or even taste them. But now there are millions! It's simply staggering. The NDEers are likely the largest undeclared religion in the world!

"Furthermore," Vidmar added, his enthusiasm carrying him, "they may well be to our planet what the hundredth monkey was to his islands. You remember the story?" Almost everyone nodded, though he noted Selma seemed not to comprehend. He shook his head with some impatience, and continued, "The hundredth monkey represents the critical mass necessary to create a strong enough field for the morphic resonance of a consciousness change to occur world-wide, as human transforms to PSI-human. But," he added tersely, "they're going to need some midwifing, and some guidance as to how to run their juiced up engines—both of consciousness and the body. For they've moved from a Model T to a rocket, almost overnight. The symptoms of kundalini range from the appearance of motor-disability, heatrushes, or even psychosis in the fledgling stages, to saint and sage at maturity, with people sprawled the gamut in between. The medical schools should really get Dr. Lee Sannella to talk on *The Kundalini Experience*—the physical and mental symptoms. Even as, though the human body *is* wired for higher consciousness, the switch has never been thrown for the vast numbers of people entering these states through NDE. It could be mass culture shock.

"Without some training—and probably therapy—by sympathetic, open-minded psychologists or psychiatrists—who are willing to lay aside their own prejudicial and biomedical Newtonian models of what is normal—many of these newly born NDE survivors are going to have a hard time. They have already had a hard time getting used to having a new perspective and

using it effectively in life. The planet desperately needs these
people to be utilized—not abused, shunned, or made out to be
freaks. They, in turn, will midwife others as well as devise new
structures based on their PSI-human experience.

"Meanwhile, the traditions in Buddhism, Taoism, Yoga,
Vedanta and so forth—are really psychotherapies aimed at *consciousness transformation*, rather than the religions or philosophies we usually think they are in the West. NDE people,
literally flung into this superconscious philosophical and psychological state without a teacher, without preparation, need the
guidance from the sophisticated, elaborately precise maps and
frameworks of the psyche that these ancient traditions can offer.
These Eastern maps and frameworks of reality are coded culturally and can be adapted for the Western mind.

"Keep in mind that the founders of all the great religions
experienced reality straight, but there seems to be an inevitable
refraction that takes place—a Zeitgeist—for followers rarely
experience the pinnacle scaled by the master, and they resort
to the prism distortion—teaching hearsay evidence from the
master—as they understood it—as the truth, or as the only
true way. They set up elaborate rules and regulations, and the
information is passed down in their culturally coded framework.
However, there are remarkable similarities in all religious traditions, and the truth is there, shrouded in mystery. But it's there.
Modern physics is heading in a direction that can make this
ancient information readily recognizable if we remember a few
basics—which I've oversimplified, granted," Vidmar continued,
his face alight with animation.

"Remember that what we know of the universe is vibrating,
whether planets, cells, molecules, or atoms; even as we are starting to see that the universe is also a vast holograph, shot through
with interference patterns that code all possible manifestation
patterns. Most spiritual systems start with Creation already having occurred, out of which things happen in a certain space-

time framework. The speed of light, which Einstein said was a constant, is only one of a whole harmonic series of velocities of vibratory energy. Maybe God moves so infinitely fast, It is in all places at the same time and back again, and hence omnipresent." Vidmar raised eloquent eyebrows and resumed, "Anyhow, this infinite vibrating universe is organized according to mathematical, harmonically resonating intervals, with huge carrier waves connecting these intervals in what might be called an outward bound and homeward bound motion. Some systems call these mighty currents light or sound. But experience can prove what the ancient sages knew and practiced—that they connect these harmonic, holographically resonating intervals. That is what is meant by the so-called planes and subplanes, the heavens, hells or purgatories of esoteric literature in our religious traditions. While the various bodies, or fields, of a human being correspond to—and operate on—many levels—from the dense physical to the most subtle and spiritual."

Vidmar saw derision on some faces, confusion on others, and pointedly noted, "This is relatively incomprehensible to someone absorbed in the Newtonian model of the universe, separated from Source and the consciousness that animates us. But let's take this table here. Solid as a rock, huh?" There was a nervous titter in the group, for they knew what he was going to say—everybody knew matter was simply mostly empty space. "Yes, matter is mostly empty space, but what makes matter organize in the first place? We think that there are fields of electromagnetic energy—prana, the yogis call it—that focus atoms along certain force fields like a magnet will focus iron filings. After the death of the physical body, these organizing fields remain—subtle bodies as it were—which can operate on corresponding subtle planes. And somehow, whether in the body or out of it, we have equipment in our endocrine systems and the subtle forms corresponding to it—called the seven chakras— which can process holographically transmitted information from higher planes down into the human system. These chakras—when awakened to full power—transfigure people—change them—and they realize that the organizing principle of the universe is love, or expansion toward the Absolute." No one breathed in the long silence that followed.

He went on, "It is my experience that after the chakras are opened, usually by arousing kundalini energy, this huge current of energy in the spine is somehow also a carrier wave holographically correspondent to the Sound Current, which runs smack dab through the middle of the universe, and then turns back upon itself, homeward bound. So maybe the means to knowing and processing reality is also smack dab in the middle of your spine? I think we see the same phenomenon in the way the subtle bodies of a human being operate. The whole auric field is ovoid, like an egg, with a positive and negative current lacing it together electromagnetically. The physical body, although the only thing visible to us, can be considered something like a skeleton of the real body, which is egg-shaped. Like a universe," he mused, thinking of how he'd experienced, with his friend Bentov, the universe in the form of a cosmic egg, just like Sathya Sai Baba had told even the parapsychologists. "Such a shape is considered sacred geometry, representing the whole of Deity, at least of that universe.

"The point is that all life is linked by the law of affinity and harmonics, or as above, so below, as the ancients called it. Everywhere in nature we see reflections of the universe's sound current. The implication is, of course, that the human being is made in the likeness of God, and that the human, therefore, is not a separate self, divided from the consciousness that animates us." Vidmar surveyed the group thoughtfully. "I'll share a secret—wisdom is attained when you understand the cosmic egg. Really, in a world where the behavior of subatomic particles depends on whether or not they are being watched, we have to figure sooner or later that consciousness itself is the prime mover of creation. And it becomes the means by which we can observe and alter our own destiny. *We have a choice in our own self-creation!*" Unwilling to say any more on record, Josip handed back the microphone with a smile that lit up both his face and the youngster's. "Can I have your autograph?" the boy muttered, rummaging in his camera bag for a well-thumbed copy of *The Paradigm Shifters.* Josip complied and patted the youth's shoulder.

Selma lifted questioning, suddenly wintery eyes which met his again with a shock that jolted them both. He knew, and she knew, but neither acknowledged it by as much as a flicker of an eyelid. In a daze she walked to the refreshment area, mechanically returning the greetings of several faculty members who asked about Dr. Asgaard, who had not been feeling well lately.

Josip felt loneliness and desolation sweep over him as she walked away, despite the solicitous ministerings of the wife of his sponsoring department's chairman, who brought him crackers, liver pâté and a glass of wine. He ate a cracker and played with his wine glass, being both a vegetarian and a nondrinker, although as a Slovenian Yugoslav, he'd enjoyed his wine not so long ago.

Josip slipped into reverie for a moment. He thought of the teacher he'd found—or who, rather, found him—after years and years of Josip's hearing about him. Like anything else, Josip surmised, when you know it you know it, and enroute, you don't even recognize what it is you are looking for because you are blocked by your own mental prejudices and defenses! Josip thought himself to be open to every possible evidence for this evolutionary step forward that he could find in the Near East, the East, the Far East. And all the while, the exemplar *par excellence* he'd written off as a fraud on hearsay evidence. It would be funny, if it were not almost tragic. Well could Josip understand the resistance of ordinary people to what he represented, by seeing his own resistance to further development written so plainly in his recent past. There was, however, an old saying he took comfort in. "When the student is ready, the master will come!"

He'd heard tales of a miracle man often called the Christ of India by some, and an Alexander the Great in his ability to organize and inspire people. Some people swore this man could duplicate Christ's miracles and had even raised the dead, that he was the world teacher prophesied by Mohammed.

Yet Josip cynically kept up his resistance. While, he thought resentfully, if a yogi truly had such an embarrassing string of paranormal tricks to his name, he would be a fraud of a *different* kind, violating the spiritual law that forbids yogis and seekers to practice publicly. Whatever *siddhis,* or psychic powers, this man had, he would have perjured them! Later, when they finally met, Josip was told, "Ah, but I am no yogi, I am no seeker—this is my expression, my love, my play; it is natural to me!" As he wagged his finger under Josip's nose, chidingly, with a sweet smile. Then, somewhat more forbiddingly, he rebuked, "You did not recognize me in all my guises and disguises! I am every jivan mukta you meet, every true teacher, every blade of grass. Call me by any name-of-God and I will answer!"

Meanwhile when Josip thought of him, he reasoned that surely if this man were so successful at defying physics, science would have discovered him, trying at least to accuse him of fraud! Somehow, it also escaped Josip that it hardly followed that a charlatan with millions of followers would start universities and primary schools, trade schools, eye clinics, create a good works brigade of boy and girl scouts, and collect devoted followers from the highest echelons of government and education who implemented his Education for Human Values program, in most of the states of India. During the forty-odd years of his teaching, this program permeated almost every district in India, graduating four generations of intellectually and spiritually educated people. He taught that *dharma* was foremost in human affairs, dharma being the practice of making right choices and practicing right doing with love being the ground rule of Reality. The graft-infested, eroded dregs of Indian classical culture which had bred with the worst of the modern West were now being spiritually reborn largely due to his influence, through a return to dharma.

Over the years, Josip continued to meet people who had been touched by this man, touched so deeply that often their lives had been changed spontaneously, overnight. As if somehow simply being in this man's presence had triggered an awakening at some deeper level of their being. Josip resisted direct encounter until Bogdaya, 1973. Then, he had taken a room near the monument commemorating the Buddha's enlightenment under the Bodhi tree. Meditating in its shadow, he passionately focused on his own desire for that great enightened state and responsibility. He was on his way to Dharmsala, where he and one other European had been given permission to study with a renowned student of an exalted Tibetan Rinpoche, due to arrive at any moment from Nepal. Josip had been waiting for the fellow professor for several weeks now.

Because he was sick, he spent most of his days in a small dreary room. One day as he lay on the bed drenched with sweat, wondering how much longer until his companion arrived, a knock sounded at the door. Confused in the heat, dizzy with the effects of dysentery, Josip stumbled to the door to find a small, graceful man in swami orange. Despite his small stature to Josip's six feet, he somehow met Josip's eyes steadily in the most charming and radiant of exchanges, as he handed Josip a telegram. Josip was somewhat taken aback, for since when did a postman look like a swami and wear an Afro hairdo—in fact, when did swamis wear Afros? At which moment, an electrical storm surged through Josip's being in a startled knowingness of *who* stood before him. Josip shook like a leaf in a wild storm of recognition that racked him innerly, into which he dissolved.

The soft voice spoke tenderly, "Surrender is the sweetest way, my dear one."

Then the vision in orange with the beautiful face and the look of father, the presence of immense authority, as well as all radiance and all goodness was gone, leaving the charged atmosphere delicately jasmine scented. Tears on his cheeks, Josip clutched the telegram. His colleague was not coming after all. Josip packed his small bag, heading for the train station. Embarked, he traveled deep into the interior of India. Days later, unshaven, stinking in the heat, but radiant with joy, he reached Bangalore. Upon inquiry, he was told that a cab was the surest way to travel to the ashram, Prasanthi Nilayam.

It was August 1971 when Josip and his driver started out on what began as a road, but which soon was less than a path through the empty red clay hills. Hours later they drove into the straggling little village of Puttaparthi, his taxi careening into the ashram proper, morning pink stained the hills. It was already hot. In those days there were just a few hundred people living or visiting there. Josip silently joined the knot of men clustered to one side of what he surmised was a temple. The women were grouped on the other side. Suddenly, the man he sought appeared, seeming at first to be surrounded by a large, sun-colored flame in an arena of white sand. Then Josip saw the man inside the huge aura gently swaying, and was riveted by a connection which started in his heart and spread through his whole body, embracing the whole assembly as well.

The teacher began his circumambulation of the arena, going first to the women's side. An already brilliant sun almost whited out his form against an equally brilliant expanse of sand, until suddenly he stood in front of Josip in that serenity he wears, his hair fairly crackling with power. He conveyed the leashed power and grace of a dancer, as well as bull-like strength and the elephant's steady, implacable will and immensity, although he was not tall. His forehead was broad, eyebrows heavily drawn above wide-set brown eyes, the blue-black of the closely shaven cheeks belying an almost feminine delicacy. Josip scented jasmine as he had in Bogdaya. The firm, delicate brown hand made what Josip would come to know as a characteristic motion in the air, gray ash appearing in his right palm which he extended to Josip. "Eat it," he said in Slovenian, "It will be good for you," he continued banteringly in the home dialect of Josip's village of Dragočajna. Humor and joy was in their homecoming and mutual recognition. Josip laughed with delight, smiling at the man who had been his teacher all the time, Sathya Sai Baba, and all the other names addressed to him through history; but that was yet to come. Josip remembered the day.

While now, far away in America, another chapter had begun at the reception as he again met another being—long awaited yet unknown until today. Her name, Selma Rieseseg.

• • •

Now, he intentionally drifted over to where Selma stood absently sipping a glass of wine. The group that surrounded him moved, too, unaware of anything but the random cocktail flow. He watched her watching him, and felt her making a decision, closing him out as dangerous. But he knew she would speak. She shook her head, as if to clear it, oblivious of the people crowding around Vidmar, some of whom were becoming aware of a certain drama playing out. Those who knew her, knew there might be blood, for she could be cantankerous in her way, very set in her views. Not for her the implications of a quantum physics of consciousness! To Selma, mysticism or any taint of it was unscientific. So what was to be made of a man like Josip? She challenged him of necessity, her resistance rising up in her, bringing out the Norwegian accent that only emerged when she was upset. She queried, "How do you *know* this?" Meaning by what authority did he speak? She marshalled her defenses.

As she spoke, her eyes had gone almost hostile, hopeless, gray as winter, belied by the childishness and charm of her hair having again slipped down over one ear. Her hands drew the neck of her sweater closer, guarding her throat. So, he thought, she's not so secure, but she is going to fight. He was so close he could see the down on her cheek, the creped skin of her throat draped gently, but not unbecomingly, upon the muscular column in the most astonishing mixture of old and young in one person he had ever experienced. It devastated him, this vulnerability of the body to age, suffused and interpenetrated by spirit that most people never know until they are released by death—and then they forget—reborn once again. This unknown woman, whatever else she knew or did not know in the realm of intellectual knowledge, knew nothing of the wisdom of her true nature, nor even of the subtle bodies in which she and he had already met, or the special space in him that only her frequency fit—no other.

He sensed correctly, that Selma was not much for the sacred. In her world, the sacred was either properly contained in those edifices the ignorant utilized to habitually attend formal church services, or was dismissed altogether. So much of human activity, Josip thought in unaccustomed despair, is merely unexamined nonsense, merely a reaction to something someone said before, often a parent, which is then accepted, or rejected, often repressed, then reprojected. The resistance or acceptance comes around in new disguise, monitored by consensus with the time lived in. Selma was different only in degree and kind from those who absorbed prejudice totally unconsciously. Somehow he'd hoped she'd be different.

Josip chose his words carefully, anticlimactic to the air of expectation in the group. "If Madame would but be so kind as to read my work first, before lodging her . . . ," he sought for a word, kind, but firm enough to deal with this kind of resistance, which was ever over-stimulated by journalism's rash interpretations of his theory. These days no one read books for accurate information, they read reviews.

Josip finally found the word he wanted in English, after having exhausted the slavic languages of his birth, Spanish, German, some Urdu, as finally, the English word came "... complaint? You will share your complaint *after* you have read my work, yes ... ?" His black eyes questioned quietly, well within his rights. It was after all, a reception for his book that she was invited to, nor was it compulsory that she attend!

Although Selma had spoken for the group, emotionally, especially for the Divinity School, everyone knew a rebuke when they heard one. They stepped back from her like school children pull away from the one the teacher is reprimanding. Josip also noticed a mood of mean satisfaction that Selma had been silenced. He wondered if it did not partially derive from some of the men's jealousy that she would not deal with them? Her cool remoteness had not escaped him, nor that she was the local character who usually got away with it, but now suddenly had not!

Josip took away the implied rebuke with unselfconscious graciousness, which itself was a teaching, and picked up a book to give to her. Their eyes again met, energy launching between them. In hers now was a mixture of wry amusement at her own put-down, and a grudging thanks for his generous and good-natured handling. As well as perception of his evasion tactic. Almost as if she saw through his eyes, or as if he had somehow seen through hers, she observed how he had refused to play either upon, or with, her partial, mostly erroneous knowledge of his position. She knew she had no right to attack something she did not know, but she'd had to, in self-defense. But which "self," then? Selma found her hands fumbling as she took a twenty-dollar bill from her shoulder bag. With a faint shrug of his shoulders and shake of his head, Josip declined, and with a slight bow, presented the book to her which became a conferring of favor. There was a pent up almost audible sigh from some of those who had hoped for the equivalent of a cock fight. Josip tightened his lips just a little, repressing a smile, as he turned to autograph another book for someone who likely would get as far as the *New York Times* book review he knew was coming. It did not escape Josip that Selma did not ask for his autograph before she left.

After the reception, Josip Vidmar made a hasty, discrete inquiry of his friend, the NDE specialist, thereby getting Selma Rieseseg's name and some of her history. His friend lifted his eyebrows in surprise, just as discretely, at the request. The following day, Selma was not at all surprised to hear Josip's soft, foreign sounding voice ask if he might meet her for lunch, when, and if she would be so kind as to bring his book, he would gladly autograph it. Again, the presumption of the man and the fitness of it all confounded and charmed Selma. She laughed and agreed to the unheard of—to meet him for lunch at a dinner theater on the river near Seaward Point. Which is the way the inevitable began.

Estuary

The following Friday found Selma at a table in the restaurant's garden area, staring at the river. She luxuriated in an October sun as benign as August's. Deep in reverie, she started when he called her name. She smiled up at him, last week's match temporarily, at least, forgotten. The river was as blue as her eyes, Josip noted, and had white sails flagged like her hair. He was always going to remember her that way, striding the deck of her life, being the river and the sail as well.

She'd ordered tea and he did the same. A long, but amiable silence drew to completion when she spoke first, characteristically blunt. "Why did you ask to have lunch with me, Dr. Vidmar?" In that moment her resemblance to an archaic Greek statue was pronounced, Josip continued his observation, especially when the brows were drawn, the nostrils almost flared, her mouth upturned still.

"Well, Dr. Rieseseg," he bantered, "how could I not? Certainly, I didn't want to leave a lovely lady with such finality. Gentlemen are supposed to save ladies in distress, not create their distress!"

With the look of an impish, aging child taking away the classic severity of her face, she leaned onto her forearms and returned, "Then, what if the lady in question helped create that distress?" Her eyes regarded his levelly with no coquetry, or bristle, her guard relaxed. Some conversation later, the waiter returned for their luncheon order. Josip ordered a once favorite wine in a festive, reckless mood, his usually serious face lit with smiles.

Thus began a charmed afternoon of talk ranging from childhood experiences in the European tradition they'd both known in their respective fashions, then onto his boyishly exuberant sharing of his experiences with altered states. He told the dramatic stories of men and women he had known who exhibited the awakened kundalini energy—PSI humans en route to godhood, he said. Atheist that she was, Selma winced at such heresy. However, she listened in growing wonder, although sometimes she scarcely understood a word she heard, lost in a reverie induced by the cadence of his voice, caught in his magnetic presence like a moth in the flame. Her attention strayed to imagining how his silky hair would feel. Selma's heart felt jumbled, as if it were dissolving in her middle somewhere, a situation which shocked one who so prided herself on her control, now rapidly being lost. No, it was already gone and she didn't care, at least for now. His obsidian, coptic eyes, liquid as oil in the icon-like face with the perfect mouth he was so un-self-conscious of and she so conscious of, leaned toward hers, as making a point, he reached out for her hand. And didn't let her go immediately, nor did she remove it, energy throbbing from palm to palm.

Josip, rapt in delight that she would have lunch with him in the first place, which by now had ranged into dinner with the theater performance about to begin, was equally taken. Earlier they had moved inside the dinner theater, when the sun dropped and the air chilled. Now with the room filling rapidly, they decided to go.

Josip wasn't thinking quite clearly; in fact he was babbling. Nor was it the unaccustomed wine that intoxicated him. It was joy, the joy of just being near this woman he had not dared to believe existed on the earth, actually incarnated. While she who had been lost was found and sat in front of him—and now . . .

Once before, years before this, he had met her in the out-of-body state. There they had promised each other to try to meet physically wherever, whenever. That had been ten years ago. Now here she was—somewhat older, but still unmistakably recognizable. She was, as we all are, what Robert Monroe would call a curl, or a personal soul, but one whose specific frequency meshed with his. Here, in 3-dimensional reality, she appeared in a body-construct; there, in multi-dimensions, she appeared as an image, as well as closer to the original wave frequency through which beings recognized and were recognized by each other in inner plane reality and dimensions.

They both stood up to go with the same thought, mesmerized by each other, he knowing why, she not knowing anything but that he was the most devastating and beautifully perfect man she had ever known. And that she trusted him, despite his wild talk. Her long repressed hunger for heart and soul connection with another human being surfaced, a longing for total intimacy past the skin barrier with a special person—him. Sex, as conventionally understood, would seem the smallest part of their joining—this fitting together of two frequencies which amplified the other, being the larger part.

Oblivious of who might see, but no one saw, arms about each other's waists, she walked with her head down, but with a little smile on the classic face, as they went to the parking lot. He caught her to him in the dark. She sighed as they met like their hearts already had. Timidly, her hands reached up, then more boldly into his curls, feeling as well the slight stubble on his upper lip as his mouth danced off hers, then pursued more deeply. She pushed him away then, but playfully, it a foregone conclusion that he was accompanying her back to Seaward Point, where she had never taken anyone before. Almost running, she went to her car.

She sped out of the parking lot; his ponderous rental Buick followed more slowly. She waited for him to catch up, then settled into a steady pace toward home. It was twenty minutes of a decision already made, already destined. Thoughts and images jumbled, as his face, his words, blended and clashed with both her fear of and longing for intimacy. Her thoughts impacted against her husband's illness, their thirty years of faithfulness, all to be thrown over in one afternoon? Then came his angelic face again. *Kjaere Gud*—had they truly known each other before—like he said, or did she just want an excuse? Were there cosmic laws, as well as social laws to entertain? And what of duty? She stopped asking questions for now.

Seaward Point arrived and then the shore turn-off to the house, the sharp salt scent never failing to secure her. She hurried to unlock the door so as to put on the light for him, when she felt him behind her. His arms folded her close as he kissed her wildly, her neck, her hair, her face, her ear lobe. Then she had her arms around his neck, breathing in his scent as he breathed hers. An age later, he closed the door as she turned on the lamp. Like apparitions to each other, each a kind of fearful symmetry to the other's being, they stared, past words. Her jacket, then her purse, draped the chair as she felt his hands, infinitely gentle, infinitely tender as she led him upstairs. They closed the door on the world that night.

Dawn came. The sleepy cooing of doves, and the more aggressive feeding sounds of gulls returned Selma to an almost usual self with terrible urgency. She studied the man that lay beside her, this total stranger, yet the beloved, his mouth curved like a child's in sleep. With almost a groan she put her head down into the thicket of fragrant hair, her cheek to his. He woke at the touch, taking her hand and kissing it, raising himself on one elbow. Smiling, he possessed the bed, the room and her as if it were his due, somehow naturally commanded by his sheer, radiant presence. She adored it and him, but she was terrified, feeling herself shrink in the light. She threw off the thought with casual banter, a little gruff, as self-consciously she tried to cover herself, it being hard to be dignified, stark naked. They both laughed as she ran to the closet for a robe. He put on his pants.

Searching for something to say and something to do besides breakfast, and not daring to look at the tousled bed, she told him, "Let's go sailing after breakfast." He looked at her attentively, inquisitively, and agreed, sensing a sea change.

Breakfast was lovely. Selma found herself still smitten, but now her usual mind clicked back on. She heard him say some things which more than shocked her. Perhaps she had heard those same things yesterday, but not really heard them through the daze of joy, even as he had not understood that she had not understood, lost in his own ecstasy of recognition. A distance fell between them, then a silence, hers somewhat embarrassed, his bewildered at her reservation, which was compounded when she turned her head away when he attempted to kiss her. Selma knew that if he kissed her again, she was lost. "I bet you do this with everyone," she finally said. So that was it, he thought, relieved. She wanted to know if this sort of thing was common with him. Well, it wasn't. He had been celibate for years—waiting—waiting for the companion, the friend, the human partner whose essence matched his and whom he matched in turn. For years he had substituted zeal and overwork when he didn't find such a person, the memory of the dream woman he had met out traveling one night, fading.

Gently he took her hand, kissing the palm lightly, and hand in hand they ran toward the beach. Selma knew how to sail, but Josip proved an equally able seaman. The sunfish quickly caught the wind, their rapport returning in the glorious day. She laughed at the incongruity of his worn, baggy pants and his beautiful, muscled chest like a satin shield. "It's from yoga and Tai Chi," he said, thinking she meant the unusual development. He quickly understood when she ran her hand wonderingly on his breast, murmuring in spite of herself, "You are so beautiful." He traced her cheek, looking into the wide gray eyes, no longer blue—"So are you," he said softly, taking her hand until she took hers away. They lapsed into a troubled silence. For one thing, he knew he'd gone too far with her about his ideas. But he couldn't hold back at least telling her all this now he'd found her after all these years . . . Surely . . . it would work out.

The brisk wind brought them around with a crackle of sail, the two of them working in perfect co-ordination. Then Selma showed Josip a place halfway between both shores of the river, but out into the sound as well, where she said fresh water and salt meet and mix. The stain of earth in the river water thinned itself until the unbroken slate gray of the sound reached the horizon. Her face was grave as she told him, "That is you and me, Josip—salt water and fresh trying to equalize and we cannot, without mixing completely. And I can't do that."

He countered, already knowing, "What's wrong with that? Besides," he said reassuringly, "if you put a bucket overboard right here, down into the salt water where you can hardly see the river, you'd get the river's sweet wonderful water and a taste of land. The two would be one, but separate."

"No," she said sadly, "The sea would take it over eventually." And she knew it was true. He was like the ocean, primal, irrepressible, overwhelmingly like an act of nature and she so happy in the spray; but he couldn't stay on the shore, and she couldn't go out to sea.

She didn't know where to put him in her life. Nor was it fair to Rolf who counted on her for everything, or to their years together, as well as her practice painstakingly built, or to all the investment of a lifetime, including children. How to tell him all this, make it real to him, not trivial, or selfish? She looked at him, already grieving.

He said urgently, but impossibly to her ears, "Selma, come back with me to Europe, where you'd be at home, too. And we would have a home in the States as well. We would travel the world together! Work with me, let me teach you, be with me!" he entreated, like a small boy, burying his face in her lap. She wound her fingers tenderly in his hair and raised his head, seeing tears in his eyes which made her words falter, those terrible words. Miserably she told him, "I can't do as you ask. In the first place I hardly believe any of it, although I love you dearly, dearly, and in the second place I just can't pick up and leave, even if I wanted to. Don't you understand?" Her eyes implored him to try to see how it was with her situation, a banked anger in her that he asked such an irresponsible thing in the first place. Her lips tightened.

"No," he flared almost shouting, his vehemence menacing. "No, I don't understand that you don't! I looked everywhere for you. For years and years. And now I have found you and you say you don't *know* me? After last night, you can doubt it?" he challenged, then softened, taking the square, plain palm and kissing it as if she were liege queen and he a peasant vassal on her estate.

She countered, softly, the sun fierce on their faces, the whip of the sail and spray sounding. "I know a powerful man, a tender man. I know that I care, that you turn me around, but I don't *truly* know about your past life connection to me, you having actually met me before in another dimension. I don't understand any of that—nor do I know it personally, since if it happened, I can't remember it. It is just your word against my experience, or lack of it, Josip. And what of duty?" she asked as she thought of her life.

"What of your duty to yourself, Selma? To destiny, even, to fulfilling yourself as the most complete person you can be? Can you be that, here?" He wanted to add, how many lives each of us lives and dies during which the apparent concerns always seem the most overwhelmingly important. These concerns are usually domestic trivia inherited out of familiar patterns, habits, and fears, the old karmic debris cast up on the shore of the human self. When the first duty and all that ever had to be done in any lifetime was to know the truth of one's own nature, after which the right choices always fall into place. He wanted to tell her that sometimes to get to that stage, you have to amputate, or be willing to walk away from all that appears real. Well he knew. Still, it was an old old question—duty; one is never supposed to run away from one's duty, but just do it with new vision, instead of the old. If, however she would just entertain the *possibility* of a new life with him, maybe not now, but later, and at least go to India with him to meet his teacher, the very catalyst of that meeting would jolt her into her own awakening. Then, the right action would be chosen in her life. He sensed, too, that old Dr. Asgaard would not live long, he being her major tie to the old life. Although Josip also sensed that Selma's habitual reluctance of mind and conditioning would likely result in calcified choices. Without such a prod, such as he represented in her life, she would likely regroup into a new version of her old life, even were Dr. Asgaard gone.

In a softer tone, but still rebuking, he challenged her that however modern she thought herself, and with all her analysis, she was still immersed in her limits, reinforced by a Protestant background and the usual 20th century five-sense reality limiting her perspective as to what could be real. Which she couldn't help unless she chose to break out of her limits. But he grudged, it takes almost an act of faith to break free—so that you can see things for what they really are.

She snapped back, "You should talk about a five-sense reality, after last night . . . ," but the words came out woodenly. She saw the hurt in his face, but refused to yield, turning to anger inevitably as she often did, to make the pain less.

"Selma," he entreated, "you are a psychotherapist; so am I, don't you see? These new ways of seeing things have often been called religions, but they are really psychotherapies of the human soul, expressed in historical and cultural coordinates that the seer, the Christ, Buddha, or Sai Baba had to use, to make them intelligible to their times. Or to hide from persecution, as the Sufis had to behind wine and love poetry. All of these religious paths are *ways,* whether disguised behind religions, or not, ways to deal with how the higher centers are working to channel higher reality evolutionarily in human kind. *This is real.* Humans are constructed to be gods, Selma. No, let me put it the bolder way that Pythagoras challenged his people with—'We are gods'—he said. Almost derisively, he used to taunt us—Are you afraid to *know* you are gods?

"Oh Selma, if you come with me—you'll be on the leading edge of all this! And I need you by me—not helplessly, but as a working companion in the trek—both of us—fulfilling our highest potential and thereby gaining the insight to truly serve others."

Selma hardly heard him. She was still reeling from his casual reference to what Pythagoras had said. Sometimes around this man she was tongue-tied, or maybe it was that she was too embarrassed to ask something which sounded so ignorant to him, but which she wanted to ask. Like, damn it, how can he quote Pythagoras, a man dead 3000 years or more as if he had just dropped in the other day for tea? Damn the man!

She looked almost frightened, the beautiful, aging child of almost 60 years facing this exuberant, brooding, blooming man twenty years her junior. He reminded her once more of an Old Testament prophet on fire with his faith. Her cooler, sparer temperament recoiled from such passionate expression, not to speak of the content. She couldn't call it his belief system, for it was with him experiential fact, but for her?

Aware of her consternation, Josip plunged on anyhow, making matters worse in Selma's mind, her resistance drawing around her like a cloak. Softly, so softly, he began to recite softly, passionately, his voice rising and falling like the sea under the little sailboat.

I am discovered,
I have been found!
A Fisher in the mighty fleet
from God has heard my plea,
re-echoed through Eternity.
The muffled cry of endless ages in
the matter-Worlds—
"To Be
To Be!"
Oh, joy, oh jest, that this year's
cast-off leaf—I thought was me
is only segment of the tree
I AM —
simultaneous to a twig
in the Tree of the Lord.
I sing the song of a
Salvaged One.

In spite of herself, Selma was moved by the intensity and heart of this man she loved so much. She knew he was on the leading edge, but it was the razor's edge for her. She'd never catch up to him, for one thing. That was her pride—perhaps, the human part that knew she'd always be in his reflection. How then to be in balance with her own life? Her place? Her children, grandchildren? What of Rolf, ailing now, her practice—her work among the needy? It went round and round. But what of his plea that she be his companion? What of their love? What of his taunt that half-knowledge only stirs the darkness; the wise, only, let in the light? She knew what he meant. But she knew, too, she couldn't just leave it all behind her. Or divorce Rolf, God forbid, the poor old man! Or confess to him, or worse, keep it secret from him that the illustrious, charismatic Josip Vidmar was visiting her? It was a wonder that the press hadn't found them already. With his visibility, it would be only a matter of time until they were discovered. Best to cut it off now. But it broke her heart.

At first, Josip mistook her silence as contemplation as she thought things over. Then he felt her decision palpably, as advance notice of a weather shift comes in the smell of oncoming snow or rain. They headed back to shore and to the house. The night before they had driven twenty minutes of a decision already made, already fated. But this was in reversal.

Silently, they beached the boat, as silently they walked, not touching. Then urgently, he turned her toward him and bore her downward on the sand. She fought him wildly, knowing she could never leave him then, "No, No, . . ." she gasped, wrenching her face away from his urgency, the scent of him around her. He drew back, the fierce light in her eyes scaring him, raising his hands in imprecation, or as if to strike. Then, something collapsed from within, defeating him. Rigorously, he wrestled himself them. The look of vulnerability left, the tenderness was back, and rue, even a wry humor spread across the even features, leashed in a fierce self-control, she knew.

Formally, he opened the door for her when they got to the house and went directly upstairs to finish putting on his clothes, returning a very few moments later, this time totally under control. Selma was less so, her heart frozen in dread, as with lips stiff she said the words she knew she had to say—part of herself knowing she was evading inevitability, yet part of her was assured she was making the right action, given the circumstances. Situational ethics, perhaps, but she was brutally caught in the cross-fire between life positions. Her past, and possible futures.

"I'm so sorry . . . so sorry . . . for us both, Josip." And he answered almost inaudibly, eschewing pride, humbly.

"So am I . . . sorry . . . I know you well. . . ." It went unspoken that if she changed her mind . . .

At the door he took her hand, holding it to his cheek a moment, grief showing in his otherwise inscrutable eyes, her memory of the night before, letting Selma know by contrast the degree of his iron control of that yogic trained will of his. A storm of realization of her love of him shuddered through her, as with eyes closed, she sagged toward him, numbly. She loved him, but that made no difference. She had to let it go before there was any more hurt . . . before she hurt anyone else. Before . . . His arms went around her, and he held her like a child for a moment, kissing the top of her head in farewell.

When he drove away, without looking back, she leaned on the door and cried as the storm broke.

• • •

It was still Selma's weekend of January 6. Her characterization of herself as a staunch behaviorist was not quite accurate, although certainly part of her was—the part she chose to show. In everyone the hide-'n-go-seek with the miraculous goes on. Selma was no exception, circumscribed as it is with us all by what she allowed through the grid of her expectations, while the very act of expecting or rejecting continued to color the outcome. This weekend she had been deified. This day she could live forever. Here in this place she had been happy. Here in this place she had sent away the one person she could not do without, partly because she could not give up all that she had to follow him—who was also herself.

Her love of him never fit neatly into her life. Had she made the right choice about Josip? Was there such a thing as right? Six years ago she'd been the tough, practical humanist with a closed mind, the kind of person who was more tolerant of a love affair than a mental skirmish with radical ideas. She dearly loved Josip, and even though she finally refused the implications of his world view, and his powerful presence by sending him away, it was inevitable that his belief in the merger of scientific and esoteric systems would leave an impression on her. It was sometime after that the hard knot in her chest came, and stayed.

The Confrontation

Josip's year at Yale was drawing to a close when her personal situation altered drastically. Dr. Rolf Asgaard died peacefully in his sleep; Josip went back to Europe alone; and Selma solved her situation by taking up a new version of her old life. She married dear Arne Thorson, a lawyer whose wife had been one of Selma's patients.

Selma had thought then about how strange, even awesome, it had been for Arne to see his fragile, rather sheltered wife, Irma, emerge from under the scourge of her impending death into full bloom. At the end, Arne had shared with her that he had an uncanny feeling that death could be adjusted from the ground, much like a kite in the air. But he hadn't known what to do, other than to be with her. So, he sat softly stroking Irma's hand or dampening her lips with ice, and just loving her. He had quite a start at the end when she sat up and addressed Julian, their son who had died years ago at age 13. Irma's face had beamed, and joy poured from her wasted body as she grasped Arne's hand with a vigor that he'd not seen for months and asked,

"Arne, can't you see him?" And she turned back to her son remarking with a mother's prerogative on how much he'd grown, and died with a smile. Arne Thorson, in the midst of wild grief, laughed out loud. Then he put his face down and cried. From a distance he was dimly aware of someone standing in the doorway behind him, and then of the door's gentle closing.

After Irma died, Arne's relationship with Selma had grown increasingly supportive and affectionate. Although he had been discretely aware of the intensity and struggle of her relationship with Josip, Arne and Selma married that year.

• • •

When Selma returned from her Light Experience weekend at Seaward Point, Arne was immediately aware of the change in her. She bloomed, laughed more easily, cried more easily, didn't need to sleep as much, and had an air about her that, frankly, scared him. When he questioned her, she looked helpless to explain, and finally handed him a book from the increasing piles she had either taken from the public library, carted back from her father's library now at Seaward Point, or that his daughter Kate bought for her. The book was Bucke's *Cosmic Consciousness*. She'd muttered as she gave it to him, "Can you believe it? My father read that book! I found it in Norwegian and English after his death. This was around me all the time . . ." She had trailed off. Puzzled, he looked through the book, published almost a hundred years ago—but relevant now as then, she said. He could back it up with Tart's *Altered State of Consciousness* and *Waking Up*, White's *The Highest State of Consciousness*, or Sannella's *The Kundalini Experience*, she'd added mysteriously, almost mischievously, and then gone off to her office.

Knowing Selma rarely did anything without strong reason, Arne submitted in puzzled silence and retreated to his study to look the book over. Its subject matter seemed the far side of the moon compared to the Selma he knew. What was going on? For the book documented accounts of mystical experience with higher consciousness, in examples that ranged from Jesus, Buddha, Swedenborg, to Walt Whitman. All the examples of extra-ordinary humanity were described as being the vanguard of an evolutionary pattern all humanity would eventually go through. Arne was intrigued and more than a little alarmed at Selma's studied intent in giving him the book. This got into Josip Vidmar's territory, which was these days far less media visible as was he, since he'd gone into relative obscurity somewhere in southern India, working in villages like some latter day Schweitzer, after the tumultuous lecture stint in the States where he had met and lost Selma.

Arne thought she'd put Josip and his work behind her as thoroughly as Vidmar had put fame and fortune, which was commendable of them both. The match just wouldn't have worked, Arne thought, as dispassionately as he could under the circumstances. He knew there had been no letters, or calls, and that she hadn't seen Josip. So that left one more possibility, improbable as it seemed; he called Selma at her office. "All right dear, tell me about what happened to you last week!" was all he had to say. He heard her relieved, throaty chuckle over the phone lines through his own relief. Ten minutes later, somewhat astonished, he could still say, thank God *that* was all it was! He thought there had been something wrong! That night they became closer than they'd ever been. Therefore, they hadn't been prepared for what the next week would bring and the gulch it would open in their lives.

• • •

On January 22, a shaken Selma Rieseseg submitted to a routine examination in unusual silence. Earlier, feeling less than cosmic bliss and irked at having to make the drive which she felt unnecessary, Selma had been out-of-sorts. Arne insisted she have the lump looked at, not believing her forty-year history of them coming and going. By the time she entered the specialist's office, she was already in an uneasy and depressed mood which rapidly changed to horror as she glimpsed the headlines of a newspaper in the waiting room. She snatched it up, disbelievingly, and read that Josip Vidmar had been among the victims of the DC-10 plane crash in Chicago that occurred during Storm Casper, the week Tom Breacher died.

Numbly, her own situation forgotten, Selma read that he'd left India to be the main speaker at a conference on religion and the nature of consciousness hosted by Menningers. He'd gone down, along with three other conference participants. The article listed his many accomplishments as well as his work championing people who had had near-death experiences. Selma submitted in silence as the doctor probed her body, wondering who would love her now, now that he was dead? The Norwegian for the 23rd Psalm rang through her mind, "Yea though I walk . . . through the valley of the Shadow of Death, I shall fear no evil . . . for Thou art with me . . . Thou art with me . . . Thou . . ." Later, Selma would wonder if Josip hadn't already been helping her from the other side—if she and Josip and the universe, at some internal level, already knew all along what they were about—living or dying.

It was too cold for snow when she started the drive home hours later. She was numb, and got nauseous every time she thought of his body bursting into flames, or being crushed beyond recognition on impact. Until she remembered—"he would have exited the body—*before* it was killed out from under him! Remember, he was adept at soul travel—after all." That helped. But not her loss . . . which was a fresher suffering than six years before had been, this was so final. She never mentioned Vidmar's death to Arne. He, however, had seen it on the news. There was nothing to say. He tried to resume the intimacy they'd shared the day before, when she'd trusted him with telling of the Light Experience. But for now, a door had closed between them. A wall drew around Selma. She walked through the rest of the day and night absently. Arne was terribly concerned, but he understood. Things were to get worse, however.

A few days later, test results showed a malignancy that raged on almost all bodily fronts. Selma realized too late that at some level of herself she had known something was wrong. But she'd lived with it so long, it had ambushed her. This was melanoma, the dreaded galloping horror of cancer, hard to treat, often painful, but not always a killer. Yet, Selma knew that the odds were stacked against the patient if it had spread to her glands and liver, when treatment probably wouldn't make a difference. All the Selmas inside her were fighting like pigs in a poke as apathy and survival vied at the verdict, a "terminal degree" right about the time Erik would graduate. If he didn't decide to take a fifth year. She went on automatic, submitting to the medical consensus in an unusual for her, but understandable, apathy. It was as though the light had gone out of her, Arne grieved. There was nothing to do but wait, be supportive, and bury himself in his law practice to keep his wits, Arne thought disconsolately.

Two days later she entered the hospital for more tests, and started the usual chemotherapy, although there would be no surgery. It was too late for that. Dr. Selma Rieseseg was given just four months to live, perhaps less. She listened in silence, to what was now no surprise, and with a semblance of her old self, strode out the door, calling over her shoulder to the flabbergasted doctor, "I'll let you know what my plans are."

But in truth she had no plans, although the week's shocking events finally penetrated her icy calm, which she knew had to melt. Selma went straight to Seaward Point. It had been here a few years ago that she finally understood why she had sent Josip away, and that it perhaps hadn't been necessary after all. Yet, at the time certain choices had had to be made—there was a certain code, after all, was there not? But the ache never left her in the place he had been, which she knew was the start of this. What would be the end?

Again today, as she'd been that day of recognition about Josip, she was wild with fury and despair; her hands clutched the wheel in rigid control, driving Route 9 to Seaward Point far too fast. Once home she raced for the beach, not even shutting the car door. She ran with grief, weeping dryly. Sounds, hardly human, came out of her until they rose to a shout, "NO, NO, NO," she bellowed furiously. Anguish pierced her soul as deeply as the errant cells that occupied the territory of her body, as deep as love. "No," Selma cried, as she ran onto the ice toward the sea, lost in a world frozen in snow. A panel of ice cracked under her weight and broke off from the shore with a rippling groan, opening a rift of dark sea all around her. She felt it first as a dull booming sound. The ice was going and Selma had just three seconds to make her choice. Some place deep within her made the choice as Selma reversed her direction and became a blur of being in motion, leaping with astonishing strength back to land.

Safe inside her house with her grief, Selma reached for a bottle of Cabernet Sauvignon that she'd been saving for a celebration and drank it to Josip, and Tom, and now herself.

When Selma didn't come home on schedule after the last round of tests, Arne knew that she'd gone to Seaward Point. He waited until dark for a call. She'd refused to let him accompany her to the hospital or pick her up, but now he had to go and find her. Approaching the house he rarely visited, he foolishly hoped Selma would lean out and wave cheerfully, but there was no movement within.

He forced open the kitchen window, climbed inside, and stood listening. Arne started up the stairs; for all he knew she could be soaking in the bathtub. Then he saw her favorite sweater huddled on the stairway near the smashed crystal of a glass. His boots gritted on broken shards as he took the polished pine stairs

two at a time, yelling her name. He came to the room at the top
of the stairs and just stared in silence.

Time reversed itself and halted. The body on the bed horri-
fied him. Beside one armpit there was a widening stain of red
and the other arm was flung up lifelessly. Her hair had turned
bone white, no longer the silver he remembered. His grief almost
strangled him as he approached her bed. When he was close
enough, socked against a solid wall of grief, anger ricocheted
into outrage when he saw the spilled bottle of wine nestled in
the bedcovers.

Arne fought back anger like nausea, swallowing hard to
make room for relief. He stared down at Selma. Pitiless light
revealed every mark on Selma's naked, wrinkled body which
seemed to have shrunk. He simply didn't know what to do
with this situation—he'd never seen her drunk—it just didn't fit
anywhere. If ever he was to find Selma repugnant, he would have
that day. But he did not. He stood looking at her collapsed face
and gaping mouth that produced soft snores. Her eyelids were
sunken and her face had all the life sucked out of it. But it was
her hair that terrified him.

Tenderly he began to cover her nakedness. Drunken arms
reached up to embrace him and in her voice he heard the whim-
pering of children and lost souls. It broke his heart to hear it,
even as Arne recalled the Biblical passage, "He giveth his beloved
sleep," and knew that there was mercy in the universe, despite
appearances. He then undressed and got into bed and held her
throughout most of the night. In the morning, he woke to find
her watching him strangely, a little smile on her face. Something
had been decided. She had kissed him gently, but tears gathered
in her eyes and spilled over. He mistook them as tears over what
she would call alternately, her terminal degree, graduation or
final exams. But at that moment, her thoughts had gone instead
to an unseasonably warm October day a long time ago and a

decision finally made. She kissed Arne then, again, most tenderly.

Selma and Arne left the next morning for home without comment about their private travail, nor did she ever apologize or explain what had happened inside her, or out on the ice. Seaward Point was her private self and he had chosen to enter it. But her gratitude was obvious. As they walked to the car, Selma turned to again thank him for his faithful friendship, looking deep into the kind, weathered face of this dear man who proved so steadfast. They both had tears in their eyes and he had to fight to avert his eyes from the bone-white hair. Although it didn't seem fair that he had to go through this twice, the last time alone, he assured her that he would journey on, as she would in her fashion, as Irma had, as had Josip. Secretly, ruing it as last vanity, Selma found it somewhat comforting to know she couldn't be any uglier at death than she'd been that night for him, which remained unspoken. He had faced the situation resolutely. While she had made her choice on the ice and now again with him. Yet, in the split second she had to make that choice, the finality of Josip's truly being gone almost swung the balance. Then came the leap across the widening dark strip of water to the other side.

Strange, that as long as someone was alive, there always seemed a forever amount of time for making good on something gone wrong. But, that isn't true; death can come at any time to anyone, and it is so final regarding any unsettled accounts. She'd always had the notion that one day she'd see Josip again walking up the beach to the house. She'd call him her angel and her daemon, and sometimes her imp. He'd call her his Muse. Now that could never be. She'd never written him to come home, trusting he'd sense it despite what had happened. But equally, she knew he couldn't, after what she'd done to him when she wouldn't go with him, when she'd sent him away and then so swiftly remarried. For weeks she let the phone ring unanswered.

Once she'd picked it up, weeping, hearing the crackle of trans-Atlantic static. Then came his voice faint, but recognizable, "Selma, Selma—listen to me, we can work this out!" She'd gently put down the phone, knowing who it was in every ring, until one day the calls stopped.

• • •

It was February 27, the day of Selma's last chemotherapy session, before she talked to her family about the Light Experience at Seaward Point. January and into February had presented bizarre symptoms of what was going on to everyone. Chaos and anger were thinly veiled. Selma stayed secluded. Mark and Erik had been called home against Selma's will, "I'm not that far gone that you have to gather for a pre-funeral," she'd shouted. Arne's daughter Kate briefed the boys, but was handicapped because she didn't know of the Light Experience. She knew, however, the same day Selma had her cancer confirmed, she'd found out Josip was dead. What that meant to Selma, added to everything else, she could only surmise from the effect, because Selma didn't talk about it to anyone. Selma just sat, staring vacantly in space, slept or read. She was so different, but then who wouldn't be? Kate ached for her.

Kate noticed Selma's depression would occasionally lift to where she seemed almost high spirited; in fact she was on a reading binge these days, Kate observed, and of the damnedest things, too. Well, Kate thought philosophically, there is such a thing as karma and a pattern to life. And though we don't live forever, the right actions necessary for each person's balance of life and death need to be paid attention to. Nor do you give up hope, least of all the feisty ones like Selma.

Meanwhile, Selma unquestioningly plowed ahead with regular medical cancer interventions but with none of the alternate therapies, which appalled Kate. Kate, like many of her generation, was all for modern medicine, but in moderate doses heavily diluted by every possible whole body, whole mind alternative that the counter-culture could produce—from acupuncture, Rolfing, the Alexander technique, mantric science, visualization, homeopathy, kinesiology, crystal therapy (which is said to augment the etheric body's energy processing) and cancer prevention diets from catalytic water to macrobiotics—the list went on. She just didn't understand Selma, who seemed to be two women in one these days—the conservative and free spirit, almost a new-ager.

This was a Selma Kate had never met, maybe because Selma, too, had only met her recently. Which probably explains many of the inconsistencies in Selma as the old vied with the new, and the front line was disease. It was going to come to a head. Kate saw that the struggle going on had nothing to do with cancer, overtly anyhow—but everything to do with death. The connection eluded her, however, which was, of course, the Light Experience which redefined the borders between life and death. Impulsively, Kate went over and hugged Selma, this still beautiful, complex and queenly woman, who usually didn't seem very huggable but suddenly looked vulnerable. To Kate's surprise, Selma took her in her arms for a long moment, sharing energy back and forth, as they rested like birds in a nest. They both were moved at the sharing. Kate was again amazed at Selma. The kids knew, boys and girls alike, the power of hugs, but grownups usually didn't.

• • •

Vertigo, nausea, diarrhea, and a devastating weakness ravaged Selma as both the cancer and the chemo killer cure galloped through her system. No one promised her the treatments would work, even in the private context of her drastic re-alignment in the Light Experience, although she had some hope. "All patients do," she thought ironically. There is also such a thing as karma to which first Josip, then Kate had clued her. The law of cause and effect plays out from past life inheritance while predisposition to events forms the script for this life. She wished she knew more about possible past lives.

Josip had alluded to a major lifetime of theirs in Greece, which no doubt, if it were true, set much of the quest and function of this life spinning subliminally, anyhow. In this business of assessing a life, hers in particular, and using these new landmarks, one had to consider the function of each life and its biological duration in relationship to genetics as well as the karma, or energy patterns that created the genetic inheritance. There is also free will to "override" the patterns. While she sensed that one comes into life with a mission, as it were. And when it's completed, your time is up. Hers was coming due. But not yet.

At first she'd allowed the doctors to take control, never seeming to question their authority. But when the whole family had been upset by the results of the liver scan, the red-headed Kate exploded: "Mom, why do you do it if it makes you so sick? Your lymph system is gone and now your liver . . . they're your body's defenses. Can killing more tissue and creating more waste do the trick?" Kate looked away as she gathered handfuls of Selma's hair that had fallen out during the shampoo, then got the scissors to crop the rest of it close to her head, like a child's.

Kate's fury helped shock Selma into a semblance of her normal good sense; she decided to stop her treatments, since they obviously weren't working for whatever reason. Maybe the Light Experience was all she needed, and Josip, though he wasn't here. Was it time to go? Was it going home like her father had always said? Since all three children were back, she decided to level with them the next morning at breakfast. It was February 27th.

Selma gathered the family in the living room and without preamble began. "For two months we've been pussy-footing around, not talking directly about this cancer, as well as some other things that have been going on, which also haven't been shared. I'm the worst offender. Well, I've decided that I'm not going for any more treatments, gang. I'm going to do this in my own way. Today, I'm taking back a part of my life, what's left of it. I need time to sort things out, and I know that I won't get it in between treatments . . . I'm losing time that I don't have. I don't know why I started them in the first place; an old feeling of trusting doctors more than myself, I guess. They're not miracle workers and are only human!" I should know! she added angrily to herself thinking of her own conditioning. She knew now she was going. She'd admitted it by stopping treatments.

Although everyone else was relieved, her decision outraged her oldest son, Mark, who'd come back especially to talk her out of any such decision. His usual cool expression was torn apart by conflicting emotion as he accused her of a death wish. She tried to keep calm when he yelled, "I suppose you'll tell the doctors off and go to your god-damned Seaward Point. I came all the way out here to see you before you . . ." He stopped in horror and confusion; he was about to say the terrible word. "Before I die, son," Selma said softly. "You said it, buddy-boy," and Selma laughed, breaking the tension somewhat. Everyone smiled nervously. It would help now, she thought, to be able to talk to them somewhat more freely. But can anyone really talk about their own death? And what about the Light?

Needing privacy, Selma absented herself mentally from the angry and concerned passion of the family encounter. She recalled how she'd taken other people through similar crises. Now it was her turn, although she had an arsenal her patients hadn't had and a glimpse of the Other Side.

But secretly she knew she hadn't dealt with her fear. It still clotted in her heart; it haunted her in nightsweats, even when there wasn't pain. She came back to the scene in the living room with a jolt, and for a moment wondered where and who she was. Then she addressed the family's concern that she needed the medical community, Mark's position, as well as Kate's well-meaning, but ill-timed alternative recommendations. Selma wondered why she had to explain so much to them. Didn't they know it was over? She was weary with all this. She wanted to go to her room. Although, since so much had happened in two short months, much yet unshared, this upset was to be understood. But why then was she apologizing? She knew the boys thought the treatments could save her life. But she wanted to tell them how secure she felt to finally dispose of this chemical death as one way to control the uncontrollable which was rampaging on its own terms, uninvited guest that it was.

Goddamn it, there was the matter of style, after all, to the way one lived one's life and the way one went out of it into the next. She insisted on that. She would fight to die with dignity and awareness, not like some trussed or sedated animal. Though she didn't know how! *Kjaere Gud,* she didn't know. Oh God, she'd changed so much, nor had it all jelled yet in her. She was still chunks and pieces of the old onto which the new was grafted. She didn't have the information that she needed yet to either live or die! While, there *had* to be some way to do this—this dying business—since life seemed to be casting that way, remorselessly. The dream she'd had of Tom Breacher that fateful weekend came back to her. Duty pulled her back from panic's precipice. Yes, there was much left to do with her life and her death, and love.

Relief flooded her as she remembered her experience with the Light. Right or wrong, she had chosen a road. Selma was completely quiet as she looked at her family with affection, staring thoughtfully at each in turn. Then, calmly, carefully, Selma told them what happened at Seaward Point that weekend after the conference. How it started with the call to identify Tom Breacher's body, how exhausted she had been that night. Then her astonishing walk across the room into the Light that lasted about one minute, but changed her forever. She was certain that it had important bearing on her dying and now cast the shadow of her life.

When she had finished, the room was quiet. Everyone was stunned into silence—except Arne—who kept quiet deliberately. Everyone began to share their feelings. Kate whooped with delight, at the incongruity, Selma . . . of all people, slapping her thigh for emphasis. "If that doesn't beat all! The most conservative pragmatist I know. You did it, Mom, and you didn't have to die or even nearly die—you went out-of-body, I mean you got the Cosmic Consciousness!" she said, lowering her voice as if she'd announced Selma won the lottery. "My God, I'm proud of you. Do you know how many hours I've spent in meditation trying to get a glimpse of what hit you broadside? You should have told me sooner: I'd have told you all about it, given you a reading list. So *that's* what's been going on!" Kate's green eyes and red hair fairly crackled with excitement as she all but pounded Selma's back. For a moment everyone forgot that Selma was dying.

Erik, the youngest, looked awed, as if Selma suddenly were a creature apart from him, while Mark characteristically glowered and stared at her, somehow angry that his mother talked about flying around the room and using another body, as if that stole her prematurely from him in some fashion. Arne had heard it before; he just looked at her with love and some trepidation.

Selma looked to be at peace, but she knew the confrontation would have to come first. Six months they gave her until she would graduate to that initiation they called death. Or was it four? She supposed terminal degrees were no different than any other deadline—you could push, shove, and bargain a bit, but not forever. But then, no one lived forever; she was almost sixty, after all. What was the saying? No one gets out of this life alive. But push or not, death meant a lot had to happen in a little time. She had to trim off fat from what was her life. Get to what counted. And all the connections. When even past lives come in

for examination. So far, other than Josip's allusions to Greece
and the Pythagorean era, she didn't have a clue to explain Josip—
the fiery meteor who had flung across the horizon of her life—
or Rolf, although he'd been more like a father than a husband,
and therefore explainable outside pastlife delving. Or Arne—his
steadfast presence—as if he'd always been in her life, and she in
his. Nor did she understand how she'd come to try to live three
lives in one, or why she had let Josip go.

Afterward, while she had the strength, she found these
reunions with her family blessed, real connections with what
mattered. In frequent family meetings, there would be evenings
studiedly spent with each other doing ordinary things. They all
agreed it was rotten to have waited so long to discover each
other's specialness. "But I thought I knew you, Mama!" Erik
had said with a sigh, petting the hair that reminded him of a
white poodle. Selma, on the other hand, was humbled at her
unintentional neglect of real feelings and sharings. She hadn't
lived the examined life, the now moment. There is something to
be said for living on the edge, she thought ruefully. But why does
it take a gun at your head to wise you up? And the confrontation
with mortal terror? She hadn't dealt with it yet. It was coming,
and then somehow she would be totally free to live until they
said goodbye. And maybe, by then, she could fly away like Josip
had.

After the February meeting with the family, Selma was
exhausted, needing the solace and privacy of Seaward Point. By
the time she abandoned the Volvo at the beach, she was in
complete rout, shaking with terror. "I have to get control of this
fear," she said desperately to herself as she walked the familiar
shore in the dwindling afternoon. She walked the beach like a
child taken by the hand and led through the stations of the cross.
She came to a field of what looked to be blue, broken, sprawled
butterflies. The shells lay as butterflies do in spring—panting,
still moist after emerging from cocoons. She brushed a gloved

hand against her feverish face, the contact of leather cold, the shells shattering underfoot. She shivered; only the sea moved, sounding a white noise in this very held, very silent space of everything contracted from summer.

She crunched her way through the astonishing appearance of millions of blue butterflies, mottled with gray, that died underfoot with crystalline chimings. They poised in upswept piles along the shore, ready to take off in droves, the illusion of life perfectly maintained, even as a gull wheeled in to dine. She walked on. A beached log, like a white whale, rose up in the distance, and blurred. Then came a desolate no man's land of beach, more beached shells, blue as robin's eggs, the shore edged with coarse ground ice. Nothing stirred.

She gained the dunes. The path still shown through the saltgrass. The only sounds were the sea, her breathing, and the occasional squeak of dry winter rushes rubbing against one another. She remembered the summer sounds when she came to the hidden sandglen that she sought—in winter it was heinously exposed—like the inside of the shells.

Repressing memories from long ago, she saw the ice of the tiny channel frozen in mid-wave as it mounted the wind-listed straw of seashore grass. She crouched down and took off her glove, putting out a finger lightly to the glaze of ice, touching it to her lips . . . faintly salt. In a jumbled rush of sensation, memory, image and feeling, it all came back, as she remembered salt on his lips and then hers—she wrenched her mind away, pulling her finger from her mouth as if it burned.

Suddenly sweaty, Selma pushed back her hood, the down of curling white hair like that of a snow bird ready to fly. She walked unsteadily past the seawall, past the last few cottages bundled up against the cold. A few random flakes of snow drifted out of the sky; she thought she would never be warm again, but then again, she knew she would. *"Kjaere gud,* dear God, guide me,"* came the humble, unexpected words. She walked toward home, hands folded across her chest to keep in the faltering warmth, where the bird that threatened to fly away also nested.

· · ·

Event piled on event. Erik went back to college, but would come home on weekends. Kate stopped by each day. Mark returned to Seattle looking frustrated, his face like a clenched fist as he hugged and kissed Selma goodbye, but wouldn't look at her. Selma had a hard cry after he'd left, knowing she might never see him again.

Selma watched herself going through most of the Kübler-Ross five stages of predeath psychology. All except denial, although she bargained well enough. Her anger subsided, only to be replaced by an acute loneliness. Once before she'd felt such an estrangement. During her pregnancies, her sense of herself had altered with her body's internal shifts, while even the conditions in the family seemed to change in proportion to the size of her stomach. She wondered if the same thing would happen as the cancer progressed and showed itself?

By now only a few friends stopped by; but then she didn't really want to see anyone socially. Instead she filled her days with research, trying to find answers to questions that she didn't yet know how to phrase. Her nights were often filled with pain that worsened when she put her attention on it. Sometimes the pain lessened when she directed her attention elsewhere. Eventually then she could drift off to sleep.

Selma wanted to put her house in order before she died, so she made all the legal arrangements and forced Arne and the kids to deal with the most taboo subjects head on. Such as money and wills and divisions of property. They had a mock auction one weekend, Mark joining in by phone reluctantly. But he got her piano, anyhow, and even laughed a little at drawing lots for it, although he decided to leave it with Arne. The strength of her relationship with her family increasingly helped her through the pain. She wanted to die at home among those she loved. She'd never realized before how much she loved them all.

Selma decided to call Dr. Tuchman, just in case. She might need a special ally to give her painkillers in this last skirmish, or if necessary, to ward off technology's methods of prolonging life. She made the necessary arrangements. Later, she totally reconsidered her position on drug usage, unless she was in the direst straits. There were alternative pain control means which would not muddy her mind and consciousness.

"Let's agree to keep as much control over the process as possible, Arne," Selma said softly and broke down, weeping helplessly, as the wall between them went down, melted by their tears. In the weeks that followed, she went many times into her husband's arms for long comforting moments. Their relationship reached into the areas of erotic poetry, lit with a directness and immediacy that left them awed, as they touched the finger of life to the finger of death.

• • •

Later, Selma talked to Kate about how laboring women can control fierce pain and even turn the pain into joy, as she had while giving birth to Erik. But it had been hard work to turn her focus from flight to participation, she recalled. Damn hard. Selma felt that there must be a similar way for her to do the same with death. These days no one teased Selma about her intense preoccupation with death or how to do it. Actually this last investigation of hers wasn't much different from other passions she'd submitted to in the past. Papers and books were piled all over the sunporch and her study; the house was an utter mess.

Kate looked at Selma speculatively. Even in illness, Selma had an air of goddess superiority, the skin pale, the classic profile still beautiful, her hair down-white. However, even in adversity, she still could be cantankerous, half-humorous, half-contemptuous of anything that she didn't understand or agree with. She was a formidable queen of her territory. Yet Kate also knew that Selma was exceedingly vulnerable now. Carefully, after days of consideration and some research, Kate suggested yoga as Selma's way out. She at least could use the breathing and relaxation techniques to get further control of the pain, and maybe get out-of-body, Kate advised her.

Yoga! Yoga was Josip's way. Hadn't it all come full circle? Selma mulled over this yoga idea, giving Kate a very serious faraway look. Kate let out her breath slowly, still rather amazed that Mom didn't hit the roof, or scoff her down. Selma agreed to try it. After all, she remembered how Lamaze techniques had helped with her pregnancy, and Kate had just told her they were derived from Hatha Yoga exercises. She'd done Lamaze alone except for the nurse who got her back on track with her breathing when Selma had lost it. Could she get out of this world with a semblance of dignity without support? Support like Lamaze was supposed to provide? Maybe yoga was the final clue to assist her to keep control, at least.

As an inner floodgate let relief flow, she knew it would be far, far more. There was a definite link between yoga, the Light, and some sort of departure procedure from physical life into death consciousness, as well as this "soul travel" business Josip's friend Paul had taught him, which he called a far-out kind of yoga. She wondered why she had neglected so long to walk the bridge of yoga, of whatever vintage, to Josip?

It was March 7 when Kate drove her to the YWCA for the first yoga class. Gingerly, Selma took a cross-legged pose on a foam pad and stared at the exotic lady instructor. Mrs. Dee had a quiet dignity that hung like the thick glistening hair around her shoulders. As the class gathered, she didn't speak, except to greet them with a smile as they filed in. Mrs. Dee took off a long woolen sweater, revealing what appeared to be a white judo suit. With no makeup, and of indefinite age, she swiftly braided the blue-black hair streaked with gray, and secured it with a band, shaking her head. In one fluid motion she sat down, crossing her legs. She closed her eyes for a moment as the class began, her strong, vibrant voice filling the room with the sweet, foreign sounds of a melodious chant. It was Selma's first exposure to the "Gayatri," a powerful mantram she would use later on.

Selma had curiosity and some dread about this woman of yoga, for yoga, according to Josip, accorded amazing powers to its practitioners. He'd claimed that Christ was an adept at this ancient art of consciousness transmutation and had studied in the East during his lost years, as well as with the Essenes, before returning to fulfill his life's mission. Moreover, that he'd been one of those "white crows," definitive to human history. Her father had talked a bit like that, too, although he'd just alluded to Jesus' lost years as training years. So Selma guessed that yoga wasn't so alien, seen in that perspective, although most churches wouldn't accept that aspect of Christ any more than they would reincarnation—any more than a behaviorist would turn transcendentalist, eh Selma! All things are possible.

So here she was, at a yoga class. Maybe Mrs. Dee could read minds? Or walk on water? Josip had told her astonishing tales. In actuality, Mrs. Dee looked relatively harmless, although Selma felt she was in the presence of someone who knew something special; it was reassuring. The dark quiet lady silently became part of Selma's life, guiding both her reading and the way she would come to think about her death. Because of Selma's circumstances, Mrs. Dee began to teach Selma only the gentler physical movements of yoga, the mental techniques, and the basic breathing exercises.

· · ·

That night she dreamed she was walking up the slopes of a vast mountain whose crown disappeared into the dark cobalt of space. Wreathes of fog and snow drifted across its granite slopes.

Selma felt herself effortlessly part of the narrow trail under her feet, the mountain, and sky above. She felt the harmony of nature's silent will with which she blended. No longer was she trying to escape; she felt the fog and wind as something circulating inside her, not threatening or alien and apart. So, also, space as light circulated like breath through her mind.

Above, carved into the side of the mountain, was a monastery to which the trail led, turning into great stone steps. At the top stood a figure Selma saw as familiar, rooted inside herself as well. Her sense of identity no longer confined to one body, she embraced the figure as herself and was embraced, piercing light flooding from each pore and atom in the airy wind circulating through her. She was simultaneously everything she saw in that vast spherical sight. The figure Selma saw was herself, her mouth curved in a tender welcoming smile. Her panoramic vision trembled as the scenery, figure, monastery and mountain violently stirred themselves forming and reforming, cause and effect. She saw her soul streaming endlessly back through tissues of light, through which time passed, and each life lived was a bead on a string connected by the endless tissue of light which enveloped and connected the materializations. This wind of light embraced the whole cosmos of her being, past the sharp etched outlines of particular events, exquisitely subtle in radiance, which in turn blazed into being by some yet farther Source which issued from her nucleus to every pore and atom of the universal construction. She cognized immortal nature in a radiating splendor that abided in her own heart.

Selma woke with the wind of life fusing her with all things, including pain, despair, and the fear which dissolved like sugar in water. She knew, beyond a shadow of doubt, her own source. Laughing and crying, the feeling of her own royal self like a perfume all around her, a scent, a flavor, Selma knew she no longer reached outside herself when she took an elder's hand, for they were One. She knew she would take up the challenge to know herself as God, albeit, conceded her Selma mind, God-the-smaller.

The Education of Selma Rieseseg

Every six months or so, as long as Kate had known her, Selma turned over a new idea which she would passionately research, as she now researched her impending death. There were many secret sides to Selma Rieseseg that Kate didn't want to mess with. Sometimes she wondered if all this tough behaviorism nonsense had just been a put-on? Under that crust, Selma must have a very sensitive skin. Or else, how could she have had a Cosmic Consciousness experience? Jesus, Buddha, Mohammed, Emerson, Lao Tzu had experiences like that, not one's step-mom! Boy, the Case of Selma is an odd one . . . and it isn't finished yet, thought Kate, in a mixture of wonder and rue, for the "inoculation of immortality" of the Light Experience had just started to take. Fondly, she looked at the strong, firm profile bent toward the book, *The Doors of Perception,* in the dim glow of the overhead light in the car as they drove to the YWCA for Mrs. Dee's next class.

"Listen to this, Kate," Selma read imperturbably, as they drove. "Huxley is asked by his wife if he would be able to die alone, remembering to do all that was necessary. And Huxley replies, after considering the question for some time, 'Perhaps I could—but only if there were somebody there to tell me about the Clear Light. One couldn't do it by oneself.' That's the point, I suppose, of the Tibetan ritual—someone sitting there all the time and telling you what's what.

"There's the problem, Kate, spelled out—you need a guide, a coach," Selma said. "And if Aldous Huxley, with all his experience with altered states, felt that he needed assistance, then I surely need my situation and solution spelled out for me! I suppose the *Tibetan Book of the Dead* gives the guidelines for the psyche, of that culture anyway. Which needs to be done for our culture, as well, because we are all human, whatever our culture, needing guidance and rite of passage. But this process hasn't been presented for the modern 20th century person, mainly because few know it's necessary. In fact, we are so besotted by a five-sense reality quotient, we've forgotten that any other quadrants of our nature exist. No one even considers the death moment important any more. It is seen as the end-point, the body being the only reality in most people's minds. No one sees death as part of our birthright, a new phase of existence.

Instead, a person's death is stuffed away in a room, or intensive care unit, or slept away in drugged dreams. The whole field of thanatology leads up to death—but leaves the moment itself to handle itself, thinking that the job is done if they just get the patient to that point as humanely as possible. All well and good, *but not good enough*. For usually the moment of death occurs under such aberrant conditions that, I ask you, how could one's experience of death not be adversely affected? By environment, by loneliness, by pain, by fear, by drugs, by grief— none of which are fitting to either meet or accompany death. And that doesn't even include accident death. What does a good Tibetan do if a gun is at his head? *Kjaere Gud,*damn and double damn!" Selma subsided into uneasy, angry silence.

Kate drove a while, thoughtfully, cutting over at the Silver Street exit to the YWCA. A long depressed moment slung between them. Slowly, hesitantly, Kate broke the unleavened quiet with: "Selma, do you think *you* could put together an instruction manual for a dying person? You've had this wild Light Experience, so you know what you are aiming for far better than a person with only a near-death brush with the Tunnel and the Light and all that. You probably even went deeper into the experience than they did, too. You are not a yogi, but Mrs. Dee could help, I bet." Kate's voice gathered momentum. She didn't have to wait for Selma to answer; her face was eloquent enough.

"Whoopee!" Kate shouted. "We are on the way to a yoga class—where we can learn relaxation techniques and God knows what else! But I betcha it's just what we need to know next!" Her eyes were shining in the darkness, lit by oncoming car lights.

Selma smiled to herself. Yes. She would do that. A manual, indeed. Audacious. Yes. But she'd give it a try. She almost laughed as she thought of her, of all people, a person who loathed shortcuts and TV dinners—putting together a "fast food version" of the *Tibetan Book of the Dead!* But short orders were all there would be time for. She'd give it a try.

So—there was something left to do, some reason to be in her life. A function. She'd taken other people through their crises and now had to find the means to take herself through the last crisis—into the great "crossing over wisdom" upon which all highly evolved beings depended at death—liberation in its wake. But that was to come later. At this point, she was aiming at self-help, more at a minor league level. "Boot-strapping," she called it. "As for now, Missy, let's get to that Yoga class," said Selma. Which is very roughly how two remarkable women would get to know each other and how the idea of the manual was born.

Mrs. Dee seemed to have expected Selma's request for help, and provided the missing link in the research for a good death. Now all the pieces of the puzzle were available for solving the unknown "how to die?" A Tibetan emigré, Mrs. Dee told Selma that her people had a tradition of right dying, which also effected a good re-entry into the next life. When she heard this, Selma uncharacteristically began to weep in relief. The pieces were falling in place. When Mrs. Dee brought Selma *The Tibetan Book of the Dead* in the Evans-Wenz edition, with a foreword by C. J. Jung, Selma knew for sure she was on course to put together some sort of guidance control system for her own take-off, called death. She recalled what Josip had said the day of the reception for *The Paradigm Shifters.* Actually he'd challenged her with his eyes somehow, when he wished someone would do a Reader's Digest version of *The Tibetan Book of the Dead*. She wanted it now, too, with all the heart and soul she was newly rediscovering. It can be said that all learning is a rediscovery of the known.

• • •

March had gusted, alternately blowing between winter and spring, like Selma. Tempestuous, inert, sulky and mild, she'd have good days and bad which followed in a pattern like the trough and crest of waves. She learned to use the momentum garnered on failing days as rest stops, like a surfer waiting for the wave upon which to travel.

Among the real things in her life, she included the simple mystery of dawn, as well as the shenanigans of the first robin and three cardinals that lived in the backyard all winter. Nature had always been a joy to Selma, but death had heightened her awareness of its moods, to which she likened her own seasons. Now she watched her last spring. Her body had stabilized; it wasn't in constant pain, but it wasn't much good either. In the last months, Mrs. Dee's teachings, which were going into the manual notes, helped her to reduce her pain by teaching her to relax and consciously control her body. And she talked to Kate a lot, knowing that Kate and her dad would be the ones to help in those last days. "Mrs. Dee planted a real bee in my bonnet the other day; listen to this," Selma said as she took out a series of quotes, shuffling them like cards, and read them to Kate.

"No master of yoga ever dies in the normal manner," read Selma from John White's *A Practical Guide to Death and Dying*. "That is to say ignorantly or full of resistance being the 'normal' manner," Kate commented wryly.

"Just wait—there's more," Selma went on. "No one, neither priest nor scientist, seems willing to affirm that dying can be an achievement, that the art of dying is as difficult as the art of living, and he who would master the first, must first be the master of the second. That a person can know when to die and can die at will, intentionally, with full awareness of what he is doing, is a concept so alien to our culture that one scarcely dares mention it without an apology. One who presents this concept is accused of being morbid, of suffering from an excess of the Freudian death wish, even of openly advocating suicide. But intentional dying has nothing to do with such flamboyant acts of self-destruction as setting fire to oneself or jumping off the Golden Gate Bridge, or even with such quiet exits as can be obtained by an overdose of barbiturates. Intentional dying is possible only for someone who has attained a high degree of mastery over physical functions, who knows how to project the principle of consciousness out of the physical body, who is able to tell by certain inner signs when his or her time has come, and who is able, with full awareness and without artificial aids, to let the life process come to a halt so far as this particular body is concerned."

"Wouldn't you like to meet some of these guys?" Selma asked, and she meant it. "Listen to this—from Dr. Ramamurti Mishra's *Fundamentals of Yoga*. 'The human mind has perceptive faculties other than those served by the five senses which we share with the lower animals. But through practice of samadhi, other worlds are revealed that are uncommon and eternal. Once the real eyes of the student are opened, he has an extension of his perception as stupendous as that of a previously blind man when he first acquires sight . . . By following the principles of Yoga, one heightens the power of concentration, arrests the vagaries of the mind by fixing one's attention on different chakras, and one masters one's soul in the same way as an athlete masters his body.' "

"Now, that's my kind of guy," Kate commented.

"Mine, too," said Selma. "I wonder if I can get anywhere near the mark, though, starting this late? Yet, something will be better than nothing."

Yet, Kate thought, since we all do die, we all have to practice the art of living mortally in the shadow of death, in order to open up in ourselves a space to more fully live. A space that had been formerly occupied by fear of death. And then, if we can get that one under our belts, we have to learn the art of dying. What a trip for this 20th century that won't even let you get old!

Selma leaned back and looked at the attractive young woman standing in front of her, arms akimbo, "Well, what do you think?"

"Well, I think you are on the right track, but you'd better stick with using this stuff to put together a system for people a bit less talented than those who go for the big time in that book," Kate mused.

Selma had been thinking the same thing—how to simplify this for just plain folks. "Just by using a kind of conditioned response by which you can teach the dying person to relax every part of the body by contraction and release—on command—you will have some major control over the person's attention, under whatever circumstances. Again the coach would be crucial in the operation," Selma went on.

"I remember during Erik's birth. When the contractions really hit, I would have lost my focus altogether if a nurse hadn't stepped in and talked me back. Thank God for that nurse who had done pioneer work with Grantly Dick-Read, for in those days, all they wanted to do was put you out, and bring the baby out from under a cabbage, or for the real romantics in the crowd, by stork! She kept me on course. Similarly, the waves of emotion and thoughts of the dying person could foul the lines of a good death.

"Coaching will help let go the dying person's fear and tension—thereby at least letting nature take a proper course. I don't think fear is the proper way to meet death."

"Then actually you don't want to just coast, you accelerate and jump right out-of-your-body like a bride into the bridegroom's arms?" Kate teased.

"Well, something like that," Selma concurred, "that's even the analogy St. Theresa used, and I believe, St. Francis," she said solemnly. "Anyhow, I'm too dumb to die, yet!"

The next yoga session was crucial for Selma's handicap. Mrs. Dee gave her a powerful mantram, the Gayatri, which she had chanted at their opening session, and a meditation exercise to develop a steady mind which could concentrate under any circumstances. She also agreed to come out to the house to teach Selma in the following weeks.

Mrs. Dee told Selma that the death process releases many experiences from the dying person's mental archives besides the review of the former life's events. These then project into seemingly objective manifestations, often demonic or angelic. The visions occur depending on which access route to the Mind, positive or negative, one triggers in the dying process. In other words, a negative emotional environment at death produces a "bad trip" somewhere, somewhen along the line. This possibility can be offset by coaching and by prayers for the dead, even if the newly dead person is either ignorant, uncooperative, in coma or an infant.

These visions must be seen for what they are, never fled from, which is the best way to deal with them, if you are aware. Mrs. Dee called this process "seeing," being the witness. These images and sensations should always be embraced as the content of one's own mind, no mean assignment for even an experienced meditator, Mrs. Dee told Kate and Selma. They swallowed hard and got the point that the support person was most important, or some sort of reminder of "what was what," as Huxley put it.

Mrs. Dee then lit a candle in front of Selma and told her to train her eyes on it. She was to see it as either the absence of everything material, or as *empty-mind,* or as the presence of everything in potential, *empty-mind.* Mrs. Dee assured Selma that light is the best symbol for the Void, as well as for introducing meditation to a beginner. She told Selma to practice twenty minutes morning and evening.

She was to gaze at the candle flame with half-closed eyes, keeping her spine straight, sitting either cross-legged on the floor or bed, or in a chair. Then she was to look at the flame with half-closed eyes, then close them. She was to retain the image of flame in her inner eye. Mrs. Dee urged Selma to feel the flame inside her, especially between the brows. Soon, Selma could hold the image. Shortly after, even when she only thought about the flame, she could feel the connection internally.

The next stage was to slide the feeling and/or image of the flame down into the lotus of the heart, illumining the path from pituitary gland to the pacer node in the heart and back again to the head. "When the feeling of luminosity enters your heart, imagine that the petals of the lotus open out one by one, or simply feel luminosity spreading behind your eyes. This feeling of light sometimes will flare visibly. Bathe every thought, feeling and emotion in that light," Mrs. Dee said. "Let there be no space for the darkness or disease to hide! Let the light become wider and brighter.

"Let the light then go into your tongue so falsehood vanishes. Let it rise back up into your ears and eyes, and dark desires vanish. Let light suffuse your head and brain and wrong thinking vanishes. Then imagine the light is in you more and more intensely and let it shine out of you, spreading from you in ever widening circles. Let it take in loved ones, friends and companions, then your enemies, and then strangers, then all living beings, the world, the solar universe, and the systems of higher universes that this universe is a part of, to God Itself. You will come to know divinity directly through this practice," she continued. "And when you go anywhere, try consciously to see the light of pure consciousness, *in every act of yours,* or anyone's, whether in human or animal nature, or in positive or negative situations. I assure you, it will change your life and your death," Mrs. Dee said softly, remembering the many times this meditation—in conjunction with the Gayatri's mantric power to amplify energy—had healed the sick, or provided the means of full consciousness at the moment of death to those who had been killed in Tibet through war, assisting as well the fortunate who experienced peaceful deaths.

Mrs. Dee told Selma that eventually the candle could be dispensed with, for the Light was within, the candle being only a training tool. While there are also certain psychic benefits derived from flame, whether that of an open fire or burning incense. Such an atmospheric cleansing was especially useful in sick rooms, or where there has been the expression of hate, or strong anger. Mrs. Dee also shared with Selma that they had been taught to use this exercise for self-protection. By recognizing the spiritual light in all sentient beings, friends or enemies, and truly feeling it, many miraculous things happened. Her family's guru taught them this life-saver along with the Gayatri.

For instance, as her family was escaping from Tibet, a squad of drunken young Chinese soldiers had intercepted them, with rape and murder on their minds. The whole family, even the youngest, had intensely practiced seeing the young soldiers as light, the Divine Unity Itself. While, in her case, she had tried to see them as wearing her teacher's face and hair, which was her preferred kind of meditation. The effect was instantaneous. Abashed the squad leader politely waved the family on its way, unmolested.

Curious, Selma had inquired who her teacher might be. With shock, but again peculiarly, with no inner surprise, she recognized the name of Josip's teacher—Sathya Sai Baba. Oh God, life comes full circle, she thought. *Kjaere Gud.* In a muffled small voice, Selma asked where they had met him, since he was supposed to be in central India someplace far from Tibet.

Quite simply, Mrs. Dee told her that he had saved their lives long-distance. He came in a dream to her young brother, Kalu, warning that he and his family would be killed by Chinese soldiers in seven days if they didn't leave their Tibetan village before then. Kalu balked and stalled at telling of a dream warning so dire. Several visitations had been necessary to persuade Kalu. Finally, at the eleventh hour, she and her immediate family left for India. Their village had been destroyed exactly seven days from the night of the dream.

Eventually the family went to thank the man to whom they owed their lives. He'd acknowledged bringing them warning, then counciled them to relocate in the States. He gave them the Gayatri mantram and the Jhoti light meditation to add to their own prayers. The two syllable chant, SO-HUM, with one syllable on the inward breath, one on the outward, would tune the consciousness, whatever tradition one belongs to, he had said. Mrs. Dee's family now represented a mixture of three traditions—her Catholic private school upbringing in India, the influence of Hinduism, and the family's practicing Buddhism.

"It is all one guru, one God, one inner master," Sai Baba had said in their home dialect. "Yet, there is love and destiny in the bond of recognition between master and student, outer and inner in the paradox of God. I AM come with all of my children already in my heart, as cells in my Body of Love, to which you only seem to be drawn. In truth, you only align with Me, which is simply aligning with your own inner Reality which I enjoy constantly, and for which you search. And now have found.

"Yet," he chuckled amiably, "How can a finger on your hand, heart in your body, or hair of your head ever be lost from you, since it is part of you? Likewise, you can never be lost from your own inner spiritual nature, which, however, you imagine you have lost and are therefore looking for! This is the paradox of human and divine life. Resolving it is the only function of any true teacher."

Although Selma did not take easily to needing any spiritual teacher—for it went totally against her do-it-yourself grain—she found this one's ecumenism and non-sectarianism a refreshing change in the midst of most religious groups' claim of exclusivity. Thank God, the fellow wasn't starting another religion, but only combining them. She remembered, however, that tuning forks had been the way Josip described the process, how one fork can set off another by resonance when it is ringing in proximity.

Whatever, she owed Providence, or someone, or something thanks for sending Mrs. Dee to her. Where would she be without her? *Kjaere Gud.* Out loud she said, "Why do you suppose we met, dear?" half knowing the answer.

Mrs. Dee's black eyes regarded her blue ones steadily, as she answered, "Service—dharma—as you give up your life to find it." Mrs. Dee replied. "And my small part is like a link in a necklace."

"Or a lifeline, lady!" Selma retorted, musing out loud, "We must have had many loving lifetimes together, for you to come all the way to help me—die." Selma laughed shortly.

Mrs. Dee smiled noncommittally, and continued, "When my teacher told me to come to the States for further education, there was the feeling that there were also people I had to meet over here, and that both karma and dharma would be served by my coming. I know now," she said softly, "I was to meet and assist you in your quest for the good death, Selma. Even as you will meet and assist others by assisting yourself with your manual. For this no doubt we were born."

Mrs. Dee's liquid black eyes were eloquent testimony of the love they both felt. "Call me any time, if I can help," she said, "although this is our last class before I return to India to see friends and family. I'll be back in a month." It went unspoken, she'd also see her teacher. It was equally unsaid, although both understood, Selma might not be there upon Mrs. Dee's return. Spontaneously, both women opened their arms to each other, embracing tenderly, tears in their eyes, for their affection was firm.

Gruffly, Selma managed to get out that she wanted Mrs. Dee to thank her teacher for sending such a lovely emissary of hope and freedom to her, just in time. She figured she owed him that.

• • •

March had come in like a lion, but soon the early crocus and reticulate iris were up. Swamp cabbage blossomed at Seaward Point. The mallards were back; the swans would soon arrive. The raccoons would soon stop robbing garbage and go back to swiping eggs. While Selma read how-to manuals and handbooks of whatever came to hand that Kate found for her. Selma was looking for a name and a style for her handbook, and she toyed with *How to Die—the Ultimate Manual,* and *The Everyman's Guide to Right Dying* which she disqualified because of inadvertent sexism. The deathing/birthing analogy was stirring in her mind as by the end of March to mid-April she went from the featherweight to the heavyweight tomes.

But Comper's *The Book of the Craft of Dying And Other Early English Tracts Concerning Death* was also not adequate for Selma's need. Or use. Or influence, except by default. It was as encrusted with the barnacles of the medieval mind as *The Tibetan Book of the Dead* was encoded by both the cultural and arcane lingo of its Bon religion and Buddhist tradition. She saw a hint of Guru yoga at the death moment, however, in the practice of whispering Christ's name into the dying person's ear as he or she expired, or shortly after. While the practice of prayers said and candles burned in the name of the deceased is a form of the Tibetan lama's guidance control and intercession with the new dead's trafficking. Selma also found out that the word "hospital," "hotel," and "hospice" derived from the same root word. Where would you rather die? Enough said, Selma thought.

By the end of March two forms of Selma's intent were visible—the theoretical and the practical. A handbook would be born of what she *already knew* from direct experience of the Light, plus what she had learned from Mrs. Dee and from her reading. She would put it together for herself, but with the idea of making a short, "how-to" book for the dying person and friends to use, after she had done the test run, so to speak.

She'd be the guinea pig to try it on. At best, it would work as a "liberation launch," using relaxation, body control, mental focus on letting go, as well as guru-yoga or name-of-God at take off. At worst, it would be simply a psychological sop to herself and the family for the trying situation death presents this culture. Yet, it couldn't hurt, she figured, and it would keep the family— not to speak of herself—occupied, and keep everyone from feeling so helpless. Or from splattering her with their grief or guilt when she died. Yet even as she argued through her disbelief, she was finally "getting it"—the six techniques of her manual would actually work. She'd had her own experience of being out-of-body and the example of the NDE people as proof that the consciousness principle was going somewhere at death. Which was as much as anyone could know without actually doing it.

She knew, too, as near-death research had proved, that the dying, if comatose—or even those declared clinically dead— could hear. Hearing, therefore, would likely be the last sense to go in death so during that transition time, she wanted her body to "hear" the right things. She devised the idea of a script she'd record to be played to "herself," wherever the body was. She would include the Sixth Technique as well as other instructions for guidance control. How many days one would play it de- pended on how long it took the consciousness principle to leave. She didn't know how long that would be but she wanted to use it for the three or four day period most traditions assigned to the "lying in" before burial. After that, surely she'd be securely in the secondary body and Arne could play the tape at home so he could monitor any afterlife considerations that would come up.

Why there was direct communication between the dead physical body and the secondary, astral body, Selma reasoned, had to be based on the quality of "deadness," or degree of breakdown of the five elements of the physical, as well as how far along the etheric body was in its disengaging process. Likely, according to conditions surrounding each particular death, the stages overlapped, she figured. She'd play safe and have her script of instructions first played or recited near the body. But, additionally, since she had the feeling that poor departures had to do with "scrambling" the signals between the physical, secondary body, the supportive biofield, or etheric body, she'd ask Arne to keep it playing.

Selma had been getting the picture, to put it mildly, that to have even a slight navigational strategy in this dying business was to her advantage. And to anyone's—just as it helps to have a destination in mind and to buy a ticket before a trip. Equally, she knew she didn't have a prayer of a chance to gain total mastery over her mind and body, like an athlete, in time for this excursion called death. By April 1st, she unabashedly accepted that even if a student trained for years in meditation, most usually they bailed out on a guru's name. So that left her most humble.

• • •

In the succeeding days, Selma felt frustration and outrage at the increasingly uncivilized situation she was beginning to see modern humanity in. She felt terribly alone as she plodded on with her notes. She started a script, using her own voice over various selections of sacred music to instruct herself as to "How to do it," which Arne would play at least four days, but hopefully the entire traditional Tibetan forty-nine days. Frankly, she was doubting if she could do it in four days, so she hoped he was patient and persistent. Nor was she at all sure she could by-pass the etheric Hades area, either through fear during her dying, or awe-filled fear of the Light—if it were stronger than what she'd got her feet wet with in the Light Experience at Seaward Point. Either situation would "knock her out" for three days, for sure. On her own. Alone. She had to have override. She recalled that Mrs. Dee had twitted her about not being too proud to ask for help—but she was so tired.

The Ginkgo Tree

April saw the Seaward Point house opened to everyone at last. Arne was no longer surprised at anything. All along the Connecticut River to Seaward Point the twigs had thickened and buds swelled. The bare willows were filigreed with delicate green along their branches, like tiny baby peas when the pod is stripped. By the third week, daffodils and forsythia co-existed. While in her maritime forest, within sight of the sea, bloodroot, spring beauties, Dutchman's breeches and trillium were in full, subtle bloom.

The leaves unfolded a bit more every day from their look of green, hanging, folded umbrellas to snapped-upright green flags. The world had a look of intaglio enameled green, thought Selma, everything done precisely by a cosmic jeweler. The lush of high summer is so different, so extravagantly spread, where this is tentatively drawn, unfolded, new, like babies. Granted, she had birth on the brain, still looking for the form the manual would take. Books on midwifery, childbirth, and videotapes on water birthing piled the sunporches of both houses. At the Middletown home, little Jon, a neighbor's child, came visiting. Seeing all the books on childbirth, as well as Selma's enlarging stomach, he went home to tell the neighborhood that Selma was having a baby. And so she was. In her own fashion.

. . .

Then one day in early May when the lilacs were heavy and the pre-dawn chorus of sleepy bird calls had sounded, Selma tried to get up. But her body would not move, wrapped in a torpor that would not respond to will, a ghastly weakness Selma had not felt since chemotherapy. She was terrified. The weakness was all-encompassing, pressing tendrils upon her intent to rise, dulling her cell by cell. The lines were closing.

Two hours later, she was able to struggle into her bath. It had been her morning companion for years, the water laving her flesh and spirit. But as she sagged in the tub, her spirit faltered; she knew now what she was up against, and that it soon would give no quarter or respite. Her belly appeared stretched as in early pregnancy, the color of old velum; several lumps had appeared elsewhere. Grudgingly she relinquished to this unknown kinsman its territory, but she insisted, as well, on hers—she would finish what she had started, even as then, it would finish her. But death would be elegant, and her burden, light.

She thought of Pablo Neruda's poem, "The Heights of Machu Picchu." The loneliness of that high place was upon her, her life vast structures of wind and snowdrift. She was a traveler, already embarked for a distant shore half-dreaded, mistily recognizable, half-awaited, but a high place.

Lying in the bath, letting go into the warmth like a safe uterine sea, Selma was finally able to mourn the passing of herself. February 27, at Seaward Point, she had almost touched this same desperate space. Then she had walked along the shore, her feet squelching through a boneyard of shells like live butterflies, to face mortality. Now a voice she thought, or was it herself, already in that high place, reminded her gently, "All that is born must die, but you are loved."

Often and longingly now, she thought of the ease and freedom of life in the alternate body that she had consciously experienced six months ago. Then her physical body had been in such a deep state of exhaustion and stupor that it could have been dead, but she had been assuredly alive, conscious on, and of, a multitude of frequencies. Soon she would be there once again, like a stack of Russian dolls, Unity's children, but this time for keeps. Seen from that point of view, death was quite nice after all. Or if you saw it as a limit, similar to a sonnet form in which you would write your life poem, limits are not all bad. Sometimes they are focusing devices—magnifying glasses, or a means to create brandy from life's blood and wine. Did Selma's knowledge of her other realities make her careless with physical life now? She thought not—quite to the contrary.

Lately, life had been especially poignant, her will to live whetted far more than usual. She was often appalled at the irony. For she knew it was her run-in with the past that had created this legacy called cancer, not her new-found immersion in the moment. As she looked at her belly, she thought, my road not taken is in that cancer, that's all. And then she understood it was all right. She accepted. Her dead-shell butterfly self was able now to fly away. But first, she insisted on finishing what she started.

Life wasn't easy. In fact, it took a warrior's courage to get through the ordeal of a day—the pain was constant. She wanted to go one last time to see the swans that bred in the breakwater by Seaward Point. She remembered at morning light always a few would rise in the air, but sometimes she'd heard the thunder of a hundred pairs of wings or more, fanning skyward. She wanted to see them spiral into the sun again. Then she could return home to her secret self—she'd never leave it now—after all, her four months were up.

Except she couldn't go. She knew she wasn't done yet. Desperately she needed to tap into other sources than the failing physical body in order to keep going. To learn how to go. She knew her father and Mrs. Dee had tapped universal *prana* to sustain their physical bodies, it being the life-force that sustained the worlds and all life, the breath of *prakriti,* Mrs. Dee called it. Could she tap it? Oh God, she had to. But how odd that the biofield, the rascal in a breech death—was the conduit and placenta to nourish her now.

This subtle pranic force could be siphoned from the air by the breath, and from the earth by the body, Mrs. Dee had said, as well as from the trunks of trees, mountain tops, and bodies of water which store it like batteries. Although Selma had practiced the breathing exercises as part of her regular routine with Mrs. Dee, now she turned to the Earth Mother in desperation, as well as to her tree.

Behind the house, facing toward the east and the sea stood a tree that had long been her favorite—a species called Ginkgo that originated in China. It was at its roots that she placed herself, back pressed to its trunk, sitting with her knees drawn up, with hands flat, palms down in the native American way one of her patients had shown her. She concentrated upon the psychic centers along her spine, using an inhalation breath to draw energy upward from the seat of generation into her head. She felt an expansion in her heart, as she came together in that place. Later, she would use this exercise as her "Withdrawal of Consciousness" technique, and would ask Arne to help her.

Power and life flowed through her as she practiced breathing up from the earth and then out the top of her head in a rhythmic, circular fashion. She later called this the "hoop" breath. Continuing, she lay down, then, in the presence of the Ginkgo tree. As she let the earth soak into her back and the sun soak into her front, she knew herself balanced between the two in that composite called a human being. She had both earth frequencies and solar frequencies bonded by spirit, independent of either. But while she was here, she was child of earth and sun, so said Mrs. Dee.

She lay in deep torpor and exhaustion, yet contentedly in a highly alert state, feeling something about to happen. Afterward she recalled that at one moment she was dissolved in the sunlight in which she basked like a lizard on a rock, with the earth and moss comfortable under her—the next she was sucked up behind her eyes and spiraling out the top of her head. She had just enough time to think "Let go," as she mentally closed her eyes and "jumped." As when at the swimming hole, the child Selma, flaxen-haired, stark-naked sexless limbs flailing, had held her nose and jumped, eyes wide open, trusting she would be fine. One has to cultivate a similar abandonment and trust for all life, Mrs. Dee had told her, especially in sleeping, loving, going out-of-body—or dying. Make all your preparations, then never hold back—just let go and do it when the time comes. And so she did.

Rapidly she poured herself up through the same image of blue-refracted diamond-design she recalled from the first night the Light gave her pain relief. Mrs. Dee would call it a mandala. Selma called it a design of some sort, like the old test patterns on television. They were one and the same. Prelude and consummation.

Then rapidly, across her inner vision which was also outside herself, witnessing, came swift images, but with no fanfare. She saw a journey across a bridge. There was a light burning on the other shore. It appeared to be an ordinary bridge across an arm of the sea not unlike that on the way to Seaward Point, but it was either only half-built, or had been half-destroyed. People crowded across it, spilling into the sea where it broke off, drowning in their own ignorance because they had no bridge, no reality construct to cross over from this shore to the Other Side, from one reality to another. The image disappeared.

Next she saw what appeared to be a television program superimposed upon the design which again filled her inner vision. A program flashed at super speed, similar to news clips. People of all races, creeds, and nationalities died, as people tend to do eventually. Some of these deaths were accident deaths of various kinds, natural catastrophes and war. And she was every man, woman and child who ever died. Most made it across, swimming the empty waters to the other side. But the deaths of skeptics, disbelievers, and materialists created disorientation, stupor, horror. All of these seemed lost, confused, scarcely even knowing they were dead, caught up in what looked like a thick gray fog. She knew it was the Gray Place. She heard herself ask, "What can be done to help these people?" And a voice answered, "Build them a bridge."

The screen went black, then tuned to another vision. Where the former had been as coolly objective as watching television, this one was subjective and hot with anguish.

She, too, now, was shrieking inside Tom Breacher's mind when the truck hit him. She experienced the full sensation tangibly, the pressure and crush as the truck smashed into her, for she was he. In astonishment, however, she noted both felt no pain, only the awful fear of what was about to happen that overwhelmed him, right before the Mack truck hit. Actually it was a Peterbilt, she noted, not missing a thing. Someone said, "Stop horsing around and really pay attention." She thought it was Josip's voice.

She snapped to, then, and noted that when Tom Breacher made impact, his energy field, the etheric that surrounded the physical, had become terribly contracted, not expanded which is the normal state. She knew experientially that the contracted etheric field was the deciding factor that had precipitated his light body, like a slingshot flying a stone into the thick, gray fog of confusion for an indefinite amount of time, until he was rescued by calling out for his father. Who answered. Was that part of the secret—that you had to ask? Electrified, she saw that it was the Sixth Technique that had rescued him, the technique she would need to use at death.

While he was lost in the crossing, she felt his horror, his anguish sucking her in, his misery was her own. With great effort, she extricated herself from the cloying darkness of his mind by following a familiar well-loved voice, or she might never have broken free. She heard herself asking in great agitation, "Well, what's to be done? Well?"

Josip answered, "People need to expand, not contract. Fear is not an appropriate response to death. Rehearsals for death are missing in Western culture—figure something out—a short cut if you want to. . . . Crisis death gives you one to thirty seconds of reaction—preparation time. Remember and record."

The screen went blank. The mandala "test pattern" returned, a hot, blue cobalt ring around a brilliant sun, diamond-white and ice-blue surrounding the pulsing, strobing blue of space. In alternating pulse beats, various faces of the world's spiritual heroes appeared in the sun core, blinking alternately with the various faces of many more whom she didn't know— an army of realized, enlightened cells in the Body-of-God, many of them saviors. Face to face, she experienced the Cosmic Buddy System, as tier after tier of enlightened cells blazed Light of Realized Beingness. *All* breathed infinite love for humankind, for soul Itself. Infinite wisdom and compassion expanded into all the universes. "Rest in Me!" sounded unconditionally, echoing out of time through time, spiraling into space, melding limits holographically. "Expand into me. Rest in me. Call my name, in any of my guises and disguises, any name of God you reverence, any name of God you cherish, any of my sons . . ."

When she came to, surprised to still be in the physical, she felt the presence of the holy multitudes like a fragrance. Selma was still under the Ginkgo tree—her cheeks slightly sun-burned, wet with tears. Awe and gratitude, and holy unspeakable joy supplanted her last encounter with mortal fear. She looked at her watch and sat up, slowly trying to piece it all together. Forty-five minutes had passed.

The first vision seemed clear enough in intent, "Build a bridge." While ample reason to build one was inherent in the shared experience with Tom. She couldn't escape a shiver. The cloying psychological glue of that gray etheric fog was a million times more unwholesome than the feeling of dissolution of her body, occupied by a parasite-guest called cancer—which was rapidly becoming the host to which she was guest! Then came the mandala with that enormous company of Cosmic Light-givers, all blazing and pulsing in perfect rhythm and accord. She had much to ponder in the meaning and application of both visions.

• • •

These days she found herself self-destructing as in a speeded up form of old age, with the tension of edges, precipices and high places to it as well. Living was something like taking a fast curve, half in a skid, half a banked turn, where you have to trust to forces past your own ability to control events. To let go . . . of control is the ultimate control, Selma realized. But this is hard to live through, she admitted. Although things could be worse. For instance, she could lose her wits before she got this job of deathing herself done!

Well, even if my brain were gone, she thought with a vestige of her old feistiness and in macabre humor, Arne would remind me—for "I AM still here, even when the equipment of the body is beyond repair." While, so far, her bodily functions were still under her control. Sort of. But even if they weren't, and one had to go back to wearing diapers, like the old menstrual rags women wore before the days of sanitary napkins—one gets used to anything, one adapts. The whole secret is "I am not the body, noway, nohow," she said to herself with a mixture of grimness and steadfastness. And in immense courage. Though she faltered when she thought of pain totally taking her over, if it came she'd deal with that, too. For now, she put the thought aside, put fear away. All the same, she made her resolution. Her weakness, and the catalyst of the visions of bridge and mandala galvanized her into action.

By the time Arne got back at noon that day, Selma had decided three things: 1) ready or not, she was finishing the manual and tape recording that week; 2) she was going to put herself and the family through trial runs of deathing, a "training" as it were; and 3) the concept of right dying, American short-order style, was to be called deathing, the counterpart of birthing.

• • •

People have asked, how did Selma cut through illness, despair, pain, and increasing weakness to do such an immense job? Because she had to, she would have answered. Because nobody else seemed to be doing it. Besides, *she* needed it done, as a means of instructing Arne and Kate as to how to help her die well. Simple enough reasons, no-nonsense reasons.

As for suffering and grief, she believed, like Colette, "that there are more urgent and honorable occupations than that incomparable waste of time we call suffering." Even though Selma now felt considerable pain, and although all too real the feelings about suffering, grief, and pain, those very real feelings were just not useful. Even as fearing death is not useful, except inasmuch as it urges you to prepare for it.

Yes, Selma had her Spartan streak; she knew a backbone was better than a wishbone—when you were about to enter unknown territory—like death. She also knew that most people are willing to do anything but work hard to be successful at anything. So she worked harder than she ever had before to gain the last success, the good death. Josip had quoted Pythagoras as saying that an individual's birthright was summed up in three goals. One should plant a tree, sire or bear a child, and know the good death. So it had been, so it would be.

She had put herself to the task of finding out how to die. And the Universe had answered. Before hand. Not letting her rely solely on on-the-job training, or the old pap that death will take care of itself, which in a highly unnatural society like this one is unlikely. At least not so as to let death happen very naturally, kindly or well. You almost have to teach a method of being natural, she mused, just as natural childbirth is a very studied approach to the process of birth. Birth or death, neither should be approached willy nilly.

• • •

Selma's manual was written by June 1—the bootstrap part of it anyhow—for she had still not quite made peace with the function of the guru at death, or the principle of "calling Central" via the name-of-God or enlightened teacher that would eventually become the Sixth Technique.

On June 6, however, the cosmic mandala with the heart-of-the-sun came once more, which persuaded her, let's say, that such a pilot, navigator, or captain (however one wants to call any realized, enlightened being—whether Christ, Buddha, Krishna or any of the thousand names of God), wasn't too bad to have around in an emergency take-off!

It wasn't the particular enlightened being that counted, although admittedly, she'd seen some as ten watts, some a hundred, some two-hundred-fifty watt bulbs in her visions. But it was the principle such a one represented, an access code to the Source—the Clear Light—the World Ground, Deity. Into which she or anyone plugged—by calling the Name, or visualizing the form of that realized being. Simple enough.

But could she put it across so everyone, even the churches and intellectuals would accept it? God, she wished she knew more physics—because of all people, it was people like her former self who were running businesses, universities, churches and nations who needed this information so badly. Having given up prayer for Lent the year she left home, she now prayed earnestly for guidance. Then she'd joked about what she and the 30's generation had in those days considered a futile, puling gesture. Faith. God. Prayer. The joke was on her.

It had all come round full circle, like her resistance to and misunderstanding of Josip. How much of life is only our argument for our limits? Well, she hoped the college kids and her colleagues would eventually read the book, anyhow. It would assist them, whether they believed it or not. And Selma realized she wanted her manual to help others after she had gone. Arne would see the book into print somehow, or Kate would prod him. She smiled briefly into the future.

Bearing Witness

During early June wild apple, plum and sprays of dogwood floated in a sea of greenery. This season always seemed more like Easter to Selma than the assigned "Resurrection time." Well, Pass-Over was going to take precedence now. And soon. Selma's body had stabilized; it didn't pain her overmuch, but it wasn't much good, either. She now addressed the question of, "Where is death?" And, "When will it come?" to herself. Then she realized she had put it into her bargain to see another cycle of the seasons before snow time.

So she waited. It seemed a good thing, after all, to make the circle. And like a child playing tag, waiting to be "It" she stalked death and let it stalk her. Or, as if standing on the seashore, she let the water come up over her ankles, then her calves, then ducked away again, to let it find her once more. So she practiced submitting, seeing "It" in all things having beginnings—and therefore, endings. Here all things change. Therefore, though it was foreign to her nature, she studiedly practiced letting go, under every circumstance, until she was "It." One day she would have practiced letting go enough to let It come, and It would be there.

The last wave of people began their visits to her, of a different sort than before. Word had gotten out that she had something to offer the terminally ill, something strange but rich with promise. In her, the dying came to one of their own, for comfort, for insight, there being no theory or analyst-to-patient role in their exchange, nor at this stage any talk of remission. Additionally, they wanted to know what she thought it was all about? Life and Death, anyway. The word spread, and they all shared.

Members of the AIDS community found her almost at the end. Selma listened quietly as they spilled out their anguish at death, at society's treating them as pariahs, and at their own confusion about the karma involved with this particular disease. She met Mark and Michael when both men had come to the house to talk. They had heard of what she was doing from someone in the ECAP program at Yale/New Haven Hospital. She surprised herself that day because she talked about the Sixth Technique, except it was no surprise when she saw their faces.

Before they came, she had planned to discuss only a rational, do-it-yourself approach to protect her reputation among the local humanists, medics, and psychologists, all her scientifically trained colleagues. Her intellectual posture went down before the faces of the two young men with the naked, suffering eyes. There was no deceit, no guile, no cover-up in their appeal to her. Wisdom opened past defensive self-protections in her; the hell with consensus thinking. These people needed help.

Without preamble, she spilled everything she knew about how to dial "central" at death and before, via the name of any realized being, or a favored name-of-God Itself. Simply, she told what had happened to her, how the manual had come about, how she discovered that guru yoga, her Sixth Technique, could help people die well. She halted, breathless, waiting for their response.

Michael smiled wanly at her half apologetic air, depreciating her need to make excuses for Buddha, Jesus, Rama or Krishna— or the existence of enlightened states of consciousness which were the backbone of the Sixth Technique. He said, "Kübler-Ross sees spirits and has visions, Bernie Siegel at Yale/New Haven Hospital has spirit guides—my mom belongs to a new age religion and does out-of-body travel—and you have a fuzzy-haired avatar swami for a teacher. I'll run with it, lady. These guys know the ropes; I don't. So I'll ask to travel in their company—hitchhike as you put it, the fail-safe way. And I pray *one* of them picks me up! I don't care who!"

She hugged and kissed him, not knowing who consoled whom, and gave him some of the precious *vibuthi*, the sacred ash that Mrs. Dee had brought from India. They left the house, the one supporting the other, moving as feebly as old men. She called to them, "Fail-safe!" knowing they would never reach another spring.

She was embarrassed; she was still shocked at herself for spilling the beans about the Sixth Technique. She who despised proselytizing! But wasn't she born again? Didn't she help them? So just bad for yourself, old girl, Selma told herself wryly, merely bad for your proud self-image of clear, calm and collected Dr. Rieseseg who never went out on a limb! But such limited parameters shrank in the Light. In the Sixth Technique, she knew she described a Cosmic Principle, whether to two or two million.

The young men were the first outside her family that she'd told of the Sixth Technique; Michael was first to practice it with Mark as his support. He died before she did by just two months. Mark reported back that the death had been peaceful. Exhausted as Selma was by then, she listened carefully and took notes for her manual.

He told her that first he had had photographic enlargements made of paintings of both Buddha and Christ. Michael had decided on both of them as drivers of his get-a-way car. Selma smiled at his vivid translation of the idea of "hitchhiking" with an avatar to be a "get-away" from a robbery. But, at 23, she knew he felt robbed.

They'd placed both pictures at the end of the bed in tandem. While in Japan, he'd seen paintings of the Far Land where the Buddhas live that are placed within eye range of the dying. Having your destination constantly before your eyes is considered an authentic one way ticket. The idea is that the dying must remember *where* they are headed—at all times. And with *whom*. So, he did the same with the Buddha's face, and a favorite picture of Jesus Christ. A fresh vase of flowers and a candle to remember the Light was kept by the photos.

His mom had wanted to add her teacher, too, for good measure. But Michael had no draw to him, while he felt pull to both Buddha and Christ. "Guess I've incarnated as a Buddhist and Christian and trust both," Michael shared good-naturedly. He also felt that too many images at this late date would be counter-productive.

Additionally, Mark taped his dying friend's voice repeating his own mantram, that of linking up himself and God to his own higher nature. They recorded it over and over until it extended the length of a tape which was then played constantly at the last, and at the lying-in. Mark kept it going, then, for a month after his friend's death, as well as prayed on his behalf. Selma was somewhat astonished at the dedication, application, faith, and plain old yankee ingenuity the young men exhibited. Michael was a medical student, too, she mused, how astonishing.

Partly shamed by their example, and partly due to her own integrity, this marked the end of her being such a coward about standing by the Sixth Technique publicly. The word continued to travel and she began to get calls from AIDS victims around the country. Most of her day now was spent on the phone, since she was no longer able to see many people.

Three Hospice workers dropped by—interested in the idea of the manual, as well as several more AIDS patients and their support teams. Since the concept of support, or buddy teams, is well established in the AIDS network, they caught on readily to the usefulness of the manual. By then, Selma had completely dropped all reservations concerning sharing the Sixth Technique. Nor did she any longer care if she sounded "too spiritual" and not "scientific" enough. She would have gone on the Donahue Show or Good Morning America with it! In actuality, she met with very little skepticism or resistance among the ill, for people in such situations are too desperate to play the usual mind-games that ordinary people who aren't dying tend to. People who came to Selma wanted help in their dying, or the dying of a dear friend.

History was made when two RNs who worked Emergency at Hartford Hospital talked with Joseph Tuchman about Selma's project. He'd told them about Selma. They drove all the way to Seaward Point to meet and talk about the idea of deathing, wanting copies of the manual, as well.

The two presented her with an excellent idea of condensing the instructions down to a mini-manual which interested staff could then apply in a hospital situation to the newly dead person. The RNs stressed that losing a patient under crisis circumstances, such as Emergency Room presents, makes many of the nursing staff wish that there were another step, something else they could do for patients after they had lost them. As well as something to make themselves feel less helpless. Then the one young woman confessed to Selma that she astral-projected, actually going into the Tunnel and approaching the Light with a patient! Selma was dumbfounded.

Thus, she said, she was able to nudge, cajole, and coax out the newly dead who "got stuck" in a constricted etheric, who couldn't, or sometimes wouldn't get out of the dead, unrepairable body. The new dead that she met in Emergency are often furious at their deaths, the RN told Selma. For instance, there was the case of a cyclist who'd gone one block from home for a loaf of bread. And wound up dead on arrival—with a ruptured aorta, body mangled. They'd spent five hours trying to save him and then gave up. Psychically during this time, she knew he was desperate to live. But there was no body for him to come back to! So, she had talked him across—talked him out of the shambles of his body—and into the Light. Selma listened with deep respect to this innovative, caring and gifted nurse, who showed the way of the future.

The three of them also conceived the idea of "Waiting Rooms" that someday could be added to hospitals, even as screaming rooms for the bereaved had already been added in some due to the efforts of Elisabeth Kübler-Ross. But the function of the waiting rooms would serve the dead, not the quick. They would be a place where the bodies of the newly dead could be given a few hours to rest in peace in order to withdraw energies from the physical body after the traumatic events that brought them to Emergency.

A waiting room for the newly dead would be especially necessary under traumatic departure conditions, to safely and effectively disengage the patient's different levels of being in that process called death. Nurses could act as a support system, if in-service programs for deathing were taught, somewhat in the same capacity as the astral-traveling nurse. As long as loving, firm guidance and instructions were given to let go to the Light, it would not matter if most support people were not as talented as the woman in Emergency.

After the nurses' visit, Selma added instructions to the manual for crisis deaths, suggesting how to give permission to the departing person to LET GO TO THE LIGHT, IT'S ALL RIGHT, in the name-of-God. The little jingle was to see her through as well.

Nor did she omit the Sixth Technique when she talked with the astral-traveling nurse. A practicing Catholic, the nurse had no trouble with the principle of evoking the name-of-God or Guru, which she called Christ, for her charges in Emergency. Nor did she have any resistance to throwing in, as she put it, Sathya Sai Baba's name, as well as a Tibetan or two if they showed up for duty.

• • •

In herself, Selma saw the phenomena she'd seen so often in others who were dying. The physical was waning, but the other aspects and quadrants of herself were swiftly unfolding. For instance, long she'd tried to successfully practice getting out-of-body to little avail. But now it was almost easy, as the rind of the physical softened through infirmity, thereby softening the etheric sheath as well. She knew that others like herself who were terminal, or those with advanced senility, Alzheimers, or in coma, were also already operating partially out of the secondary body, before the physical died, either for karmic reasons, or simply because they needed adjustment time to splice both worlds. As did the survivors.

She made practice flights to the Other Side getting ready for boarding, making short OBE flights out the *nierika* or the third-eye area, like an eagle sorties from the nest. Some movements were so subtle she hardly knew them as flights, and rather thought of them as dreams, or imaginings. Others were unmistakable, along the line of her original OBE at Seaward Point. In one experience of that order higher than dreams, she was overjoyed to meet Josip, this time not just hearing his voice as before. She knew then it would not be long.

Blossoms

Selma and the family remembered the so-called rehearsal of the manual as a day of blossoms. Later, they had dry runs once a week, like fire drills in grade school, Kate joked.

It had been after lunch when Selma lay dozing on the divan on the sun deck off the study, half in shadow, half in dappled sunlight from the huge flowering plum tree out back of the Middletown house. She wakened to the gentle settling of blossoms pelting her lightly. Behind her closed lids, the petals in which she was buried made her think she was already dead. It was silent and wonderful. She felt her last fear of dissolution let go, like a melting chunk of ice. Her last, "When I have fears that I shall cease to be," vanished, leaving her ecstatic. With difficulty, then, and some regret, she realized she was assuredly still here and opened her eyes, blinking away the blossom's cool, tender touch, the air thick with a shower of pink and white, ground and divan littered with flowers. She looked up in new wonderment at the old plum that overhung the porch. Ugly in every season but this moment which it was now shedding, it relinquished itself in this shower of blossoms in which she was covered, her dandelion fluff and white-flag hair sequined with pink and white. A brisk wind from the river stirred through the laden branches as slowly and with difficulty, pregnant with herself, Selma swung bare feet onto the deck, dislodging some of the petals. Slowly she took in her breath so as not to disturb the atmosphere of joyful wantonness, the scent overpowering. Bees hummed, extracting the last secretions before it was too late. Their buzzing hum sounded "home, home, home, home," as they busily hummed the sacred mantram of the universe.

Selma felt her bare feet press down petals, damply, fragrance all around her. How gorgeous, she thought. She laughed aloud, which is how Arne found her, having watched the whole episode from the doorway. Seen her body outstretched and watched it become slowly covered, utterly grown over with petals so that her features, in an illusion of cherubic youth, no longer showed on the fragrant bier. Terror rose up in him and then he let it go. Nature was showing them all how to do it as surely as Selma's agile intellect and caring heart tried in this last good work, wilder than skydiving, higher than flying. How rarely we listen, or look, or pay attention to a moment like this, which is why books and poetry were invented—like live and die and live until you say good-bye, he thought.

Now the look of her was that of a child, an aging child, he thought, past joy, past despair. He buried his head in her lap as she comforted him, petting his lank hair, his arms around her, the hard distension of her stomach against his cheek like a pregnancy. It seemed smaller. But just as they had agreed to let fear go, they'd agreed also to let go hope of cure. Just to let be. Life teaches something other than hurrying after something. This moment sufficed.

People had bitterly criticized her for not submitting to aggressive measures like surgery. And he was criticized for his defense of her decision. But could there be anything more than this moment, he thought? Would hospital life these last months, and a maimed body, or amputated limbs, be better than a petal bier on a June day? Each person had to decide, Arne thought, as the petals came down and fragrance contained them both. Kate broke them out of their reverie, gently. "We are all ready, Mom, Dad . . ."

As Eric and Kate pushed the portable divan into the living room through the porch doors, petals streamed behind them. All remarked on the wonder of it all. Selma's eyes brimmed almost to overflowing. It was almost too beautiful to bear, life, she thought—this wonderful gift of life. And too sweet to hold. The only secret is to let be each moment, she thought. And then let go every breath and moment, so another can take its place. How to say that to these children from whom she was about to be swept away? To tell them that she was content?

Selma had the best part of the living room, positioned facing the open window, air moving gently against her face. She looked past the porch littered with the nuptial finery of the old plum tree into the sensuous emerald green haze along the Connecticut

River. The most lovely of seasons. What a strange time to die, she thought; in spring, but a perfect time. She had it all worked out that she was going to make transition in oh, two weeks anyhow . . . it was getting on toward graduation time.

Rehearsal

As if she were teaching again, Selma rallied and swept her eyes around the room, then allowed herself a bit of mischief. In her most important voice, she said, "Well, class, have you all read the assignment?" For by this time, she had the manual done. They all roared, relief channeled through laughter. But now that it was actually the dress rehearsal moment, everyone had stage fright. Except Selma.

Selma said, "By now you know how it all started with pain, at least this manual how-to part of it. I turned to yoga with Kate's help, and then Mrs. Dee's, to learn to relax my body, to better control it, thus reducing pain. Out of this came bonuses— expansion of consciousness and some out-of-body experience to act as a back up to my understanding of what happened the weekend of the Light Experience. And the Sixth Technique.

"Before we begin, there are a few things I want to share with you and they are heartfelt. A prayer and a warning. Death is a rite of passage, I am convinced. It won't yield to intellectualizing when you are experiencing it. I pray that this idea of deathing, even in its preliminary form, will always be directed to the whole person interacting with it—whether by reading about it, or practicing it. Let us lend enlightenment to the process of transition— to the death moment itself—in this methodless method I call deathing, which will always follow being born. It serves the same function of dignity, control, and life affirmation as does prepared natural childbirth. Pregnancy produces a baby. Deathing may as well, the baby of pure consciousness meeting the Light of its own beingness.

"My modest aim for myself, and others, is to take care of the death moment itself, although I am sneaking in the next four days afterwards, and ask you to play the tape I made for the rest of the forty-nine days, just in case I may be slow or forgetful. But, my real point in the manual is the death moment itself. I know, if I take care of that the 'baby' will come."

She paused a moment, looking at them intently, her blue eyes shining, a few petals still caught in the fine spun wild nimbus of hair. In her blue dressing gown, her low, passionate voice could be that of the prophesying pythoness at Delphi, Kate thought in wonder.

"Kids, *Go with the flow* of the situation, *no matter what!* Let love, even humor . . . expand, *never contract* your efforts, all of which will affect my efforts and ability to keep expanded, not contracted, when facing fear, pain, anxiety, or even awe of the unknown. I have complete faith in the Sixth Technique— knowing I have Arne's support and your assistance." Selma exchanged a glance with him. "Whatever happens at my death, no matter how bizarre, or different from what we expect or prepare for, fair or foul, *it's all right!*" She admonished fondly. "Remember . . . it's all Light in the long run, though it casts shadows. Any day is a good day to be born or die! All of us together will achieve the good death of ol' Selma.

"But for now—just understand that *fear* contracts the firing action of either getting out-of-body, going to sleep, healing, making love, or dying well—and creates bad effects. In the case of dying, constriction of the energy field through negative thoughts or fear causes bad dreams. While love expands your energy, and mine, and my navigator's as well. Love accelerates the natural process of the evolution of both individual and universal consciousness and brings good dreams, or lives, scripts and worlds in coherent, illumined harmony. So remember what I'm going to say now.

"Let love flow through your heart to me, from your mind to me, through your voice to me as you LOVE ME AND LET GO. Follow the instructions in the manual, watching for signs of where I'm at—or guess where I am in the withdrawal of the consciousness process. The stages don't have to be sequential, for it's likely that things will be either slowed or speeded up, not unlike the time difference in childbirth.

"Next, keep affirming for me to go into the Light, let go to the Light, whenever it intuitively comes to you to say it. Use your sixth sense like I will the Sixth Technique. Say 'Go Deeper into the Light, relax into the Light, let go to the Light. You are the Light, etc. You are all that is; flee from nothing; be all you see.' And be sure to alternate these injunctions with the name of my captain, the enlightened Being you know I'm training myself to remember as much as possible in my life, who will assist me in my efforts at death as well.

"Using the Sixth Technique is not a spiritual welfare program, however. I am responsible for doing the best I can on my own—but my teacher will help me. I no longer feel like a failure by asking for help in an area I have no experience of—so much for pride. Any questions?" She paused.

"Remember—it doesn't matter which savior you call on— or even if you don't believe it works. You don't have to know how to make a telephone to use it, do you? But, you do have to have it connected! In the Sixth Technique, connecting means knowing the name, using the name as a reflex, automatically, all the while being open and loving to that being. It works like two tuning forks that resonate to each other. And the more you love God the better, but you *don't have to love*. I guess they have enough love for you to cover for the deficiency.

"As for me, I use a linking of my personal identity with his liberated identity as my formula for a personal mantra. Anybody can use the same formula with their teacher." She trailed off, more to herself than them. The bizarreness, yet naturalness in talking like this moved everyone. The room was full of feelings, of care, love, and concern.

"And as the days pass after my death, play the tape I made several times a day. Simply say or think, Be the Light, Be God, You are God, when thinking of me. Don't address me by name, although you may call me Soul-of-Selma. Time will not be linear where I am. Although the Selma package is unwrapping itself, the old coordinates will still exist, for nothing is ever lost in reality. The Selma you knew needs to be busily adding unto Itself by experiencing the letting go into death process, and resultant illumination, so help me by linking my old identity with the real Self that I am.

"After a while . . . in five to six days, you will no doubt feel my vibration for I may be coming around, occasionally, visiting in my Light body. Continue to tell me not to be afraid of anything. Tell me that what I see is only the magic pictures of the universe, while I am the projector and film. Go to the Light, it's all all right, and be Light, be Light, be Light.

"As my last request to you, I urge you to train yourself, in your own life to remember your favored name of God to hold in your heart and mind while in life, and to use at your death. *Start now* to practice seeing all life as an expression of divinity. If you can do all in the name of God, you are no longer the actor acting and taking the credit—or discredit—for the action. Take action without needing the fruit of the harvest. This is called karmaless action, and will help you to progress spiritually, as well as prepare for death. For in a sense, all life is only a preparation for death—or illumination.

"But, you don't have to die to do it. I know I am speaking cryptically," Selma apologized, seeing Erik's open, but frankly puzzled face, as she continued. "See everything that is physical as merely solidified light, or as Light-in-form. Other than my abiding love of you all, this is all I can leave you." Silence meshed with the tree frogs' sunset song as petals continued to litter the porch with finery.

Test Case

One day late in July Selma tried to get up from the lawnchair but her body would not respond to her will. She knew terror, but realized it was her body's terror, not that of her real identity. Selma understood she had to visit the terror intimately now. She knew that as the disease progressed, increasingly she would have "mock ups" she could practice "ego death" upon, which is actually what death is, and what meditation teaches. Both are the cessation of the body-mind's dominance, as well as a transfer of attention to the higher processes of psycho-spiritual reality, a closing of the gap between object and subject. Meditation teaches you how to let go of stress, in preparation for the final letting go.

Mrs. Dee had urged her to go down into dissolution of her body and the resultant terror that she would cease to be. She was to submerge in the fear and the pain so she blended into it, not desiring its cessation, nor recoiling from it. The same process would occur at death, as the various elements that made up the body dissolved into each other. Then she was to watch the process of dissolution as she had her pain and terror, extinguishing its hold upon her by neither recoiling nor identifying with it. She was to be both the witness and the participant in her own death, diving deeply to get to the eye of the hurricane. She would not cease to be.

Time and again, Selma thought she'd finished with mortal terror, but here it was again. She rattled and shook, agony pouring through her veins like a heat wave, but something being born as well. Wracked, she thought she was surely dying, the pain being such she couldn't do it quick enough to suit her. Pressure and pain like a ravening beast gnawed and chewed at her vital parts, shrieking up and down her spine, exploding in her head. Even if she could have moved to get them, she didn't want to take the prescription drugs she had, or alcohol, which she used moderately, for that would cloud her consciousness, if this was "it." Her consciousness had to be clear in order to die clearly, into the Clear Light of Day, she knew. But oh God.

In desperation and despair, she cried out for Arne, but no sound emitted, as in a nightmare, her body pervaded by a deep, painful fog and immobility. Though she couldn't draw in a breath, nor even think of the top of her head, much less find it through the burning mental haze, she remembered enough to cast about to anchor somewhere positive. Involuntarily, spontaneously, she cried out for God. At that moment, for the first time, she knew the identity of the Sixth Technique—for her—and had mind for nothing more. The memory of the flame and the face with its tender smile, stroked her heart, almost smothered in pain.

She anchored on her name-of-God as if harpooning a whale, it both pulling her out to sea and reeling her in. Then the sphere of light shown like a little sun by her chair. His human form came into focus, alternating with that of the sphere of light, then back into focus as human once more and pain and fear stopped short. His look of infinite compassion had a quizzical air, as if to say, "You called? I answer! Do you doubt it?" She no longer doubted, even in the finest crannies of her heart and mind. That, she admitted, was quite a feat and marked the finishing off of the "old Selma" that had vied with the new all through this strange journey into Light.

At which moment, on a day when July basked like a lizard on a rock, her exemplar of the Sixth Technique faded away into the sun in her eyes. The pain went with him, leaving peace and well-being, the scent of jasmine and wisteria lingering in the air. "Why, it works!" she cried out loud and began to sob; test case over. Even as she realized that the lines had closed, and her body would soon die.

That day Selma celebrated her good fortune to share these last poignant months with her family, and accepted her own great crossing-over wisdom. How strange she really hadn't known until now—at almost the twelfth hour! As her realization came to full bloom in heart and mind, Selma felt her body slowly respond once more to her will, feebly, but with some compliance. She lay back, then, looking up at the blue and glass-clear sky in a peace that passed understanding.

Retrospective and Requiem

The last of July and into August were days of blue sky, sea and sand, blended with a horizon that reached the high place Selma was going to. While goldenrod and cornflowers, plus armloads of zinneas, marigolds, and her huge Russian sunflowers all delighted the eye.

Gone were the luxuriant scents of wisteria and mock orange, summer rolled over to the beginnings of fall, a dreamer turning in sleep. Greens darkened and deepened, the haze cleared and skies became blue as corn flowers. She practiced letting go as she dozed by the sea, allowing the waves of her consciousness to pattern with the waves of the sea. Pain came, then letting pain go, joy came, then letting joy go; equanimity came. And stayed. Storms had passed, trials come and gone, childhood, youth and maturity had been experienced. It was a good enough life, thought Selma though she knew that the quality had sometimes been patchy. Yet, she had followed her own bent, commendable at a time when women usually were totally formed by circumstances. Nor had she hurt many people, she had loved and been loved, even though hurting one person was too many. And she had done that out of fear, fear of hurting others as well as herself. Fear, then, not love had dictated a major decision. The life she had walked away from had come back to her. She and Josip met once more and she and Arne were almost caught up to where he had gone. Soon, now.

She had worked hard to play catch up—with herself, really—to gain the last success. She had worked harder these last
six months than ever before to gain the lost birthright which had
to be re-won—the good death and transfiguration.

She let her mind wander, and wished she had the right, like
Socrates, to drink the hemlock. But she was wise enough to
know she could not do that. For ordinary people, suicide makes
it impossible to keep the necessary focus on positive images and
thoughts, for a part of you knows you are cheating life's hour-
glass, defying the allotted time, the number of breaths coded
into your vehicle, the garage for the consciousness principle. The
Cosmic Plan would be defied, not deified. While the conscious
dying of a yogi who knew his time and place was a whole
different matter. Oh, it was so complicated; she really was too
tired to think of it properly. But she knew for her to do it right,
death had to ambush her, like a deadline, or choose her like the
moment on the ice had almost chosen her. And then she would
let go.

The Walk

It was her month, on a day much the way she looked, with blue
eyes like October skies, the hair turned to white clouds flying.
Selma wondered, like a child waiting for a birthday, was it today?
Would it ever come? She was gay and celebrative, expectant . . .
tremulous.

Along the garden wall roses nestled in ivy, as flaming sumac
punctuated maples and oaks that drifted bronzed and golden
leaves along the path to the sea. Outside the bay window, Selma
saw the birds at the sunflowers which drooped their heads now,
spilling seed. Selma lost herself in the vision of the seeds falling
every which-way when the birds flew away, and had the idea—
now, just this minute—to go for a walk in the fallen splendor of
the leaves. It was October 7, two weeks before her birthday.

• • •

To see Selma would shock anyone who had not been around her for some time, like her son Mark who decided to come home once more. He hadn't told his mother yet. Erik warned him how fragile and see-through luminous she was, her bones as thin as sticks, the blue, fading eyes immense, looking often into the distance, as if waiting for something. But he had not told him that she radiated an acceptance that embarrassed him, nor did he make much mention of her manual, not to speak of their fire drills. All of the above would have effects.

At noon, Mark arrived at Bradley Field having missed lunch on board. He grabbed a sandwich at the airport and drove toward Seaward Point where Erik said everyone would be for the weekend. Mark had told Erik he'd be there around two o'clock, but to let it be a surprise. Mark knew it certainly would be for him, he hadn't been near the house since he was 16. His mother had put it off limits for him then, and never relented.

Mama had always let them have their way with the shore house as children, playing on the beach, digging for clams, cookouts and picnics. But when the teenage and young adult years began, as they wanted to be with friends and the picnics turned to beer parties—she'd said no. Like the damned spot was sacred or something, Seaward Point was her special place, Mark thought with a trace of the old anger at the banishment. For she really hadn't welcomed any of them after that. Which is what made it all the more surprising to him that suddenly the whole family was invited to Seaward Point.

• • •

Selma made preparations to take her walk. Everything these days was such a production, she sighed. She regretted being so weak. Very carefully, so carefully, Selma swung her legs off the divan. She didn't want to fall at this stage of the game, no sir! Her vision swirled her about like a merry-go-round as she sat, gripping the divan as if it might run away with her. Carefully she focused her attention outward, pulling it from that inward place it liked to dwell these days. Ah, good. There, it was back! So now she dared to move.

Owlishly, she cocked her head, blinking her huge blue eyes rapidly, the look of an escaped child pronounced. She noted with satisfaction that no one was about, although Kate was baking a quiche in the kitchen. Maybe someone was coming for dinner, who could it be? Selma felt slightly naughty, for she knew Kate would scold her for going out alone, but she had to go right now. It was calling her. She went out the back door, stopping frequently to both rest and listen for pursuit. Satisfied she wasn't being followed, she felt adventurous as she passed the carport without mishap, holding onto the bushes occasionally for support, then cut through the scrub grass and sedge to the seashore.

Oh, good, she thought, the sea was talking to itself and to her as usual. She greeted it with affection, thanking it for all these years of service and joy when it had been the only sustainer during difficult times.

The wind felt tangible, even as it was audible, singing companionably, "home, home, home," through the tall Norwegian pines. She smelled their rosin in the sun and the loam, rich and fecund from the leaves of maritime oak, maple and elm. Peering ahead, she thought she saw the glen, just over the lee from the dune and swale and sea, the pond in the distance like a metal shield, light pouring off it, almost blinding her. With a little sob, her joy vanished as she recalled Josip's saying how her coloring perfectly matched October.

She found her joy again as her feet found the overgrown path along the shore that led to the glade. Scuffing the fragrant, loamy leaves under foot and drawing in a deep breath, holding it as long as she could, she passed the Ginkgo tree, and looked back. Ah, it was her tall, stately friend of all seasons under which she could sit most intimately in another world, a world carved like its wonderful leaves of ancient green jade. But not today. Today she wanted the wanton, unraked fallen leaves underfoot fresh and crisp, pungent with earth, the pleasure of stepping on them like the pleasure of biting into a crisp apple. She kicked leaves about like a youngster, reeling as if slightly intoxicated. She squinted at the light, the brilliant yellows, reds and greens incandescent, nature putting the frame of intense blue sky overhead and decided she would not go all the way. It was the feel and smell of the leaves she wanted, the rough kindly bark of her favorite trees that she wanted to touch, to lean against for a moment, just a little moment before she left.

Turning back meant turning around, reminding her of spinning when she was a child, spinning round and round for fun. Panting, slightly dizzy, her breathing light and shallow, she oriented herself, her hand grasping a small sapling. She realized she'd forgotten to tell Arne and the children the most important thing of all. It was to be happy. That happiness was maybe better even than love, though you can't have love without happiness, she guessed.

Kjaere Gud, she was so happy! Yes, that was it. Very, very happy. Tripping over a branch she could not see, her body felled in slow motion as she stepped out into space with the sun in her eyes, so very happy. Falling played hide-and-seek with up and down to finally settle her body softly into a leaf pile.

Part of her lay still, listening to the restless October wind hum harmonics. Playfully, the companionable leaves covered her; she was a child again, burrowing into leaf piles and laying mysteriously quiet, smelling the ripe smell of life itself. No one could ever find her, except Papa.

Perfect happiness and light did not distract her as she lay on her back, the sun in her eyes . . . "let not thy mind be distracted, go to the Light, it's all right." Ha, the Light was right there all the time, everywhere. See, it's so bright, she had to squint. She'd have to tell Arne and Kate, they'd be worried about her. She should have told them to eat supper without her. The leaves now half blanketed her body, slowly settling russet in her wintered hair, sun in her eyes, now, all she knew . . . Light there all the time . . . how odd she hadn't noticed. She'd have to . . .

• • •

Kate was the first to notice that Selma was missing. As she hurried to check the front yard, Mark drove up with a big grin, although his face was strained. He'd picked a lousy time for a surprise visit home, she thought, even though she hugged him warmly and enlisted his help.

It was Mark who found her first, almost covered with leaves, her white hair tumbled untidily. He fell to his knees in shock, screaming for help, waving frantically. But no one was there. Desperately he moaned, "Why me?" Why did he have to find her looking like a sleeping, aged child, but like no one he had ever known before? "Oh God," he cried. In terror, he reached to lift the frail body. When Selma suddenly breathed, Mark almost dropped her. "Mama, Mama, Mama," he cried to her for help, not knowing where else to turn, scared, wanting to be anywhere but here. He had to get someone. That's right, he thought in relief; call a doctor! He took off up the path to the house, sprinting for the phone, unthinking, just reacting to his terror and abandonment, begging the operator to get a hospital, any hospital. Dimly from the yard, he heard Kate yelling, "No, Mark . . . No!" Not knowing what she meant.

• • •

From a long way away Selma heard herself say, "Let not thy mind be distracted. Go to the light, it's all right!" as Mark knelt beside her body in the bed of leaves. Querulously, she plainted, *Kjaere Gud,* boy! Why are you distracting me so with all this? I was so happy . . . why didn't you leave me be? Didn't I tell you never to come in on me unannounced in four situations without knocking? First, when I was bathing, on the pot, in the bedroom, or with a patient? Now, I'm with a patient, dearie. ME!

The moment Mark touched her, she helplessly dove back into the body, bagged, almost blind, dumb, but not deaf, half-in, half-out of the body. As they hurried her down the path on a stretcher, the sky lurched above her, dipping first to blue, then to spilled light everywhere, spinning, spinning, spinning . . . round and round, still playing hide'n go seek with up and down.

• • •

One hour before, as Selma's body pitched over onto the leafy path, a part of Selma had zephyred high above Seaward Point. Ecstatic, she saw the estuary spread a brilliant blue below her, met with the river, its banks lit with the kelly-green and burnt-sienna of fall, the heavens above. Then, more immediately, from a position in the Ginkgo tree, Selma had seen Mark racing toward her body, his mouth shaping the words, "Mama, Mama, Mama," which bellowed in her head, noisily, gusting her with his grief and terror. She felt no surprise, or distress—except she didn't want him to break in on her now. She was busy deathing herself—couldn't the boy tell? Couldn't he leave her alone, since she was doing so well? She flitted away.

From her yet new perch and vantage point in the tallest Norwegian pine in the glen, she continued to watch Mark run up to the body of Selma that lay sprawled among the leaves. "Why, it works!" she thought exultantly, referring to her ejection from the physical body so easily. Although she'd had every reason to believe it worked, when the second part of the Light Experience in January had sent her skatting all over the universe.

Now she watched, curiously, as Mark ran up to the little ragdoll mannequin of herself sprawled on the path. She saw him touch her, and she plopped back into the leaf pile. That, she hadn't planned on. She hadn't reckoned that once out, mere touch could draw her back! Why, she should tell that to Dr. Tuchman and those nice RNs. They'd better know that. *Kjaere Gud* and double damn it anyhow, though. That meant complications.

The pressure was suffocating her now with what she'd have to call pain, for everything in her was riddled with disease. She stopped her mind short, rearing it back onto its haunches like a runaway horse she was riding.

Guiltily, her mind fretted and stewed, for she knew she wasn't to think anything negative, or dwell on anything but Light, especially not a ghastly image like being a sack of bagworms. "This is dangerous territory, Selma, old girl. You are not properly dead yet; there are things to do, so pay attention!" She scolded herself, forgetting all about God, or her navigator. It upset her that the physical body that was breaking up would affect the secondary body differently than a mere out-of-body experience. In fact, this was almost totally different, for now she was not only flotsam and jetsam to the world of thought, she was also on the receiving end of physical effects. *Kjaere Gud* anyhow.

Big Time

She'd learned while birthing Erik that when labor got intense it was imperative to concentrate. For once you let the birth/labor process slip away, the universe began breaking over your head, like a tidal wave. But she gained freedom, control, balance and even ecstasy when she had used her breath to ride and surf those huge waves, the contractions that ebbed and flowed, no longer a victim of the body's demands.

Now she'd had her first set-back in this dying business, equivalent to losing control in the birth process—now she realized that death might well be far more subtle than the kind of physical dominance that occurred in birthing, and thus trickier to monitor, harder to keep her mind clear of distractions. And where was this Light, anyhow?

Nothing new seemed to be happening. Everything was in slow motion, the Eternal now yawned forever, as Selma, half-in and half-out-of-the-body, saw Mark still running toward her, although she could have sworn he'd already touched her. While wretched pain was building up in her chest.

She hurt so to draw in breath that she decided not to breathe. Peevishly, she wished she wasn't back in the body. She'd enjoyed, nay, adored the utter clarity of being in the secondary body. Yet, how to get out there once more? Time was all so confusing. She guessed she had to pack her bags for keeps, in order to stay out.

Once she got out again, by damn, she'd withdraw all her energies, using her breath to roll them up toward her head like Mrs. Dee taught her. That would pull the plug, all right. If she switched to the secondary body again before that happened, she would submit that body to the Light as well, to dissolve in splendor.

But she was scared; she felt like a little girl lost. Be brave, be brave, little girl, she told herself. Then her partial Selma-self came back on her . . . stacks of Russian dolls and selves without number and she was falling and spinning every which way. She noticed she was starting, despite the pain, to get euphoric. The same thing had happened in early labor with Erik, probably endorphins pouring in at the crisis response. She recalled now, with some humor, that in early labor she'd also congratulated herself, thinking, "What a cinch, this isn't so bad, a little breathing here and there and all is well." Then, heavy labor knocked her silly. *Kjaere Gud,* she'd better be alert for more counterparts in the deathing process.

But, my oh my, she felt exhilarated. This was it. Big time, no more tests. Having prepared for exams, she felt like she knew enough to do well, but even so, there was an area of ambivalence, a gray area which could throw her low or high—if the wrong situation occurred, were she not to have the answer. Just then, it happened. Again.

Mark reached her, weeping, touched her cheek, and then— even worse—tried to pick her up, and of all things, next, took off running for the house. She had a terrible feeling that he was bolting, and would call Emergency, which of course would send an ambulance to take her to the hospital, and then the fat was in the fire. Her helplessness while in the body infuriated her. She wanted to run after him, and drat, tackle the kid—even though he was a grown man by now, acting like a little, lost, panicked boy.

"Don't do it, Mark!" she heard Kate yell. Selma yelled, too. Then with a sigh, for she was standing right by him as he dialed, Selma saw he didn't hear either of them. So now we'll have to go through all this, she thought resignedly, more to Selma-the-body, than to herself.

Then Kate flung down on Selma's body, sobbing, and Selma in and out as she was, wanted to reassure her, and pet the tawny hair, but she couldn't move her hands. Her frustration popped her out-of-body again, where she drifted over to the Ginkgo tree one last time, hanging in its field like a hummingbird. With rather a shock she felt it say hello and good-bye, as its energy greeted hers on the same wavelength. "I love you, I love you . . ." she called as she returned to body consciousness, just as two orderlies were strapping her on the stretcher. They took off at a swift trot, the sky lurching above her, dipping first to blue, then spilling into the sun, light everywhere, spinning, spinning.

Selma was loaded unceremoniously into the ambulance where the perfectly odious orderly and his buddy started chattering. With a start, Selma realized neither had yet spoken. It was different than what happened with Mark; he'd been screaming. Oh, Oh, that complicates things! I should have guessed this would happen . . . telepathy . . . Now not only would Arne have to monitor her incoming and outgoing images, and modify them for her, as per plan with their little jingle about "Go to the Light, it's all right," acting as white noise, he'd have to override their physical nonsense. But, oh dear, she'd still forgotten the most important thing. Oh God, where *was* Arne? She strained to open her eyes. He had to remind her what to do.

The orderlies' thoughts broke over her like a tidal wave, almost smothering her feeble station. Anything could happen now, Selma thought, almost extinguished, finding herself flung here and there on his ugly thoughts. She had the problem not just of her own, but theirs. She hoped that, like a radio station she didn't like, she could tune them out, once she got the hang of it, but she was starting to doubt it for they were so strong. While the attendants hadn't even opened their mouths yet. When they did, their mouths were even worse than their thoughts. She clung to body consciousness, for she didn't dare flit away— she might just drift, if she forgot where was she going . . . her awareness was so fragile. She had to wait for Arne to remind her of something.

Querulously she asked, panicked, where's Arne? Where is this Light anyway? Maybe there was no Light to make everything right, and she would be stuck like this interminably, or doomed to run around in this other body she knew she had, invisible, drifting through walls unseen, like the ghost she would soon be . . . how horrid . . . to see and not be seen . . . she had to get used to it. *The Tibetan Book of the Dead* warned the departed spirit that this would happen, and that you were not to attach any importance to seeing your family there without you, crying, or your goods being divided up, or she supposed, even new mates running in before the bed sheets were cool, although that wouldn't be her lot. Her mind jumbled.

At last, faintly she heard Arne say, his face close to hers, "I love you, Selma, I do love you." She felt vast relief that he was there at last. She focused all her strength in her two fingers to press his, just a little. To tell him she'd heard and to thank him for everything. Though this wasn't the way they'd planned it.

• • •

Arne arrived home just as the attendants were loading Selma into the ambulance. Her face was white, gray eyelids shuttered over sunken eyes. She looked incredibly old. Arne's heart wrenched. Kate and Erik were crying in each other's arms.

At first the orderlies weren't going to let Arne ride in the back of the ambulance, but the outrage in his eyes wore them down. As Arne got in, he looked over at Mark with the unspoken "Why?" He heard Mark say in a small, quivery child's voice, "But maybe she won't die."

Arne understood how it had happened, but God help them now. He couldn't refuse to let them take her, because they'd been called. Soon they'd reach the Emergency Room. Oh God, this isn't the way they'd planned it. With anguish, he realized as the ambulance careened out of the driveway, that he'd forgotten to tell Kate to call Dr. Tuchman to meet them there. Now, there would be no ally to help them ward off heroic, well-meaning but misplaced measures.

In the close quarters of the ambulance, the road turned into a nightmare for Arne, the bridge across the arm of the sea was passed at full siren. In alarm, multitudes of swans mounted into the sky, their silvery, sun-burnished wings making a sound like rushing winds or high tide as they flew ahead of the ambulance. "Goddamned birds," said the pimple-faced driver. The other fellow caught Arne's eye sympathetically, sharing both his plight and the strange, beautiful phenomenon of the swans, whose hoarse cries cut through the wail of the siren.

As the attendant prepared to place the oxygen mask over Selma's face, her huge, trapped, pleading eyes met Arne's. He shook his head. He knew what she wanted; he felt overwhelmed and out of control. At that moment, for the first time, in total submission, with nowhere else to turn, he prayed to God for help, and unabashedly wept as he begged Selma's captain to help her, Josip's white crow. He threw in the Christ of his childhood and Buddha as well. To please do something to help him assist her. To take care of her dying. He started to say her captain's name and felt Selma relax somewhat.

Feebly, he patted her hand, fighting off the gag of sadness that threatened to overwhelm him, and forced himself to remain calm so he could function for them both. That was the whole point of his being a support person, he told himself, shakily, so shape up! He was glad he'd assisted at Kate's birth; he was glad for the rehearsals that Selma had insisted on. For he had to stay calm. He was her coach.

He felt a strange, lonely exultancy building in him, as he began to repeat the Gayatri and the Great Death Defying Mantra which Mrs. Dee had said to use at death. Then he said the Lord's prayer of his childhood, and her mantra, as they had planned, linking her identity with that of the avatar. He recited the glorious 23rd Psalm, in a stirring whisper—"Yea, though I walk through the valley of the shadow of Death . . . I shall fear no evil, for Thou art with me. Captain, my captain, I cease from my song for thee . . ."

Furtively, Arne looked at the orderly next to the stretcher and groaned. Selma was stretched out flat which made it difficult to breathe. Helplessness turned to outrage as he thought, My God, she's tied down like an animal, surrounded by a screeching siren and strangers. He saw she was drawing up her knees painfully, trying to turn over on her right side, to get into the Lion's Pose, where she was to rest her head on her right arm. With amazement, he saw the straps suddenly slacken.

A part of Arne wanted to laugh, for this was the first miracle, for he hadn't loosened them, nor had the orderly. His swift elation fled as he realized he couldn't remember her instructions, his mind gone blank. Panic washed through him and ebbed, as he remembered and leaned down to her ear to whisper, "I love you, I love you, Selma," knowing she could hear him. Then, with a start, he remembered he had to begin telling her to let go to the Light of pure consciousness, to let it merge with the consciousness principle in herself and not just indulge his own feelings, or even hers. Big time.

Arne's feelings of helplessness cleared as he took stock of the situation. He figured they had twenty minutes before they got to the hospital, maybe less at this speed. Maybe, just maybe, he could get her across in that time. He'd have to, God willing by any name. Hesitantly, but with new resolve, he took off her mask and leaned toward her. Selma's eyes fluttered open again and he could have sworn there was a flicker of amusement in them as she looked up into his grim face. He felt power working through him, and he was in command, every motion planned and choreographed in some other space than here, then activated through him.

He adjusted her arm under her head and whispered into her ear, "You are dying, Selma. Disregard all the sirens and commotion. Soon you'll be getting into the Light. Remember your teacher, your captain, and keep his name and form always before you, and breathe through his image in and out, slow and easy, yet letting your energy rise up and out the top of your head like an upside down waterfall, or the geyser, Old Faithful. We have twenty minutes. You know better than I what that means, right?" His face was earnest, drawn, haunted, but had an expression of growing confidence.

"Give me a sign that you understand what I'm telling you. We have to hurry. You can do it. Our only chance is if you can do it in fifteen minutes; otherwise, technology is going to take the day. Please, can you hear me?" She moved her fingers twice, deliberately, under his hand. He was overwhelmed with gratitude; it was going to work.

Triumph of Life

Yet it was the train at the crossing that saved them. Arne had never once had to stop for a train in all his years in that town, but there it was, a train from nowhere. The ambulance like a beached whale by the tracks for long minutes, the siren shrieking the whole time, Arne managed to make it through the whole list of suggestions for the dying which she had made him practice with her, his head bent very close to Selma's ear.

The attendants couldn't hear Arne telling Selma to go to the Light of her own nature, or to let go through the grace of the guru to the Light. The noise of the train and the siren was decidedly enough to cover Arne's sing-song chanting, "Let go, let it go, let yourself go to the Light, it's all right," interspersed with the Gayatri. Nor did they hear his entreaty for her to be God and merge with the Clear Light, Soul-of-Selma.

He put his hand on her diaphragm to remind her to start the withdrawal of consciousness by using the hoop style breathing. She was to focus her breath and attention on each section of the body her energy was to vacate, starting feet first. He heard her ragged, dragging breath and felt her struggle to hold her attention on the internal energies, first at the feet and legs, then to the base of the spine, and the first chakra, breathing out the top of her head, to begin again in the circular, hoop-like motion. She would rest at the navel area, gathering power to make it to the heart, she would pull up to throat, to crown, always thinking up and out.

Her eyes flickered and her breathing evened out somewhat. Now, with his face very close to hers, he continued whispering, "Slow the breath—that's it—slow and easy, get your rhythm, find your pace. Now slowly roll your lifeforce upward with each inhalation, letting it go out the top of your head as you exhale. Then hoop down and start again. It's the reverse of having a baby. Use your attention and your breath to close off an energy switchpoint chakra behind yourself, when all your energies are gathered above it, like locks in a canal. Okay, let's go again, Selma—use either hoop style breathing or pretend you are breathing in through a straw. You found the straw approach easier in practice . . . let's go. Move out from the base chakra, I'm breathing with you!

"Oh, baby, keep it up. Oh nobly born, let not thy mind be distracted . . ." from anything, Arne thought grimly, "especially all this," as bedlam from siren and train continued. "Hey, Wake-up Committee, all the Light Brigade, Lord Krishna, Lord Jesus Christ, Lord Buddha, Baba, all the saints and adepts, help her, help me to help her, please be with us!" Arne prayed.

"Your body may be getting cold, or hot, or feeling like it is dissolving or exploding. Let go, let it go. You are not the body, you have one which you are leaving behind as an old worn-out garment is left behind when it has served its purpose. You know your soul has other bodies. Let go, my darling, lightly, lightly," he intoned. "You may hear the sounds of disintegration, the tugging apart of energy fields, and the disintegration of the body sheaths composed of the five elements. Let it all go. Let the ice of the failing body system break up like ice on the river in spring melt! Feel yourself dissolve into pure energy, pure consciousness, peace and bliss. Keep calm, serene, be happy. Relax into the Light with every breath now, tug more and more of yourselfness upward with every breath now, exit with every exhalation. Use the slow, gentle breath as a way to control the mental waves of your mind, focus on immortal energy, resonate with it," Arne chanted.

"You're in the Light, it's all right," he chanted over and over, as they'd planned. The singsong blocked the volume of the other noise and distractions, blanketing her with his voice like white noise, even as the din covered them. The Gayatri was chanted in the same fashion, establishing a higher presence than mere physical circumstances.

"Oh Selma, Selma," his voice broke. He laid his head down on the pillow by hers for a moment, cushioning in the nimbus of her hair, soft as thistle down. Arne knew he hadn't failed her before and he wouldn't fail her now. The orderlies completely forgotten, he kept breathing right along with her, matching her long dragging breaths, and blending with her, holding light and love in his own heart which opened into territories heretofore unknown between them.

When her mind would drift off, saying the word "Light" or her captain's name would refocus her. She had to *consciously* withdraw from the body, rather than let it become the evacuation that takes place when your house is burned down. She had to keep her attention on letting go to the Light via her captain, or Light alone. In love, in acceptance, in joy. She had to let go her definitions of selfhood, sex, age, disease, nationality, family—in order to be able to merge with the Light. Her own real Self, then, the Consciousness Principle, would dock at the Mothership of All. Or as the Tibetans say, be as a child welcoming and being welcomed by its mother. The manual really helps. Bless you, dear heart. I finally understand. We seem to be addressing right dying, but we are truly addressing immortality and our immortal nature in a mortal shell, Arne thought silently to Selma.

Arne prayed once more that she would make transfer within the next ten minutes, or sooner. He asked that it be so, he knew it had to be—if the train just delayed them a bit more. The driver cursed the train, and got out, futilely waving his fists. Arne smiled thinly, and went back to maintaining an appropriate attitude for death, assisting her thereby.

• • •

Selma had warned him how responsive to stimuli she had found the secondary body to be—which she would likely switch to as she got close to death, or more likely, move in and out of. The secondary body wafts about on thoughts, which become objects and events. How far that process really went, only Selma knew, as the orderly's disorderly, vulgar, disrespectful thoughts had already proved a hazard that Arne's white noise of "Go to the light, it's all right," had covered for.

She had real fear, however, that any thought or random image rising up in her that she unwittingly put her attention on could disturb her exit procedure, impede her, or worse, detour her. He *had* to keep covering for her, she had urged, utilizing the Sixth Technique for security. And she needed the Gayatri Mantram to evoke a higher reality than environmental stimuli, thereby providing a positive reception for death, and an automatically positive rebirth in which her higher consciousness would be of service to all, not just herself.

So, Arne went on breathing with Selma, blending with her, holding love and faith and belief in his heart. A growing sense of Presence spread through the ambulance, as if there were more than four people in the cab. He sensed she knew it, too. He knew it had to be her captain. Relief poured through him. They were going to make it. It would be a tight squeeze, though, he thought as he saw the caboose of the train in the distance. He knew the minute they got her into the hospital they would try to pull her back. "You're dying, Selma. Don't come back once you are out, my dear, no matter what they do to you!" he whispered fiercely. "You have no body to come home to. Fly away home!"

Arne was again in command, the relief the tangible Presence in the ambulance evoked in him firming his heart's resolve. He wondered if she could see him? Surely with death having thinned down her five senses, she would be using the senses of the secondary body to navigate already, although she looked so white and cold and old. He saw the faint flutter of pulse in her throat, while the slow, dragging breaths she rode like a horse still persisted. He saw the orderly noting she still breathed, frowning at Arne's having removed the oxygen mask. But he let it go by.

Everything was improvised, but isn't that life? thought Arne. His confidence grew. He was grateful that Selma had chosen him as her midwife in this birth and recognition of herself as unconditional Light. He repeated the Gayatri once more as part of the coordinates for both her departure and arrival, as more boldly, he checked her vital signs. Her pulse was getting very slow, but she still had a good grip on her breathing, although there was a longer and longer wait between breaths now. He saw the deep, racking drags of air that she was taking in continue to slow as she willed herself up and out with each exhalation. Soon they would stop altogether. Then clinical death would occur, but he'd keep invoking the Light and her captain's help to assist the deathing of Selma. Consciousness would lightly return Home.

The ambulance attendants seemed oblivious, except for that one glance. The driver still had the radio on which bellowed into the siren, "Will you kiss me and stop me from shakin" in a high whine. Arne leaned over to touch the driver on the shoulder, something he'd never had the disregard of social conditioning enough to do before, and said mildly, with admirable control, "Maybe you could switch to the classical station, Mister?" Surprised, and not a little embarrassed at Arne's request, the driver did as he was asked.

The deep, rolling strains of "The Moldau" pouring through the ambulance, quieted everyone. "Great," thought Arne. The wonderful surges of a river turned into music would lift her spirits if she heard it, as stimuli, and help her catch a wave. He had learned that certain music helps create an atmosphere of expansion, joy, and liberation.

Now Selma's neck corded and arched and her fingers spread, then her body relaxed, consciously, a frown of concentration furrowing her brows. Her mouth was open, breath rattling unevenly, but still under control of her will which hauled each breath along, slowly, ever more slowly. They were close. He touched the top of her head, reminding her to let go—up and out. He whispered again, "Just keep breathing that way, Selma, and then stop . . . and fly away home, just slip away my darling." Love for her suffused him and gratitude that he was calm in the middle of chaos.

The moment of total submission was coming, to be submitted to fearlessly and with love. He started again the singsong words they had created together, keeping them up like they had planned, the powerful lyrics blocking out the siren, and riding on the strains of the river and his love. He found himself chanting "Light, light, light," as the ambulance started up with a lurch and turned and twisted down Route 9.

•   •   •

Selma was no longer Selma, but she was still she, and cold, very cold with hardly any feeling left in her lower legs and torso. That was good, quite predictable, but so frightening. Then she heard the music swirl and realized the surge of a beloved piece of music. She knew she had to use its musical swells to help her exit, and not be side-tracked to Czechoslovakia or something, to the river by the same name! In a world where thought rapidly assumes the reality of things, you must monitor thoughts, she admonished herself. With a great effort of will, Selma realized she really was going to have to put her total attention on this dying business. "You're dying, Selma," Arne said. "Fly away home. Be Light. Be God." Love for him suffused her as her last conscious physical act was to deliberately roll her eyes upward to remind herself to think up, to the crown and out. To Arne, her lids were half-opened on blue-white slits. He knew what she was doing and why. "Just let go . . . we've had some complications . . . can you die quickly, Selma?" he begged, apology in his voice. "Can you make transfer in the next few minutes, to be on the safe side?"

She tried to grunt an affirmative; nor could she press his hand. Holding the deep ragged breaths together took all her strength, slowing them from chaos and panic. Oddly, she didn't feel oxygen deprived, except her body fizzed, electrically. Now her breathing wrenched itself away from her control. It became the body's business, it knew what do without her now. With difficulty, she quelled panic, and with intense effort focused all her attention to know where most of herself was. Ah, her life force was in her heart area already. Well, shoot for the head now, pull up and out with each breath and exhalation transmute energy to pure consciousness. Her breath pumped itself like a bellows now, dragging her along with it. She heard Arne breathing right beside her; he didn't know her body rhythm now paced his. She blessed him silently.

His fingers were stroking her throat gently to draw her attention upward, in case she forgot. When he did that, she felt an immediate rush of energy to her head, the sensation sort of curling up into her sinus bones. More little sunbursts spattered her interior vision, little strokes in the brain, she dimly discerned. But where was this Light? The Real Light of interior reality, not just biochemical fireworks? Maybe there was no Light to make all things well, maybe she was just a fool for wanting answers so badly.

The weirdest hallucinations beset her now, she knew they weren't real, just effluvia from disengaging elements impinging on her mind. Let go. Let go! She experienced floods and earthquakes creating tidal waves in her head. Then all went yellow, shifting to white. Selma felt very thirsty, despite the whole universe being flooded with water. Faintly, again she heard a familiar piece of music . . . it was, yes, water, the Moldau, surges and swells.

Then she remembered she was dying. How peculiar, she kept forgetting. Ah, that was what was happening. She was supposed to grasp that all this was a creation of her own mind. She tried to hold to that, but again she slipped away on the water . . . drowning . . . light . . . then fainting into coldness, as she forgot everything.

His fingers brought her back, this time, lightly, feathering on her crown, and his singsong chanting, "Light, light, light." More little sunbursts occurred and now it was night as her left eye went, too, in a splendid light show, firecrackers crackling through her nervous system in lazy displays. She fought against the fascination of running with the pretty patterns . . . pretty . . . pretty. . . .

Then Selma heard him say, "Light, light," and again, the sweet name she'd forgotten. Say it again, I must remember the truth, she thought.

She had to be exiting soon; her house was in ruins. Since her sensations were partially monitored through this failing system of body and brain, she'd soon be senile at this rate, and unable to consciously help the deathing of Selma. So, hurry. Are you there? She called out for Him, now, in earnest. Where was her captain? Where is Truth?

Her breath went slower yet, as images rose and fell in front of her interior vision like molten honey in water. Time was so slowed down that she could watch the gestation of these thoughts and pictures, see them flower like a kaleidoscope fanned out, and then collapse back, folded as if into a handfan, which would then fling out again with a different image, in and out, in slow motion. She heard a long exhalation and knew it was her own. Her breath stopped and did not resume.

The Moldau was behind her now, the orderlies long forgotten. Superimposed upon all exterior sounds came the throbbing rhythm of the sea from deep inside her. It throbbed, resonating through, over and beyond her body's interior sounds, groaning like ice wrenching loose in the spring thaw, as the high harmonic of the sea sounded far away. She went with the process. In the faint edges of the galaxy of her mind, she heard Arne chanting "Let go, let go, let go to the Light!" interspersed with her captain's name. "Don't worry about the sounds, this is only the etheric body pulling loose . . . use the energy to get up and out the top of your head. LET GO, LET GO."

A sucking sensation began somewhere inside of her, gathering momentum. She relaxed and let it have its way. She had heard none of the really terrifying sounds she had expected to hear in this farewell, perhaps because she had let go to the process. But the cacophony of interior music persisted. Then the high, sweet piping again drew her attention, a harmonic throbbing hum that coordinated the departure fugue of herselfness. She felt her heart give a shudder and let go.

She let It pull her now, this melody that danced and boomed inside her, peace and delight emitting from her stilled heart. The body winked out—was gone. At last she heard Arne's triumphant voice, "BE LIGHT, BE GOD, BEGODBEGODBEGOD—I AM GOD," and she sang past the corridor of infinite night into the Light. Breaking free of earth's gravity like a jet stream from a pressure cooker, a sharp spray of dazzled incandescent honey burst into the starburst of herself, to rendezvous Light with LIGHT. It flooded her with herselfness, as ahead of her, yet both inside and out, the great Light of herself bore her onward to ITSELF, that was Herself, as well.

Stretched endlessly, the tunnel connected the levels of herself through time, filled with beings she had loved through many ages, as she spanned from the hearts of stars to the animal kindgom where once she had dwelled, now to occupy the human frame, house abandoned, now occupied—always participating in unity, in multiplicity, and multiplicity in unity.

Soul-of-Selma passed by, rising higher as all the worlds and universes beckoned, each with their colors and different frequencies, circle within circle, a white hot core, with cobalt rings of orange, red, yellow and green, luring her on. She knew to keep to the center of the road, to head for the heart, the bright white of the core of the mandala, no detour.

Truth's voice kept her on course. Just as she left Time twined in a double helix far behind, she passed through Truth's face, right between the brows, and came out the Other Side. Now, a clear and shining beloved form was all that stood between herself and the unutterably perfect heart of a diamond-of-Light at Tunnel's end. She remembered to see all as God, all as herself, all as Truth, and remembered to press on. When Josip stepped aside, smiling, urging her onward, wearing Truth's face, she knew she would meet him at the marriage feast afterward and hastened to the Consummation. Then two LIGHTS plummeted toward each other in waves ready to crest upon each other's breast, and embraced as One.

• • •

Selma surfaced on several occasions from the oceanic splendor of unconditional love and perfect wisdom, a Godsea of sun and luminous waves laving her own heart. The four days prismed the Clear Light into colored aspects which she visited in and out of, recognizing all as God and as herself. The tape recording they made before she died also helped her to remember herSelf, while Arne's personal loving, caring injunctions, repeated daily for each of the forty-nine traditional days of the journey between, also helped her remember her original Essence.

Emerging out of the splendor of the yellow Light on the third day, the tape recording of her own voice met her, telling her to have no fear, and to follow the Light, Be It. She, as Soul, the Consciousness Principle, was to recognize It as Herself in all guises, positive or negative. She told herself never to flee the Light, but to fling herself toward the brightest, most awe inspiring, and therefore terrifying expression of Light that ever revealed its face to her. For it was her own, face to face. She had not been able to completely merge with her beloved, the Light, but was that not also plan? Nor in the succeeding waves of varying perfect Lights and corresponding opportunities for grace. But is that not also grace?

It was on the fourth day of discrimination, or level of consciousness, that all was seen as it is, in a red landscape with stark red rocks, and brilliant gloom, where there was no place to focus. She heard then, as from a long way away Truth's voice singing, "Aum, Bhuh Bhuvah Svah, Tat Savitur Varenyum, Bhargo Devasya

Dheemahe, Dhiyo Yo Nah Pracholdayat!" as the Gayatri from Arne's tape recorder. And just then she remembered her captain. Just in time she focused on his name and anchored there before she flinched away, recoiled to Hades or the Gray Place, or ran to take a body, carelessly, anyone's, anything . . . just to fix the Consciousness Principle somewhere.

Instead, in her longing, suddenly he was with her on the red planet, his brilliance lighting the gloom. She no longer was lost in the crossing. Anchored upon Him, which was Herself, she finally remembered Him totally, He who was the form and formless she sought, often called Light, but in a more accessible form, not unlike herself.

Another time when she surfaced, she hardly believed the secondary body's senses, although she knew Arne was right on course. First, she saw her body in the casket, laid out in blue satin in a bronze box which she hoped was only borrowed, since she was going to have the body cremated. But it was not her thin face, faintly smiling, nor the blue eyes closed forever in that body, that astonished her. What amused and astonished her was the tape recorder poking out from under the sedate, funeral parlor blue satin pillow upon which rested her pristinely chiseled head, her usually untidy white hair neatly combed for once, spread out over, but not really hiding the little tape recorder. Valiantly it spun out, most noticeably, the Gayatri Mantra repeated over and over again as background to Selma's own voice giving herself instructions to go to the Light, to flee nothing, to accept everything as herself and hence God, and to pay no attention to what was going on at Seaward Point or the Middletown house!

Selma watched people file past the casket, paying their respects to the dead Selma, their faces a study as they first saw the tape recorder and then heard her familiar voice giving cosmic instructions for the voyage home! Arne had done that touch a bit deliberately, for he could have hidden the recorder much better, had he wanted to, and toned it down! She smiled, she had not even thought of putting the tape in her own casket!

She saw Kate and Erik file by, pale, but with resolute, tender faces as they looked into the casket. Selma stood behind them with a hand on each of their shoulders, sending them love and thanks. Then Mark and her newly pregnant daughter-in-law filed by. She sent her love to the couple, and would have liked to share the joke with them. Granted, it might be on her, for she didn't know what kind of a father Mark would make, not to speak of grandfather. But she had a feeling that by the time they met again he would have mellowed considerably, partly through his wife's kindly character. While the forty more years at Seaward Point she'd seen when peeking ahead in Time would bring out a gifted environmental architect, displacing today's investment banker. Although the flax-en-haired tot named after her own grandmother, who indeed was her own grandmother, would live in the southwest, she'd spend summers at Seaward Point with Nana and Grampa. And so it would come full circle once more—and the word is love, until you get it right, Selma knew. Little Jon came and put a cornflower tenderly by her hand. Selma said "hello" to him, and he looked up sharply, then smiled broadly and made as if to run to her. She shook her head slightly, putting her finger to her lips in conspiracy, as they had done in games in the past. He understood, and hesitated a bit, then filed on by with his parents, looked over his shoulder at her and tentatively waved. That no one else could see her was no surprise, so she prepared to submerge once more into the Godsea, right on course.

• • •

It was on a green Sunday after the fourth day that she surfaced once again. This time she was drawn upstairs to their bedroom. The tape recorder was still on, devotional music in the background. Arne sat reading the manual. *The Tibetan Book of the Dead* was on the table beside him.

She gazed at Arne's back, seeing the thinning hair, the dear, stooped shoulders, and was overwhelmed, not with poignancy, but with tenderness. Her radiating love, gratitude, and triumph spread through the room, and unfolded inside him. Arne put down the notebook. "Selma?" he thought, hesitantly. Tentatively, he called her name out loud, an expression of wonderment on his features which rapidly changed to, "Selma, you old rascal you! I can FEEL you. You're right here in this room, aren't you?"

His voice trailed off wistfully, for in this exchange only intuition operated, at least from his side of the fence. But this is love, Arne thought, experiencing the warmth and the feeling of a "shift of state" inside his whole body as "herselfness," somehow, tucked inside his body like fruit inside a rind. And then the feeling was again outside in the room. And then it was gone, leaving an afterglow. But she knew. And he knew.

• • •

It is not how to end, but where, in a story like this. There could be many other chapters in this beginning. But, for now, you can join three people in the small plane flying high above the Connecticut River carrying an urn of ashes that they intend to return to the sea, or the sound, as you chance to define your position from above the estuary. But remember—in a story like this, you must go higher than flying.

PART III

THE MANUAL OF DEATHING

Great is life . . . and the real and mystical . . . wherever and
   whoever,
Great is death . . . Sure as life holds all parts together, death
   holds all parts together;
Sure as the stars return again after they merge in the light,
   death is as great as life.

Walt Whitman
Leaves of Grass, "Great Are the Myths"

◇ ◇

CONCEPTS FOR DEATHING

At death, the boundaries of what is "real" about yourself and the world are totally negotiable. In a flash there is for each of you an automatic shift from the personal "I" to the cosmic and universal Reality, often called the Light. This infinite vibrating field—called God in the Judeo-Christian tradition, while Vedic sages call it Brahman-Atman, mystics call it the unknowable or the Overself, and modern theoretical physicists use the term, "superspace"—by whatever name, emerges for all at the moment of death.

How you meet the unconditional Reality that you each are a part of has potent effects for you. Whether this experience proceeds consciously (in full or in partial recognition of what's going on), or unconsciously, is the choice *Deathing* offers you.

You can experience death in one of two ways. First, there is the ordinary, uninformed dying that just happens when it happens, soon or late, expected (as in terminal illness) or unexpected (as in accident). Even if expected physically, such a death is an unnecessarily rude, forced evacuation of consciousness, resulting from the body's mechanical breakdown. It normally results in a recoil from the Light Experience into lesser states, with corresponding innerspace geographies and experiences, as the dying person takes refuge in instinct, not wisdom. Such a death has long passed for normal in this society because we no longer remember any alternative. It catches the person unprepared and rather bewildered by it all, or frightened, especially if he or she has been left alone to die. Often acceptance of death under such circumstances merely means that you admit to being trapped, which is not the kind of acceptance and expanded consciousness that best grants the peace of mind and heart appropriate for death's dramatic change-of-state.

Second, but of primary concern, is deathing. It is a means of making an informed, safe, responsible, and joyous transition from the physically focused "I" consciousness to the various subtle stages of life-after-death's expanded states, including humanity's birthright—full enlightenment, or liberation. Deathing, which is poles apart from merely dying, is one means to claim the lost birthright by whatever name: *Unio Mystica, Satori, Jivan Mukti,* Self-Realization, or *Nirvana.* Thereby, death's change-of-state becomes part of your VOLUNTARY awareness, activating the higher centers (or chakras), instead of it being unconsciously stockpiled into lower, INVOLUNTARY instinctive centers as is most ordinary dying.

Such a conscious death as deathing imparts allows you to utilize the death process in such a way that it transforms what appears to be a mere biological misfunction, or accident, into a spiritual art form—the tool for the transformation of consciousness that it should be. In this short manual we will strive to attain that level of competence, content to hit the mark anywhere near the bullseye. Deathing fosters the ethics and humanistic practice of a still evolving humanity, and becomes as well its midwife in the cycle of rebirth for the coming millennium. Conscious dying, whether achieved by traditional spiritual means, or deathing's abbreviated, but potent link with the Divine, has effects exponentially powerful, benign and beneficial to the individual, society and all life.

Although the information in this book can be your companion on that transition, only you can be the real coach. Since bodily functions become disturbed at the time of death, and the mind is not always in good condition, it is wise to enlist the aid of a support person, ideally. But since you ultimately are your own support, the principles of *Deathing* will serve you well— whatever the circumstances of your departure and with or without assistance from others.

Experience tells us that it is vitally important to keep positive thoughts during the death transition, either by your own efforts, or through a support person's assistance. The information taught in *Deathing* is one means to positively modify difficulties brought on by your reaction to any part of the dying process—the distractions of negative thoughts, emotions or pain—even in the event of coma, accidental or sudden death, as well as posthumously.

Ideally the method should be learned and practiced before the physical body irretrievably breaks down. But, in the event of accident death, or a death for which there has been no preparation, the Sixth Technique (see page 213) and a support person can assist even total strangers. Whenever possible, by practicing ahead of time with an eye toward this spiritual life insurance, you can increasingly live in an atmosphere free from fear and ignorance. A correct grasp of *how to die* necessarily produces an expanded philosophy of *how to live* more abundantly, however short or long your time of physical life.

When the fear of death is relieved through education and some practice of these techniques, death can be seen simply as a refocusing of attention from this universe and plane of existence to the next. Subsuming the visible universe, behind everything that is subject to change, including the magnificent gift of human life, there is the unchanging and permanent Divine including your own "wave signature," or Consciousness Principle, which some people call Soul.

Many of us are prone to see ourselves as biological thinking machines, to whom death is the ultimate disaster; for without a body, what else is there, says a materialistic world? However,

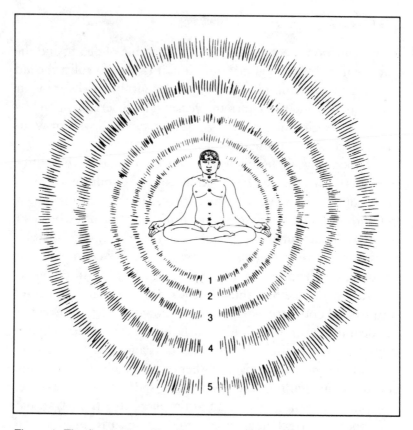

Figure 1. The five bodies. The five radiating circles around the body in the center represent five sheaths: (1) the physical sheath, the sheath of matter and motion (Annamaya Kosha); (2) the electromagnetic sheath, the etheric biofield body (Pranamaya Kosha); (3) the sheath of consciousness, mental-causal, the personality (Manomaya Kosha); (4) the sheath of revelation, intuitive laws of evolution and involution (Vijnanamaya Kosha); and (5) the sheath of bliss and reality (Anandamaya Kosha). All of this is held in Brahman (the square) as Ultimate Reality, all-pervading, interpenetrating, immanent, and transcendent. It is the One-Without-a-Second, and the other five states are submerging and merging into it. By these states, Its oneness is not broken. (Adapted from *Dynamics of Yoga Mudras and Five Suggestions for Meditation* by Shri Ramamurti, I.S.C.A. Press, Ananda Ashram, 1961. Used by permission.)

from a holonomic, mystical point of view, not only is it impossible for the "real" you to really die, but death is one means of attaining humanity's birthright—full enlightenment, Self-Realization—although you don't have to die to do it.

An examination of our human subtle anatomy reveals that there are five bodies, not one, although some systems describe seven. (See figure 1.) For our purposes, four more than one is enough to make the point that life is an ongoing process of consciousness transformation, in post-mortem states as well as physical experience. Even as the baby who was once "you" took its first breath, became the child, the teen, the adult, the oldster and will expel its last breath, so does the Consciousness Principle (that is, the real occupant, "you") expel itself in death.

The method we shall discuss here does not interfere with natural events, nor does it condone euthanasia or any suggestion of suicide! It is simply a method to be practiced before your final departure moment, a means of consciousness transference. It's a technique and an access code to the pure Light during your life, as well as the means to recognize and accept It at death, and you will learn how to reflex to It ahead of time. You can then call upon It during death's transition into the near-death areas of clinical death, then on to real-death. Real-death is when the Consciousness Principle truly departs the physical body that up until that point has housed all the other subtle bodies that sheath the real you. Ordinarily, real-death can take up to four days after clinical death, as all the elements of the various bodies disengage from the physical. *Deathing* can effect this departure almost immediately—a real advantage in a world of organ donorship, autopsies, and mortuary practices that may include premature burial or cremation—before transfer is completed. The principles of right dying are sound and can be applied under any circumstances, at any time, under any conditions—whether death comes in the back seat of a taxi, in an ambulance, during an earthquake, in wartime, as the result of an assault, in a car wreck, from a heart attack, a lingering cancer, or unannounced, when you are in the pink of health.

You Are Not the Body

You, Kinsman, are not just the individual "I am" that operates out of a given body, identity, name, form, age, sex, culture, or race that you appear to be. You are cosmic and eternal with or without a physical body. Death is a great revealer of this truth, though you don't have to die to experience it.

By practicing deathing, you will come to know that the matter of your body is part of cosmic matter, your energy is part of cosmic energy, and your consciousness is part of the Cosmic and Universal Consciousness, with Spirit, or the Essence of Unconditional Reality, being the integrating and integral dimension of your selfhood.

This proposition runs counter to current popular authority in both orthodox religions and scientific camps. The religionists maintain that there is a mortal body and an immortal soul, of a substance called Spirit. Scientists connect mind and consciousness with the body, making the brain the exclusive seat of consciousness. Nor do they often admit to "soul" surviving the body, a proposition that can be proved readily enough by putting yourself in the proper level of consciousness to find out firsthand. Modern physics now sees the interconnectedness of matter, energy, time and space to the degree that many esoteric spiritual teachings—among them, yoga—have always recognized. Quantum theory more than accepts a world of vibrating fields in which the behavior of subatomic particles depends on whether or not they are being watched. The definition of who is the "watcher," as well as closing the gap between watcher and watched—or subject/object—also forms the basis of the highest spiritual practice.

A major concept to remember in deathing is that the human mind and human intention, consciously or unconsciously, can alter the very substratum of reality out of which our physical world is formed. The mind and intention will also alter the other planes of reality correspondent to the emotional, mental, intuitional and spiritual components of our being. This is what Josip Vidmar meant when he said we all have a choice in our own self-creations. By altering your state of consciousness, and thereby the frame of reference from which you view the world, you change its behavior for yourself, here and hereafter. Deathing is such a means.

At this point, you may well ask, "Well, if I'm not a body and yet the body and the world I know somehow derives out whatever it is that I am, then what in heaven's name am I?" Well, dear Kinsman, you may well be a vibration, a unique wave signature among the many in the vibrating field of the Lord, which is also the holograph that Bentov discusses.[1] Each part of the Whole has access to the Whole, yet, as the Pythagorean axiom puts it, "the totality is greater than the sum of its parts." As a vibration, you would partake of the Infinite, which is omniscient, omnipresent, and omnipotent because it can be in all places simultaneously, and therefore has no duration. Or, It, like you, can contract and limit Itself by means of various bufferings, conditions and boundaries of the Real of Its own nature. This gamut of potential is described in the Samkha yoga model of Reality, which we will discuss later.

Your ego-consciousness (or self-consciousness) is such a construct, a tacit agreement as to what will be real for the physical form called human. *Deathing* is concerned with these self-definitions and how to manifest them—both in your life, and at the transformation we call death. I am convinced that as the evolution of science proceeds, it will eventually lead to and

---

[1]See Itzhak Bentov, *Stalking the Wild Pendulum* (Rochester, VT: Inner Traditions/Destiny, 1988), pp. 21–33.

verify the astral, mental-psychic-spiritual planes and correspondent bodies that have always been recognized by mystics and
saints. As well, this research will lead to the eventual recognition
of an all pervasive supreme Being as the ultimate substratum of
existence, already recognized in the concept of the trinity that is
sacred to most religions, which is known as Light and Sound.
For deathing, we only need be content that science has found
the biofield—that it exists.

To take this a bit further, the infinite vibrating field of the
universe is organized according to mathematical, harmonically
resonating intervals into which consciousness is structured.
These intervals correspond to planes and subplanes—called
bardos and *lokas* in esoteric traditions. The various bodies of a
human correspond to (and operate on) these various levels—
ranging from the dense physical to the most sublimely subtle.
The harmonic levels (or planes) exist not only in varying wave
lengths, frequencies or geometrical modalities, but in velocity as
well—all the way up to infinite speed—simultaneity—instantaneous omnipresence—superspace. That would allow for a multi-
dimensional reality in which all events co-exist in potential.
Under varying conditions, they would manifest at different rates
in space and time, or not at all, as the case might be, depending
on your point of view.*

These harmonically linked and interpenetrating strata all
connect with your nervous system and its subtle body counterparts. Also contained in the body are switchpoints of energy and
information exchange, as energy expressed as matter, thought,
and/or consciousness interchange. The ancients called these

---

*I am indebted to Louis Acker for a series of conversations we shared on the
nature of reality during January, 1989, for he helped me touch on important
points here. I'm also grateful to Mirtala Bentov for many inspiring conversations and for her elucidation and animation of her late husband's work via
videotapes.

switchpoints chakras, which we will discuss in depth later on. However, the chakras can be considered as organized standing wave fields in the human system, thus linking many harmonic levels of vibration through an array of shared nodal points. That would allow for the holographic imprinting of information— love, power, wisdom—from infinite and wholly spiritual levels, down to the physical body, the nervous system and the brain. As above, so below; or in the macrocosm, so in the microcosm— with consciousness itself the go-between octave on the scale, and ultimately the creator of the scale at harmonically resonating intervals.

Upon the death of the physical body "program," the intelligence accumulation of organized information of the unique Consciousness Principle that you are in this incarnation persists—as holographic information patterns in both the subtle energy field of the soul, and in the holographic records of Universal Mind. Due to the limiting contractive tendency in the lower levels of creation, one lifetime doesn't express the unlimited potential of the universal vibrating field that we each are a part of. This means that the unique Consciousness Principle—you—seek enlightenment or liberation, and reincarnate again and again. However, you can break the cycle by focusing on your original nature. Liberation is possible in this lifetime, and certainly at death—that sublime forgotten birthright. You have to let go of the limits of who you think you are as the individual "I AM" and go to the cosmic and eternal "I AM." The easiest way to do it is by means of an intermediary already resonating to the Source—the enlightened teacher.

Due to the nature of mind and the consciousness that you all are vested with, you are simultaneously expressions of Unconditional Reality, rays of Light (harmonic wave frequencies), as well as relative, conditional, reality-creating beings. You influence the outcome of your life by your thoughts—consciously, but mostly unconsciously. What you think is "out there" in the world is what you tend to experience as out there, because you have chosen to focus on that. This is crucial to deathing, and has direct bearing on why the thoughts of a person at death need to be positive.

Thoughts at the death moment—positive or negative—tend to determine the cast of both the afterlife experience and the immediate next life, because of the resonance factor. Like factors or conditions will have long-lasting effects. This means that the thoughts of the dying person need to be focused on the highest consciousness, Reality Itself, *or an enlightened teacher*. This has long been a teaching of high Hinduism (Bhagavad Gita, Chapter 8: 5,6,7), and high Buddhism, as found in early Buddhist tracts (and in the *Bardo Thodol, The Tibetan Book of the Dead*), and surfaces popularly once more in this manual. For now, it is sufficient to grasp the concept that you want to have positive thoughts at the death moment, and that you will be assisted in that endeavor by having a support person to help keep you on course.

Since there are correspondences and crossovers between the vibrating fields of the body, mind and consciousness, energy manifested as thought and energy manifested as matter interrelate and modify each other. By practicing the exercises in this manual, you start taking conscious hold of some of the processes which are normally unconscious—assumed through the usual "reality adjusting" processes of culture and education. This manual may become both your handbook to spiritually letting go to death's extended out-of-body experience and your encounter with unconditional Reality, the Light, and your training manual for healing as your boundaries of the "Real" are renegotiated by restructuring the contents of your mind.

Many of you are in crisis, or serving those in crisis, pending the gravest loss—life. Or, you have had notice of an arbitrary and perhaps premature death served like divorce papers, vouchsafed, signed and sealed by the medical establishment, so-called biological imperatives laid at your door like so many statistical voodoos in the areas of aging, degenerative disease and terminal illness. Although biological mortality is a given in the human equation, the "when" is far more contingent on conditions of mind and consciousness than is at first apparent. Deathing, in order to be most effective in your life *and* death, necessarily challenges your personal and heretofore unchallenged assumptions of what is real, if your disease, near-death experience, or biological breakdown hasn't already.

Life-threatening disease (or accident) immediately breaks you out of the everyday ordinary reality in which most people live. It is up to you to take a positive hold of this break from (and dislocation of) your normal reality that disease presents you, instead of seeing it as an abnormality to life's flow, and hence to be feared. Utilize this "shift point" as a means to maximize your opportunity for taking a quantum leap in consciousness, and thereby in your experience, whether it be that of healing, or quality dying—or both—when the time comes.

Samkhya yoga observes there are a certain number of both breaths and heartbeats "coded" into the fertilized egg at conception, as well as predilections for certain disease families, or miasmas. By removing stress, the heart and breathing rate are slowed, thus prolonging life. And if you can restructure consciousness by using various techniques—imaging, meditation, mantra, breathing, prayer, energy transference—often disease can be arrested, based on the theory that energy manifested in thought and matter modify each other.

The "beyond ordinary reality" appropriate for death, then, that deathing aims to impart, is of the same realm in which firewalkers walk fire; tumors regress instead of proliferate; yogis control the so-called involuntary processes of blood flow, heartbeat, breath; and healers heal. This is no freak phenomena nor accidental process, but a basic given in the human equation and its relationship to consciousness, mind, body, and energy. It's not an embarrassment to reason.

Quite to the contrary, reason should stand abashed at the limits it has set for its employ in our materialistic time. Instead, it could, should, and still can array itself to make a wide-scale investigation of consciousness, mind and body, the relationship of which is the *real* Doer and Maker of our realities. In the balance hangs the end of hunger, disease, war, and the beginning of a new era of higher consciousness. If we but let it, the very seat of human identity is mobilizing upward from its former lower, egoic, survival-oriented territorial considerations to higher expressions of kinsmanship with all life through the awakened centers of heart and mind. At any point in the continuum of life, death, or in-between, the relationship of heart and mind to reality tends to bring about its own fulfillment level by level. These levels holographically imprint each other, bringing each new level into manifestation, or dissolving it as a limit.

On my lake one morning, just at dawn, it came to me how all this works, if the Sun were to represent Reality, and the lake, consciousness and mind. The night before I'd played with a friend's small laser, dancing its coherent light around the living room with mirrors, or distorting it through smoke, noticing that it always stayed laser light though it went through various modifications. That morning as the sun rose, round, red like the laser I'd played with a few hours before, I noticed it was reflected as an almost duplicate image of itself in the nearly unmarred silvery mirror of the lake. The following morning I again went out in the chilly predawn, but that day a gentle wind stirred against my face. When the sun rose, I watched its now elongated, reddish, but still recognizable, distorted reflection in the lake, for the water was agitated by the wind. The next morning, the lake was uneasy, swollen with odd, run-off currents caused by a heavy rain. A remaining wind from the storm fanned the surface into waves, which broke on shore. When the sun came up, the mist and clouds parted for a moment. Now I saw the sun's reflection dispersed unrecognizeably by wave motion and wind except for the reddish bits of light dancing on the wave crests, staining them like red dye. Other than the color red, there was no resemblance to the parent sun's shape in the transposed, dispersed bits of light on the water. Were this my first experience with reflections, and had I not seen the almost perfect copy of the sun imaged in the lake's mirrored surface just two days before, I never would have believed it possible to achieve such a perfect reflection.

Stunned and exultant, I understood the current, wind, and ripples distorted the harmonic resonance necessary for perfect reflection. I saw the interference patterns of the crests and troughs, various vibratory "programs" of existence reinforcing or cancelling each other, all either coherently or incoherently stirring and being stirred by *thought,* which generates the reflective conditions for the Light. The sun is always able to mirror or manifest itself perfectly, if the conditions are right.

Similarly, the Light of undifferentiated Reality—which manifests also as the Sound of universal energy of which we are all part—generates out into the wave/mirroring process of consciousness, or Mind. It differentiates the Light—like the lake did the sun's reflection. Mind, composed of subconscious, conscious and superconscious stuff,—i.e., bits of light on the sounding wave crests of thought—reflects, modifies, distorts, and interprets the pure Light. The reality process projects out and also reflects back this interpretation, to in turn be "played back" to yourself, and thereby experienced as your reality! This is the mechanism of creation—whether of rocks, trees, stars or people—of the manifestation of worlds within worlds or bodies—the very means of creation or destruction. *All* is caused by the play of mind and consciousness in Reality's pool, the Sun the only survivor beyond its own creations. And we partake of Its nature as a ray of the Sun partakes of the Sun.

How you see and think life to be *creates* how it shows up to you! The hitch is that most of this process is beyond the ordinary reality of the waking human mind, or it is submerged in the unconscious processes that seethe like magma at the earth's core, often erupting volcanically and involuntarily in wars and cataclysms of all kinds. This manual shares various strategies for coming closer to the voluntary application, rather than involuntary expression, of the laws of mind and consciousness. So this is one way to enter the beyond ordinary realm of superconsciousness and kinship with all life.

Enlightenment of the "ray of light" (or Consciousness Principle) you all are occurs when a perfect mirroring between the mindstuff of your consciousness and the Light of pure Reality occurs. The possibility for this *always* manifests at the death moment when most of the "ripple effect" of mind and body is stripped off, or else is made temporarily quiet as you are directly exposed to the Source. If, at that moment, you can let go your mental/emotional limits and self-definitions, recognizing the Light at its own level as your own self as well, a perfect mirror effect is achieved in your consciousness. The Light can then perfectly reflect back to Itself, causing Self-Realization in the projected ray of light, the wave frequency which you are, which each of us is. This encounter, or mirroring of the Light, whether perfect, partial, or obscured by various negativities and distortion patterns, is also holographically recorded, impartially.

Not letting go of your limiting self-definitions (including the emotions of fear or shock, for whatever reason) when experiencing the Light at death creates a recoil like that of a ball bouncing off a wall. You bounce "down" into the survival centers, the etheric plane, obscured by the biofield (or etheric body), your perception mechanisms temporarily blanketed and held fast, usually for about three days. Since the Light engraves the last thoughts (positive or negative) of the death moment and adds them to the collective stockpile of mindstuff, they are later available, subjectively, to your particular and individual Consciousness Principle because you experienced that particular death moment. Later in the death experience, your individual being (or ray of light, or wave pattern) will draw toward those thoughts (along with other impressions) in the afterlife and rebirth process. These thoughts will eventually project out as part of your Consciousness Principle's subjective reality—adding to the accumulation of actions, thoughts and associations in that lifetime (and others) from which your "new" life, body and basic script will be composed.

If your last thoughts are of the Light (by whatever deity's name or form) and/or an enlightened being you know and love, a perfect mirroring occurs—enlightenment. This is the strategy of consciousness transference that in deathing we call the Sixth Technique. And if merely a positive mood or thought is engendered at the death moment, your individual Consciousness Principle experiences an opening to that positive train of thought in the subjective and collective stockpile. These event matrixes will then manifest in the afterlife and later rebirth. If a negative thought occurs during the death moment—due to ignorance of the death process, accident death, or shock—that negative thought will manifest in the afterlife experience, and equally influence re-entry of the Consciousness Principle into incarnation. Out of proportion to the micro-moment of death as this seems to be, the macro-effect on the next life occurs.

Events and choices in the afterlife, and the tone and texture of the next life, are connected in great part to the tone and texture of the death moment karma of the life before. That's why religious systems (with or without knowing how it worked) have always aimed to positively influence people's last experiences in earth life, directing them toward the "beyond ordinary" reality appropriate for death. Assisting the dying positively (i.e., right dying) and helping them to remain in a positive environment is not just humane treatment for this life—for why should our last moments be our worst?—but also benefits ongoing and incoming life for the Soul.

Some of you will be outraged that death moment karma can be so influential to the next life. First, you should be reassured that even in a "bad" death, under the worst imaginable negativities, long distance prayers for the deceased, and the invocation of the Sixth Technique on the behalf of the new dead, can result in correcting the "breech death." If you find it unfair that such a powerful process as death moment karma should be the mechanism to spring the next life into being, look at its counterpart— fertilization, pregnancy and birth! Not knowing about the "birds and bees" doesn't ward off pregnancy! *Only knowledge of the process* provides the surest protection. Knowing the process, whether of birth or death, means you can positively utilize it. That is part of *Deathing's* function.

Deathing teaches two main methods to circumvent negative departure moments in addition to a support person's intervention on the new dead's behalf after a bad death. One method is to learn how to relax, to stay calm and positive, to experience yourself as energy (the Fifth Technique). By learning this, you train yourself to RECOGNIZE WHAT IS GOING ON and to IDENTIFY everything you subjectively experience as yourself, no separation. Hence you will be less likely at death to fear anything you experience as "out there" because you will already know it to be at some level of yourself "in there." And second, by trying to perfectly mirror yourself via resonance with the Light as you quit the body, you can reflex to the name of the Supreme Reality, in whatever form or name you most are drawn to, or require. *This is the Sixth Technique whereby you hitchhike on the already enlightened "mirror" of a spiritual being!* It will free you from material concerns and engage your heart, mind and spiritual intelligence in the highest consciousness at this crucial crossroads. Call It by whatever name: the *Light, Purusha, Logos, Satnam, Sugmad, Aleph, Brahman, Dharmakaya,* or an enlightened teacher of your choice, such as Jesus, Buddha, Allah, Krishna, or any of the contemporary enlightened beings. This practice is the way to make your own tuning fork resound by putting it into the proximity of an already sounding tuning fork. Try it.

Such practice helps bypass the limits your own mind might bring to either a slow or sudden entry to the field of undifferentiated pure Consciousness (or Source Itself) that death is. Since you, too, are of Divine Nature, although obscured from reflecting your native Divinity (by limits, constructs, and tendencies of Mind), it is only good sense to hitchhike on the name and level of reality of either the Supreme, Itself,[2] or that of an already enlightened being, who by definition already reflects the Light purely. Such a being, through love, resonance and affinity helps you override obscurements[3] and aberrations in your mindstuff,[4] which frees you to more purely reflect the Light of Supreme Reality. The failsafe Sixth Technique—remembering the name of God or guru at the death moment—used in conjunction with the Fifth Technique, the Withdrawal of Consciousness, assures a safe, conscious transition at death's dramatic change-of-state.

---

[2]Supreme, itself, i.e., God, the Light of Unconditionality.
[3]Obscurements—life tendencies and associations, patterns and passions, etc.
[4]Mindstuff—i.e., *Chittam*, the ego, superego, and related material.

◇ ◇

REINCARNATION AND KARMA

There have been many attempts to model and chart the levels and dimensions of human existence through history. Some of the most sophisticated studies in consciousness have been produced by the Hindu, and later Buddhist, religious founders, avatars, and yogi-saint-scholars during thousands of years of inner space exploration. The Judeo-Christian and Western metaphysical tradition, if not the religious orthodoxy, is also rich, although heavily influenced by the Eastern traditions.

The twin concepts of reincarnation and karma are major features in these traditions and models. The doctrine of the pre-existence of the Soul was accepted within the early Christian church until A.D. 533, when the anathemas were understood by orthodox Christianity to proscribe against the doctrine. On technical grounds, reported in *The Catholic Encyclopedia,*[5] this proscription seems to have been illegal, which allows the conclusion that there is no longer, if ever there was, a closed door to belief in reincarnation for Catholic Christians. If reincarnation were accepted seriously today among Christians, life and the dying process would be treated much differently than it has been.

---

[5]See J. Head and S. L. Cranston, *Reincarnation: The Phoenix Fire Mystery* (New York: Julian Press, 1979), p. 157.

In the preceding introductory material, I've already alluded
to reincarnation as a fact, the re-entry into human life being for
each of us in great part connected to the death moment of the
life before. Since the idea of death moment karma and its potent
effect on the next life is likely to be new information even
to those who believe in reincarnation, not to speak of being
meaningless to those who don't, let me quote Itzhak Bentov's
statement as my own on the subject.

> I will, for example, handle reincarnation as a matter of fact,
> completely disregarding the great controversy that rages
> over the subject. There are two reasons for this: First, the
> simple fact that when one puts himself into the proper
> level of consciousness, one may obtain this information
> firsthand; second, we know that energy cannot be lost
> within a closed system. . . . During a (human) lifetime, we
> organize a lot of information on many levels. Emotional
> information is built up, mental information is built up, etc.
> This information bundle is not material, although some will
> say that it is the brain that contains it. What we have
> here is a "body" of information. It is a nonmaterial entity
> containing all the knowledge that we have accumulated over
> a lifetime, including our personality traits and character. It
> is the nonmaterial "us."

In life we deal, therefore, with two organizing systems,
one material and one nonmaterial. At the time of death, the
physical system decays, and disorder sets in; will the same
thing happen to the nonphysical energy system? This system, which I shall call the "psyche," is the organizer and
processor of this information, and that information is stored
outside our physical bodies. I assert that the psyche can
exist independent of the physical body, that this thinking
and knowing part of us is conserved. It is nonphysical and
therefore not subject to decay after death of the physical

body. This "body" of information will eventually be absorbed in the large reservoir of information produced by all mankind, which I shall call the "universal mind."

In short, I suggest that people having problems with accepting the concept of reincarnation consider this bundle of organized information as having continuity in time, while the physical body serves as just a temporary vehicle for the psyche. When the psyche, after having been without a physical body for a while (the period after death), decides that it needs additional pieces of information obtainable only through the physical body, it will acquire one and continue to associate with the new body until it wears out and dies.[6]

Additionally on the subject of reincarnation, there is a marvelous compilation of material from practically every religion, discipline, philosophy, literature and art called *Reincarnation: The Phoenix Fire Mystery*.[7] The introductory essays discuss the pros and cons for and against reincarnation, and provide an extraordinary weight of testimony for reincarnation from history's best minds. They cast toward reincarnation as an explanation for the otherwise confusing moral and intellectual inequality, the seeming injustice and outright evil, as well as those superior characteristics evidenced in beings like the sages and founders of the major religions.

The experience in a person's rebirth depends on the character, actions, and attainments of previous lives in an accumulated balance of debits and credits called karma, or organized energy pattern from which the new life is made. What *Deathing* calls

---

[6]Bentov, *Stalking the Wild Pendulum*, p. 507. Used by permission.
[7]By J. Head and S. L. Cranston, with a foreword by Elisabeth Kübler-Ross, published by Julian Press, 1979, New York.

death moment karma is only one form and kind of karma, of which there are many, but it is an exceedingly potent catalyst for creating the tone and texture of new life.

Though the word karma is often defined as part of a fixed system of moral cause and effect—and interpreted as stern retributions—it needn't be seen in that manner, but can instead be seen as a teaching tool for the Consciousness Principle. How fast or slow one learns to master the Self (i.e., liberation or enlightenment) depends on both aptitude and effort. Theoretically, as we are all "rays of light" from the Source, we all have the necessary equipment to do it in one life, and also have relatively the same physical form and neurological system as our already enlightened elder brothers and sisters. That leaves us, perhaps, with understanding of the process, will, love, and grace as the deciding factors in the spiritual unfoldment which often, though not always, entails the opening of the nervous system in what has been called the Kundalini Awakening.[8] I am convinced that an involuntary version of this occurs in ordinary death, but it can become voluntary, conscious, and part of the liberating process during life, in addition to being harnessed to use at death.

In the accumulation of karmically recorded memories, patterns, and associations of consciousness and mind, that organize like iron filings around the magnet of the Consciousness Principle, there is a cumulative cosmic record, toward which we all gravitate. There are also currents in the magnetic ocean around that soul which can de-bond these iron filings from their position with radical force at certain times during each lifetime. These special moments have infinite possibilities because the boundaries of the "real" are renegotiated. Death of the physical body is one such moment. Meeting with an enlightened being who has

---

[8]See Lee Sannella, *The Kundalini Experience* (Lower Lake, CA: Integral Publishing, 1987), pp. 119, 120 and chapter 10.

already mastered the human instrument of the Self is another. By putting the two together in the practice of the Sixth Technique, you can take practical advantage of the powerful moment of death to speed you past the normal, but rather slow advance of evolution, life by life, trial and error, as well as avoiding detours, which an unfortunate navigation of death can incur.

Let's again address, but from a different angle, any objection to the uncanny influence of death moment karma in the positive or negative formation of the immediate next life. Some say that death moment karma breaks the sense of justice, ethics, and morality that the doctrine of reincarnation grants—in which the good are rewarded and the bad are punished according to the Old Testament law of "as a man sow, so shall he reap." If you consider "good" and "bad" outside of your conventional ethical interpretation, and re-define "good" as coherent light, a harmonious relationship with the cosmos, and "bad" as incoherent light, or ignorant, inharmonious relationship with the cosmos, you will see that by aligning with the Universal and *coherent* Light you reap the highest good—enlightenment itself. Beings having achieved that coherent, focused state of consciousness operate out of a superior ethic, harmony and goodness, although not always conventionally.

By its very nature, the death moment exposes you nakedly to the possibility of enlightenment. At death's abrupt de-bonding, all your habits, notions, and predilections—your karmic, cosmic bank balance—are held in suspension, no matter what the debits and credits. The Light—Unconditional Reality—waits for you to either align with It, or ricochet off It. It's as if, at that potent instant you have a chance to choose between Old Testament law and the grace of the Gospel's good news—which you don't earn, except by *recognizing, accepting* and *surrendering* to it. And then effect follows cause, as every decision—conscious or unconscious—has determinate consequences. For example, to use a sailing analogy, going at cross purposes to a swift current has effects, even to that of capsizing, while going with a fast current and sailing with the wind also has effects. You do not call such a situation fair or foul, as would an immature child, but instead simply learn to sail! So with human life and consciousness at the moment of death. Deathing urges you to maximize your utilization at that moment of potential through the grace of the Sixth Technique. The New Testament parable of the workers in the vineyard can also be recalled, wherein the workers who toiled all day were paid the same as those who came and worked only at the end of the day. Does that not mean they were paid by the same cosmic principle?

The liberating potential of death moment karma has been hidden in Hinduism, so even most Hindus have forgotten it, although it is spelled out in the *Bhagavad Gita*. It has also been long sequestered in Tibetan Buddhism and recently re-released. The concept of reincarnation erroneously disappeared from public Christianity fourteen centuries ago, but is now returned to your attention so you can apply it to your life now. But as one wise Tibetan told me, rather urgently after our speaking of these matters, "Remember and convey how to meet the Clear Light of death which comes to all, but is recognized and utilized by few. Now I have told you!"

◇ ◇

THE THREE-BODY
AND FIVE-BODY MODELS

There is a complex relationship between the subjective and objective physical body—the mortal and immortal elements—which are levels and frequencies of the infinite vibrating field. We don't want to go heavily into the Tibetan or Hindu outlook here, for there are many other books you can read if you are interested in this. However, it is important to understand the concept so you will know there are different stages, states, and energy centers present in the body that relate to universal energy, and ultimately, to the Light.

Mahayana and Tibetan Vajrayana Buddhism have a three-body system (Trikaya), with corresponding inner space geographies that are called planes, lokas, or bardos. Hindu psychology traditionally uses a five-body model (the Samkhya system), which Buddhist psychology also acknowledges. (See figure 2 on page 224.) The three-body model describes the body of transformations (Nirmanakaya), which corresponds to the physical body and physical world. The heavenly body of bliss (Sambhogakaya) roughly corresponds to the astral, or secondary body used in afterlife states. It is "laced" with aspects of the mental and intuitional bodies of pure energy and light in the five-body system described by Samkhya yoga, with corresponding macrocosmic geographies and entities. The body of truth (Dharmakaya) is the infinite, unconditional field of sheer existence—Reality Itself—

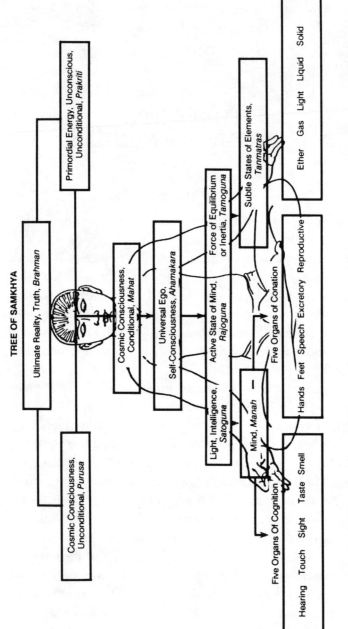

Figure 2. The Tree of Samkhya Yoga. This should give you a visual overview of what we have been discussing up to this point. If you wish to study further, read *The Textbook of Yoga Psychology*, by Ramamurti S. Mishra, listed in the Resources section. This figure was adapted from that book.

in which all exists in potency, but is manifest in voidness. This is called Brahman, or the Greatest, in Samkhya philosophy—God, Itself, the Supreme. It's beyond range of the limits of perception, ideation, or visualization. It is into this source that the Consciousness Principle dips its wick at death, and is lit; but most usually the Light is swiftly snuffed out due to the gust of awe, wonder, and terror experienced by the Consciousness Principle. It winces away from the Light of its own Self, thereby setting up a contraction and recoil response. This sends it off into lesser states until eventually enlightenment occurs somewhere, somewhen, although paradoxically, that state is always around us—in which we swim like fish.

Enlightened beings who have achieved that state *before* death, and/or have arrived back into human life via incarnation after achieving that state—such as religious founders and avatars—report that there is life after enlightenment, albeit a complete turning around of the seat of consciousness from what we normally term human. As the Zen saying goes, "Before enlightenment, chop wood and carry water, and after enlightenment, chop wood and carry water!" Though the actions of life remain the same, the space from which they are done is different. This enlightened state of being, when it is realized, completes the potential inherent in your spiritual constitution, which is already far more complete than is generally realized. You all have the equipment for enlightenment, here and now. You don't have to die to do it, though death is another opportunity for your liberation, if you so choose. The spiritual student who fails to attain total liberation or enlightenment in his or her lifetime can finish off the final stages under the dynamic impact of the death experience.

The center of our being, the Consciousness Principle (Soul, ray of Light, wave frequency, vortex, Atma, Self) is the point of relationship upon which all forces converge. Traditionally, it is spoken of in yoga psychology (in the Samkhya system) as having five sheaths, or koshas.[9] These vehicles are of different degrees of density. They are not crystallized, separate layers, but are mutually interpenetrating forms of energy and consciousness, from the finest, all-pervading, infinitely fast neumonal consciousness down to the grossest, densest, slowest vibrating form of materialized phenomenal consciousness—the physical body. The finer sheaths interpenetrate and thereby enclose the denser ones, not quite like the stack of Russian dolls that Selma Rieseseg envisoned them to be, but close enough.

1. The Physical Body (Annamaya Kosha) is the densest and outermost, is built and nourished by taking in food, and comes from the father and mother. It is isolated from conscious awareness of the other bodies and their states of consciousness and is the most limited of the bodies. It is not able to interpenetrate the other sheaths, although all the others can occupy its territory. As such, it is the stage for heaven and hell on earth. Here the mystery of the divine and the animal meet, "little lower than the angels," but able to experience the highest of the high. It is the spiritual use of the higher, pranic, etheric "breath body" in the process of conscious meditative breathing that assists this body to come awake, to become conscious as a vehicle for Spirit.

2. The Etheric Body (Pranamaya Kosha) is next. It is the body of lifeforce consisting of prana (electromagnetic energy) and is the subtle go-between to higher and lower bodies. It conveys the properties of four kinds of prana, and the information carried in those energy fields. It is nourished by the subtle forces conveyed usually by breath, which in turn keeps the physical body alive, not unlike a placenta serves the human fetus. It is this biofield,

---

[9]Alternate spelling is kósa, which is frequently found in Eastern descriptions. We have eliminated the "foreign looking" accent for easy reading.

the lower etheric body, that especially interests us in deathing. Like the placenta at birth, the biofield at death needs to disengage itself from the body and return to the elements, and to the universal pranic energies after its function is over. When it does not, for whatever reason, it causes a breech death—and obscures and delays the best experience of the Soul. It can be influenced by the higher, thought-carrying pranas. Some systems count the etheric twice, as both a lower etheric, which feeds the physical, and a higher etheric, the psychic-spiritual go-between to Atma. The semantics of many spiritual works are confused and confusing in English, which is why I remain with the Samkhya system, using Sanskrit as a referent for terms.

3. The third, next finer sheath is the Thought-Body (Manomaya Kosha), which contains the mental consciousness and personality formed through mostly waking thought in your lifetime, although it is modified by subconscious causal forces from past lives and associations. Some systems subdivide the thought body into mind and causal mind. It contains, when operating through a physical body, the five senses, five sensory organs, and five motor organs. (See figure 2 on page 224.) This body is employed in the receiving and giving of conscious, positive autosuggestions to override unconsciously accepted negative ones. An aspect of this body operates in the dream state when incarnated, and as the astral, or secondary body after death.

4. The fourth body is the sheath of Revelation (Vijnanamaya Kosha), the point of consciousness, where laws of evolution, involution, and intuition operate. This is minimally the nonordinary state appropriate for death and healing. Artists, scientists, mystics, poets, gain their "Eureka" insights from this plane of consciousness, while remissions in disease also derive from here, as the personality is restructured. This is the body of your potential consciousness, which stretches past active thought by embracing the whole of your spiritual potential. It can be fully

exercised through an awakened nervous system and full operation of the first five chakra switchpoints.

5. The last sheath is the sheath of Bliss and Reality (Anandamaya Kosha), which penetrates all the rest. It is a coming together of egoic self-consciousness and the Consciousness Principle in the Universal Consciousness. Sustained by spiritual rapture and ecstasy (Ananda), it is only experienced in the highest states of meditation, or in a state of enlightenment, and corresponds to the Body of Inspiration and Bliss (Sambhoga Kaya) in the Trikaya system of Mahayana Buddhism. The individual self-principle—the Consciousness Principle—and the Supreme Being co-exist here as Jivatma becomes Atman/Brahman, using Eastern terminology.

Readers should understand that the secondary body (sometimes called the astral body or the light body) is a vehicle for and combination of the second, third and fourth sheaths, or (2) Pranamaya Kosha, (3) Manomaya Kosha, and (4) Vijnanamaya Kosha.

◇ ◇

THE CHAKRAS

The chakras are really energy vortexes in the human subtle anatomy. They are located along the spine and brain and are not so much locations but concepts you need to visualize. They are the main force centers or switchpoints that we will use in deathing. They are energy-changeovers from gross to subtle, and from subtle to gross, or physical, states. I want you to understand the kind of information exchange and the movement of varying kinds of consciousness (from subconscious, elemental realities and programs) that you find in the first two chakras, up to ordinary human states, which includes the first three chakras. The fourth chakra starts to filter in more heartfelt and less territorial concerns for the human race. The fifth chakra, or switchpoint, is the door to superconsciousness, with the two highest chakras opening the door wide. Conversely, one source of our superconscious potential, the fabled kundalini energy, which we shall discuss later, is stored dormantly in the lowest chakra.

Some people don't understand that the chakras are partially open and functioning all the time, for they bring through the multi-level programs of our human reality, without which we can't exist. For example, the lifeforce is stored in the first chakra, our reflex to danger is stored in the solar plexus chakra—automatically activating when we feel danger. The higher chakras are available to bring through programs of superconscious re-

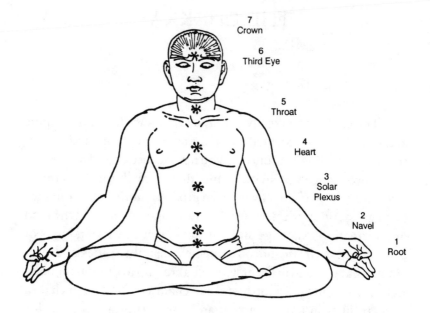

Figure 3. The seven chakras: (1) the root chakra is located at the center of the pubic bone; (2) the navel chakra is located at your umbilical point; (3) the solar plexus chakra is found beneath the sternum just beneath your ribs; (4) the heart chakra is located in the center of your chest; (5) the throat chakra is really located at the base of your neck; (6) the third eye chakra, located between your eyebrows; and (7) the crown chakra, found at the center of the top of your head. The chakras are called by various names in the Orient, depending on the tradition you study. When you die, the various energies leave your body by passing through some or all of these points. You want to direct the Consciousness Principle out of the top of your head. (Adapted from *Fundamentals of Yoga,* by Ramamurti S. Mishra, published by Julian Press, New York, 1969. Used by permission.)

ality that deathing is most interested in. For where you put your attention in the departure process from the body, is where you tend to "fix" at the death moment. To make sense of why this may be so, I suggest that chakras are highly organized patterns of energy, which harmonically superimpose and link many wavelengths, frequencies, and velocities through an array of convergence points. And the programs brought in through these access points can be directed by the focus of your attention—of your thought power, by prayer or mantra, and through the Sixth Technique. Mark this for your life and death.

Figure 3 outlines the chakras, these psycho-physical centers of our multidimensional nature. They will become major switch-points in the movement of consciousness in the dying process. As the chakras turn off, one by one, they influence the dying person's subjective reality. Deathing seeks to harness this energy, often called kundalini, which is released in the process, as well as the energy in the disengaging biofield. When mystics and spiritual students explore the chakras, they learn to move energy from the root chakra (1) to the crown chakra (7). This opens you to higher consciousness, level by level. You will be using the chakras as well as the subtle bodies when you leave your body, either unconsciously, or consciously through deathing techniques.[10]

You can use the chakras as focal points for the reception and transmission of both energies and levels of consciousness. These energies, "radio waves," or programs originate from a multitude of sources, some intergalactic, some cosmic, some solar, some planetary. Others derive from the collective mind of humanity at large, or a specific nation, or people, or from your

---

[10]If you decide you want to work with the kundalini prior to preparing for death, I really suggest that you work under the guidance of a realized teacher because without a good teacher you may not be able to handle the energy well. You wouldn't drive a car without taking lessons and working with a teacher!

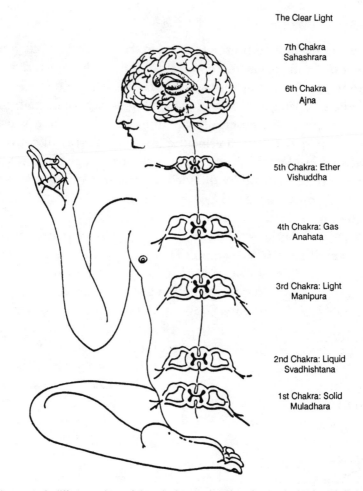

The Clear Light

7th Chakra
Sahashrara

6th Chakra
Ajna

5th Chakra: Ether
Vishuddha

4th Chakra: Gas
Anahata

3rd Chakra: Light
Manipura

2nd Chakra: Liquid
Svadhishtana

1st Chakra: Solid
Muladhara

Figure 4. A different view of the chakras, showing the path the kundalini will travel during the deathing process. Accessed through the chakras are also the four elements and ether (the Tanmatras). For example, the physical liquid of the body (2nd chakra) transmutes back into the subtle form or seed of liquid, which is connected to the quality of chemical heat (or Light) in the body at the 3rd chakra, which in turn disbands and shifts into more subtle forms. You want to go through this process so you can depart from the 7th chakra, although you can depart at either the 5th or 6th as well. But the 7th gives you a better chance at enlightenment.

own physical, emotional and mental worlds, including the past life repository. Last, but not least, the "gift waves" from already enlightened beings, or your own teachers are part of your conglomerate identity, to which you can draw closer. All of these impact upon that being of consciousness called you, establishing characteristics, moods, tendencies to illness, longevity and the like.

Nothing in the human equation is cut and dried, least of all death. The "when" and "how" is far more contingent on conditions of mind and consciousness than is at first apparent. By restructuring the contents of your consciousness the outcome of consciousness is changed, including remission from disease. Some of the most powerful methods to alter consciousness are called mantras or affirmative autosuggestions, as well as identification with and visualization of a revered, enlightened teacher, or else the "end product"—such as the outright remission of disease. The exercises in this manual are a powerful means to integrate and restructure mind and consciousness, and, thereby, your body will be influenced as well.

Traditionally, the chakras are charted in parallel correspondences with the body. Psychic and spiritual functions are evidenced in the endocrine glands, the various systems of the body, psychic nerve currents, sounds, colors and elements. Starting from the root chakra in figure 4, note the corresponding five elements of earth, water, fire, wind and ether. It isn't important that you know their Sanskrit or Tibetan names. It *is* important that you can visualize what is going to happen inside of you in the letting go process of death, which is prepared for by learning the five basic techniques. However, the means to *best* let go is using the Sixth Technique during the withdrawal of consciousness.

The departing Consciousness Principle will focus through the chakra system, moving upward through the three main spiritual-psychic currents (Ida, Pingala, and Sushumna)[11] for final release. If it releases in this lifetime, the release results in whole or partial enlightenment, and many students of Eastern philosophy study and practice to do this. At death, however, the process *involuntarily* fuels the departure of the Consciousness Principle. This doesn't result in automatic enlightenment, although death's change-of-state *can be* a conscious, voluntary means of enlightenment during the process. As the five elements release, they transmute into their more subtle correspondences (called Tanmatras) which in turn are motivated and determined by even more subtle thought processes and levels of consciousness (see figure 4), all the way up to the master control panel of the body/mind, the crown chakra. It contains correspondences to the other chakras which are activated in enlightenment, although remaining relatively dormant in ordinary people.

Figures 2 and 4 both show how the five elements (solid, liquid, light, gas, ether) relate to the chakras, or switchpoints. Chakras 1 and 2 are involved with subconscious elemental earthbound forces of nature. Your normal consciousness lies between chakras 1, 2, and 3, as fully active chakras. You probably have partial use of chakras 5 and 6. You feel your life focus in your heart (the 4th chakra). True loving on a universal level takes place in heartfelt, non-territorial kinsmanship with all life when this center becomes fully operative. Chakra 5 is the switchpoint of ether, into levels of superconsciousness.

When you are dying, the elements begin to disband. For example, the physical liquid of the body (the 2nd chakra switchpoint) transmutes back into the subtle form or seed of liquid, which is connected to the quality of chemical heat (or light)

---

[11]For students who want to understand this more, see Lama Govinda, *Foundations of Tibetan Mysticism* (York Beach, ME: Samuel Weiser, 1969; and London; Rider & Co., 1960), pp. 149–159.

in the body (the 3rd chakra), which in turn disbands, shifts, transmutes to more subtle forms, etc. As the elements disband from gross to subtle, the activating field of the body—its biofield energy matrix—is broken as well by the time the process gets to the 5th chakra, where high etheric matter transmutes to consciousness, which then can infinitely expand without limit. This process—going from the 1st to the 5th chakra—is part of the kundalini awakening that is automatically a part of death. (We shall discuss kundalini energy in the next section.)

By the time the energy withdrawal (either consciously or unconsciously) has proceeded to the 5th chakra, the body is likely to be declared clinically dead, but light is just starting to dawn to the interior gaze of the departing being. When you get to the 5th chakra, you can first eject safely and without interference, though you still want to aim for the crown chakra for this. As the inner scenarios associated with each shift of the elements in their breaking up cease, and light begins to dominate, there is a tendency to recoil, often in awe and wonder—certainly if you've been precipitated into death suddenly with no preparation. This recoil reflex needs to be overridden by what you learn here—it can be done by a support person who is helping you—so that a ricochet effect is not set-up from the discharging etheric field as it moves into the first stages of superconsciousness.

There are at least four grades of etheric energy (prana), and all operate harmonically, so fear, or a closedown of your field through shock, or even awe, will constrict it and cause it to rebound below the higher forms. The highest form of prana is the go-between for Soul (Atma), while the lowest is the biofield for the body, the go-between to the physical. The inner space that corresponds to this lower biofield is the Gray Place (or Hades) and the usual stay is from three to four days before you bounce up again into further light experiences.

By using the deathing techniques, when your consciousness passes the 5th chakra, aiming for the Clear Light during the dying process, you now understand that you may black out due to the shock of unconditional Reality upon the conditioned mind. Try to keep alert, since you have some preview of what is coming to guide you. Enlist your support person to help. It's important that your support person give strong mental or voice commands so you can recognize yourself as Light, thus letting go to your own divine nature.

By letting go to the unconditional Reality—experienced as Light—and identifying with it as yourself, you avoid reliving your former life, which ordinary people usually go through. Your life review will be seen from a higher perspective, since you are resonating to higher frequencies of yourself, thereby "who you are" has also shifted. It is important to outgrow the hallucinatory aspect of the afterlife experience and utilize it fully as a means to full consciousness transformation. How you meet the Light has important effects on your evolutionary journey.

In conclusion, you want to avoid any tendency to recoil which would precipitate you into the Gray Place, delaying your light experience after your initial experience with it. And additionally, you want to identify yourself with the highest aspect of Reality you can grasp—as Light, by identifying with a realized being, or calling on them for help. This lifts your self-identity out of the limits of human personality and ego-definitions which would cause you to think you were just dreaming. If you don't do this, then you'll sink into remorse about the dream, further trapping yourself, and all the while, everything that you felt, thought, or did in that state would be recorded holographically, contributing to your stockpile from which you would draw new scenarios. Yesterday made today. Make tomorrow beautiful.

Although deathing can effect consciousness withdrawal in twenty minutes, or maybe less, there also can be as long as a three-day lapse in ordinary dying before you reach the Clear Light while you are either in the physical or secondary body. From the crown, you move to the Void, where form and nonform meet, and where all potential is held. The 5th chakra is the first entry to superconsciousness, while the crown (or 7th chakra) will provide spontaneous awareness of the Infinite symbolized in blue sky, boundless space, unconditionality, timeless wisdom and love. Hold the state without grasping, stop all effort and motion. Just be there for the good of it all, no separation. And the word is love.

◇ ◇

KUNDALINI ENERGY

In a universe of vibration where, due to the nature of mind and consciousness, energy manifested as thought and matter interrelate and modify each other, the power of thought (and love and will) to influence the bioenergetics of subtle forms of matter should not be underestimated. Neither should bioenergy in its *localized* form—the fabled kundalini—be ignored as a power for transformation of consciousness. Modern physics now recognizes the interconnectedness of matter, energy, time and space which brings us full circle. The highest esoteric teachings have always recognized this.

The observer in modern physics is now no longer outside of what he or she observes—as scientific method used to decree—but is a party to creating that which is observed. *Deathing* urges this same participatory role for both the dying person and the support person. Intuitively we each know that we are nourished and sustained by a personal, but cosmically connected "self" whose basic "stuff" is the paraphysical energy of consciousness and awareness. But most of us fail to do anything with this knowledge. We can tune into this part of ourselves in various ways, kundalini energy being one of the ways that the incarnated personal self can understand the universal energy it partakes of in life and at death.

Kundalini is a coded "wake up" mechanism in the five-body system that switches on at certain intervals in evolutionary timing. Every time the personal self dies out of the physical body, the kundalini switch is thrown. Research has also shown us that kundalini is switched on with the near-death experience. Adepts and sages—as well as spiritual students—train this energy. Many untrained people have also experienced kundalini; for some it just happened (switched on by itself) and some people trained to do it inadequately—these are the people who could not handle it well. That's why I say that if you want to consciously train the kundalini energy long before you plan to die, you should study with an enlightened teacher who can guide you and supervise your training. And of course, the kundalini awakens automatically when you die, and when it awakens automatically at death, it will not hurt you.

Called in the East the divine fire, divine Light, or yogic fire, kundalini is Sanskrit for the coiled up subtle bioelectrical energies said to lie latent at the base of the spine. It is a term still unfamiliar to many, despite an extensive literature ranging from ancient texts to modern day systems, including NDE research. Western writers have called it the serpent fire, while Madame Blavatsky, Alice Bailey and others described it as universal electricity which travels faster than the speed of light. And light, of course, has been calculated to travel 186,000 miles per second. Both Blavatsky and Bailey were discredited in their time.[12]

However, this alleged constant, so imperative to modern relativity theory, has recently proved relative to itself, as all paradigms tend to do. As of this writing, the *London Times*

---

[12]Swami Yogeshwaranand Saraswati, *Science of Soul: A Treatise on Higher Yoga and a Practical Exposition of Ancient Methods of Visualization of Soul—Atma-Vijnana*. Published by the Yoga Niketan Trust, Muni-ki-Reti, Rishikesh (Uttara-Khand) India.

(Nov. 29, 1988)[13] has announced that an experimental physicist has proven in the laboratory what was first announced by Nikola Tesla over sixty years ago, and what yogis and mystics have known for thousands of years. The experiments into superluminal velocities prove that the speed of light is not the fastest speed of energy in the universe, but rather one of a harmonic series of quantized velocities of vibratory energy. You can research this for yourself if you want to, but the point that I make is that kundalini energy exists, and if you accept that, you can use this during the dying process.

One of the implications of "faster than light" velocities is that it is possible to reverse the flow of time, for going faster than the speed of light is equivalent to going backward in time from the point of view of physical dimension. The celebrated life review in NDE, in which people see their entire life flash in front of them—or conversely, experience future events at a personal or planetary level—is thus explained at last. While as we approach infinite velocity, we also approach omnipresence, omnipotence, and omniscience—Deity itself.

The localized or personalized aspect of this cosmic life force could be the kundalini, which in yogic tradition is called *prana.* John White notes that this "primal cosmic energy is akin, if not identical to *ch'i* (Chinese), *ki* (Japanese), the *Holy Spirit,* or various other terms from various cultures and religious traditions that identify a life force that is the source of all vital activity."[14] Neither prana nor kundalini have been identified by orthodox science up until supraluminal breakthroughs, but Bentov, Hiroshi Motoyama and others have monitored this energy. Ken Ring

---

[13]Pearce Wright, "Is Travel Faster than the Speed of Light Possible?" *The London Times,* Tuesday, November 29, 1988.
[14]John White, editor, *Kundalini, Evolution and Enlightenment* (New York: Anchor Books/Doubleday, 1979), p. 21.

says that this bioenergy—kundalini or whatever one calls it—is now recognized by its effects sufficiently that it can no longer be disregarded, even if it remains outside the accepted theories of science. Much like NDE itself.[15]

Ancient wisdom maintains that prana is "the means for raising human awareness to a higher form of perception, variously called illumination, enlightenment, cosmic consciousness, samadhi.[16] Various systems have been devised to concentrate, raise, and channel the serpent power. Traditionally it is said to move upward from the base of the spine to the brain, along the central nervous system, through the main subtle channel called *Sushumna* in Sanskrit. Tributary subtle nerve flows, the Ida (correspondent to the parasympathetic nervous system), and the Pingala (correspondent to the sympathetic nervous system) are respectively identified with the feminine (or negative) electrical charge and the masculine (positive) magnetic force.

The routing and symptoms of the awakening of kundalini, whether induced by forms of kundalini yoga which aim to create an upward flowing energy to the brain, or occurring spontaneously by various means (including NDE), or occurring spontaneously due to mechanical vibrations, electromagnetic waves, or certain sounds[17], as well as the influence of an already mature kundalini in an enlightened being, are described for the modern reader by both Bentov and Sannella.[18]

Bentov describes the physiokundalini syndrome and the coming of age of the nervous system in some detail. Sannella has an expanded version of that description, which provides very

---

[15]Kenneth Ring, *Heading Toward Omega* (New York: William Morrow, 1984). See chapter 9, "The Biological Basis of NDE's," p. 229.
[16]White, *Kundalini, Evolution and Enlightenment,* p. 21.
[17]See Sound Current/Nadam, page 247.
[18]Bentov, *Stalking the Wild Pendulum,* and Sannella, *The Kundalini Experience.*

important information for anyone who has experienced an NDE because the NDE tends to trigger off kundalini. The symptoms are so bizarre in the unsuspecting participant that they can be wrongly diagnosed as various diseases or even as mental illness. The symptoms of undiagnosed kundalini awakening relate to a radical change in the nervous system, much like adolescence changes the child into an adult, which can also be disruptive. Pain, psychological disorientation, dislocation, or other symptoms occur when the opening circuit of higher-energy-monitoring reaches areas of stress in the body/mind.

Until recently our models of reality didn't entertain anything that related to kundalini, as many NDE people learned the hard way. It is a sorry situation that Bentov and Sannella bring to our attention, and my own experience verifies this as well, for some of the psychological symptoms of kundalini awakening may mimic schizophrenia. Some NDE people have been institutionalized or given unwarranted treatment. "It is ironic that persons in whom the evolutionary process of Nature have begun to operate more rapidly, and who can be considered as advanced mutants of the human race, are institutionalized as subnormal by their 'normal' peers."[19] Bentov suggests that the number of kundalini awakened institutionalized schizophrenics may be as high as thirty percent, a waste of human potential.

In deathing, kundalini is part of the "ultimate stress release" of death, as the localized aspect of the universal life force moves through the various energy centers of the body (the chakras) in the departure process. When the chakras are energized by the rising kundalini during the lifetime, they become better receptors and distributors of the inflowing universal life force. The chakras monitor and filter cosmic programs according to the degree of activation of the kundalini energy moving through them.

---

[19]Bentov, *Stalking the Wild Pendulum*, p. 175.

According to the yogi sage, Ramamurti S. Mishra, chakras are a neurohormonal mechanism through which psychic energy is distributed.[20] He defines kundalini as the energy potential of the eternal and immortal which only partially operates in the localized state of ordinary humanity. It is this level of activity of the life force moving through the lower three chakras (or switchpoints) which consigns us to our normal territorially possessive, sexually desirious humanity. Samuel Sandweiss reminds us, however, that "Yogis believe that will and desire are the higher and lower aspects of the same attribute: for the powerful kundalini force to be directed properly, the will must be cultivated."[21] If only the first three chakras are activated, the kundalini is first directed by desire and survival. But as Dr. Sandwiess says, "as the individual's consciousness develops and higher spiritual centers are activated, when his character becomes strengthened and his intuition far-reaching, the energy is directed and controlled from 'above' rather than 'below,' by will rather than desire."[22] And, we might add, love.

Dr. Mishra observes that with certain training and education, or spontaneously—in intellectual or artistic bursts of inspiration—this kundalini force operates moderately. But it is in the enlightened one (one who is in the state of samadhi or being "one without a Second" with the universal) that kundalini operates fully and perfectly.[23] The kundalini path, then, is the "mechanism that deals with the correlations and integrations of various bodily processes, the reaction and adjustments of the organism to its environment, and with conscious, superconscious and sub-

---

[20]Ramamurti S. Mishra, *Fundamentals of Yoga* (New York: Crown, 1987), chapter 7, p. 37.
[21]Samuel H. Sandweiss, *Spirit and Mind* (San Diego, CA: Birth Day Publishing, 1985), Appendix III, p. 291.
[22]Sandweiss, *Spirit and Mind*, p. 291.
[23]Mishra, *Fundamentals of Yoga*, chapter 19, p. 87.

conscious life."[24] As a medical doctor, with specialties in endocrinology, ophthalmology and psychiatry, Dr. Mishra's comments are especially recognizable to the West, as he observes correspondences that are anatomic, physiologic, psychologic, and biologic. Kundalini has emerged out of the realm of the unknowable, mythical and mystical as the evolutionary energy of the new era, as Gopi Krishna puts it. It is an activating, neural, biological, psychic and spiritual transformative energy that allows for the expanded perception of being human. In short, the emergence of a new kind of human being—what Josip Vidmar called the PSI human, and what John White calls *homo noeticus*—is around the corner, as more and more people are beginning to work with it consciously. This transformation is happening in the millions, mainly through NDE. John White further makes a point that, ". . . the kundalini experience, then, considered from the viewpoint of individual transformation, is said to be a path for enlightenment. But if a large number of people were to appear in society at the same time, the result could well transform society itself. So the kundalini experience, in its broadest aspect, is evolutionary—a path for the advancement of the entire human race to a higher state."[25]

Ancient wisdom maintains that right dying, which is reintroduced in our time as deathing, is one major way for attaining higher evolution in the following lifetime. It is my hope that this will be so. However, the annals of kundalini literature are filled with warnings about premature awakenings before the ethics and morality of the individual have grown apace with the emerging kundalini power. In our age of spontaneous unfoldment, this is important advice, and a spiritual teacher is strongly suggested, to help students avoid misunderstanding the energy.

---

[24]Mishra, *Fundamentals of Yoga*, chapter 19, p. 82.
[25]White, *Kundalini, Evolution and Enlightenment*, p. 17.

◇ ◇

THE SOUND CURRENT
AND THE LIGHT

If we look at the universe as a vibrating field, organized according to harmonically resonating intervals, with interlocking interfacing energies criss-crossing its vast holographic nature, we find that it looks like the auric sac around a human being. Additionally, there are huge currents moving throughout the Whole, and some spiritual systems call this the Sound Current (or Shabda) upon which our subtle bodies surf by tuning into its frequency. These currents appear like the Gulf Stream, or the Humbolt current in the oceans, or astrally like the electromagnetic currents stretching from pole to pole of the Earth's egg-shaped energy field. But these huge currents are not of Earth—they are said to go out from Source and are homeward bound from Source, passing through eons of endless time in the journey, yet conversely, they can be traversed instantaneously.

Since the same archetypal patterns of creation repeat themselves over and over on each level of manifestation, whether atom, one-celled organism, seed, apple, planet, solar system, universe, or beyond, it is no surprise that Bentov makes the same point from atom to human to cosmos in his *A Cosmic Book*.

As always, there are analogies between the macro- and the microlevels. . . . Every seed in nature, whether plant or animal, has a similar current running along its axis, creating

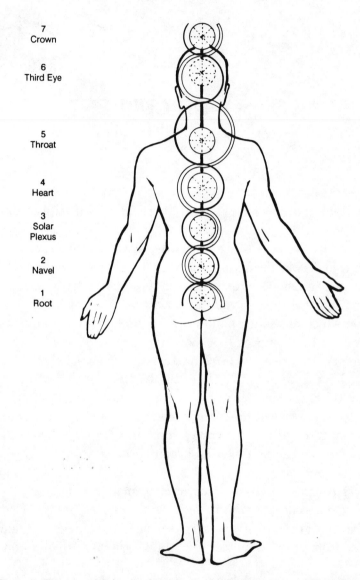

7
Crown

6
Third Eye

5
Throat

4
Heart

3
Solar
Plexus

2
Navel

1
Root

Figure 5. The tunnel going up the spine is called sushumna, while the energy of ida and pingala are represented by the curved double line and the curved single line. The energy goes up to the crown and out the top of the head.

an electromagnetic field around the seed. . . . Biologists have called this current the *organizing field* of life, which guides atoms and molecules of a growing organism into their proper positions. In other words, an electromagnetic hologram or an energy pattern preexists and determines the material form which eventually fills this pattern.[26]

In the human being, the outer form of the physical body is not what our limited senses make it out to be. Seeing the human figure is rather like seeing the skeleton of the energy system. The real being is an ovoid sphere of energy housing the subtle bodies and criss-crossed with flow patterns that the Chinese *ch'i* system describes as a "flowering tree" going up the middle, with both a positive and negative pole. See figure 5. The central subtle energy canal, correspondent to the spine, is the area of densest activity between positive and negative, like a meeting ground between Universal pranas and localized (or personal) forms. How much of this is kundalini is unknown.

The soul (or localized Consciousness Principle) and the personality composite (body/mind and its etheric and astral bodies) are linked by a stream of vibratory energy, which I call a mini sound current. Some systems describe it as a silver cord. Some clairvoyants can see it, some can't. This sushumna, or silver cord, operates rather like a traintrack and signal system in orienting the time-space coordinates of the physical-etheric body and the astral or secondary body which can roam free during sleep, meditation, or at death.

Death separates the soul from the body by snapping this connection so it no longer returns to the incarnated "track" of the body-time-space coordinate. However, in or out of the body,

---

[26]See Itzhak Bentov, *A Cosmic Book* (Rochester, VT: Inner Traditions/Destiny, 1988), pp. 39–40.

dead or alive, this inherent mini sound current is one way you can tune into the large Sound Current that spans the Universe, connecting solar system to universe to cosmos through harmonic, morphic resonance.

The question arises, which Lee Sannella brings up in his *Kundalini Experience*, as to whether spiritual unfoldment is dependent or not on the kundalini mechanism. We may find the whole controversy is one of semantics since the fundamental thing is vibration anyway. No matter what you call it. In any event, there are a number of spiritual systems that don't discuss kundalini either by name or by symptoms. Some discuss it and discount it as limited self-transcendence, or—like the various forms of Shabda yoga, or Sound Current yoga—maintain that the Sound Current (Shabda), vibrating at its different levels activates the Soul, not kundalini.

My first teacher, Paul Twitchell, described kundalini as relatively inconsequential in the spiritual process when it was compared to the efficacy and divine stimulation of the Sound Current, which could be experienced both as inner Sound (Nadam) or Light. My own experience is that one switch on the kundalini mechanism can be activated by resonance with the macrocosmic aspect of sushumna—the Sound Current. This is the organizing field of all life forms. Perhaps it is the recently discovered "Great Attractor" toward which all the known galaxies are streaming like a vast vanishing point!

In the process of deathing, kundalini will awaken, although it may have been unawakened up until that point. The deathing process actually is propelled by kundalini, discharging energy to de-bond the Consciousness Principle from the body. Because of this, I have blended the techniques of Sound Current and kundalini.

As we have previously discussed, the dying person focuses the release of the kundalini energy through breathing, sound, and visualization techniques, which brings the energy up to the crown chakra—the positive pole. By concentrating on an enlightened being (using the Sixth Technique), you balance the positive/negative forces (pingala/ida) in the central tunnel (sushumna). This overrides other lower programs or distractions and converts the biofield energy into lift-off. The dying person will also have learned about the ten major forms of the Sound Current—aspects of the original AUM sound—called nadam, which can also be seen as light. Hopefully the dying person will be listening for this during the deathing process.

The fundamental thing to remember, however, is that all life operates in an infinite vibrating field in which vibrations are organized into discrete, harmonic intervals and geometric standing wave nodal patterns that are open to the highest level of spiritual reality. When these approach infinity, all possibilities for manifested creation exist in the simultaneity of the eternal "now." Time and space only exist where there is finite velocity, or in the lower harmonic manifestations of the eternal "now." And it is interesting to understand that the evolutionary possibilities already present in the eternal now unfold in time and space in evolutionary sequence.

Everything starts with vibration, and spiritual practices all aim to make the subtle fields coherent—a quiet, reflecting pool by which to imprint the Real.

Most people cannot readily experience a memory of the inner life until they begin meditation, or some spiritual practice which trains them to see or hear the great organizing fields. This is the Holy Spirit of the Gospels, which can confer grace by simply hearing it. By changing the organizing fields of your makeup, this Holy Spirit can also dissolve sins or lower karmic imprints in the subtle fields, or restructure genetic codes, as well as healing the body and spirit. The dying naively enter a state whereby they can hear some or all sounds of the Sound Current, and need to know and recognize the incredible favor being conferred by the universe.

The Sound Current was called the Logos, the harmony of the Spheres, the Holy Spirit by Western teachers, and AUM, Nadam, or the Shabda by the Eastern. Both systems represent the Logos/AUM as the primal Sound of creation, which the German philosopher/mystics of the 18th century called "das Uhrwort." Both systems describe this original sound as both causing and expressing itself in various manifestations of noumenon and phenomenon, of sounds and frequencies, even as its other aspect, the "original Light," expresses itself in corresponding colors, degrees, and levels.

Pythagoras, founder of one of the most important schools of mystic-scientific philosophy in the West, based his teachings on the Sound Current, as the source of creation. His school was located first on the island of Samos, then in the Greek colonies c. 500 B.C.[27] in Crotona, Italy. In his teachings, which combined esoteric geometry and the human voice in advanced mantric science, he duplicated many of the powers and attributes of the solar and cosmic forces by duplicating the sounds they emitted, all of which he experienced as levels of the Logos. His wife, Theana, was the most subtle instrument in his investigative enterprises. She was possessed of a miraculous voice, which could span an awesome range of octaves, in sublime mystical-musical experience that blended music with healing, philosophy and science. Levitation, healings, shape-changing of etheric, astral and physical bodies, as well as the heightening of consciousness were within her range.

Pythagoras conducted most of his work in strictest secrecy, for fear of persecution, and to honor the code of mystery school silence. Much of his work was destroyed after his death. His use

---

[27]See visionary/autobiographical novel, *Daughter of Artemis*, from the triology *Net and Trident*, soon to be published. Contact the Ariel Foundation (listed in Resources) for more information.

of mandalas (esoteric geometrical forms which arranged force fields multidimensionally) achieved "miracles" not seen or heard of since Atlantis, or the already misty past of Golden Age India and the rule of the sage-kings. The secrets of his esoteric geometry, regretably, have been lost, but it is believed that he classified and demonstrated that each system, star, or planet—in fact each atom—emitted a particular sound because of its rhythm, movement, and plane of vibrating frequency in relation to all other vibrations. All of these together composed a symphony, a universal harmony, in which each part (although having its own function and characteristics), furthered the Whole—even as violin, cello, flute, drum, and brass, although separate instruments and sounds, can contribute to a collective symphonic sound. So did Pythagoras conceive and practice the energy exchange of the universe through harmonics and resonance, while the proper exchange between the micrososm of humanhood and the celestial realms would make of humans the gods he knew them to be.

• • •

Going back to the quantum door through which you enter life and death experience, you will be able personally to experience that everything in Reality has a voice, vibrating in the mindstuff of consciousness in which knowledge is structured. It is composed of particles of Light, noumenon differentiated into programs of phenomenon, or event matrixes—the interference patterns of what appears to be a huge hologram, the universe itself. Paul Twitchell constantly reminded his students that the universe was already created, past time-space as we knew it, to then be acted out in all its infinite display of possibilities.

Before I had his theoretical framework and experience to draw from, or that of Samkhya yoga, my own experience during near-death substantiated this. I discerned parallel universes and their event matrixes that could have manifested in this time-space, but somehow didn't.[28] Paul Twitchell always referred to the plus factor of God, that God was always creating itself, subsuming all lesser gods within it, refuting the big bang theory of a once and for all creation. The paradox is that ever the totality is greater than the sum of its parts, as more parts of Creation become conscious—and thus influence themselves. I have also experienced this to be true, as there are many universes within this cell group, each with its Creator God, all connected by a stream of energy that emits out of the Void, or Nameless Place, into manifestation, then returns once more through the black hole on a higher octave of the Reality scale.

Modern science still subscribes to the big bang theory of how the universe began. We commonly think of events starting someplace, an assumption that can also be derived by taking Genesis too literally. But what if creation is always going on, as Samkhya Yoga describes, and as Bentov describes in his "bang, bang" theory outlined in his *A Cosmic Book*?

And which comes first, the chicken or the egg? Does the organizing field, or thought of God, as original impetus come first—the original AUM sound—or does the creation come first? Bentov asks the question and solves it in ways close enough to my own independent experience for me to think he has the modern interpretation of the Holy Ghost, and the explanation for the Sound Current, or Logos, when he describes his model of the creation of the universe.

Bentov's qualifications for making theories are the same as the ancient sages—direct experience. Experience has served as the qualification for the other authorities that I refer to about these matters, either from their written works, or from interviews—Ramamurti Mishra, M.D., Sathya Sai Baba, and my first

---

[28]See the chapter entitled "Planetary Visions," in *Heading Toward Omega*, by Kenneth Ring.

teacher, Paul Twitchell. My own experience, although far more modest, has the same direction as theirs, independently duplicating enough about these principles and practices for me to confidently share them with you in this study of deathing. This is not just "word-smithing," a game smart moderns play. Nor would I "put you on," since I take very seriously that the quality of your life and death may depend on what you learn and practice here.

Bentov describes how the universe was made in a framework of many universes, which in turn make up one cosmos, and many cosmoses make up a cell group of supercosmos, etc. But the organizing principle of creation from the Voidness is the same— the Sound Current in its outward and homeward bound cycle. If we say that AUM is the original Universal Sound of All, we can also say that the HUM, or HU is the Universal Sound personalizing itself at the heart in the sacred theater of the human being.[29] It resonates to the heart of the Creator, even as AUM can be likened to the breath. Bentov's model of the universe as a cosmic egg suggests this interpretation. The two are One, AUM and HU(M), in different aspects, aspects and semantics being the usual cause of confusion and the specious arguments earnestly undertaken by neophytes on different paths. Not having themselves experienced what they conceptualize their teachers to have meant in the writings, they make an argument where there is in experience no grounds for an argument at all.

In the spiritual practices of different religions and paths, the goal is always to refine and purify the consciousness of the practitioner, so it can deal with Source directly (i.e., reflect or resonate to it perfectly, through removal of any impurity, impediment, or distortion). That is the intent as well in preparing for

---

[29]Govinda, *Foundations of Tibetan Mysticism*. See Part IV for Govinda's discussion of *Om* and *Hum* as complimentary values of experience as metaphysical symbols.

death via deathing. To attain this state, whether achieved by traditional means and teachings, or by deathing's abbreviated, but potent preparations, the same strategies of visual light-oriented exercises, or audio/vocal sound-oriented exercises are employed. Both have their advantages, according to your personal temperament, culture or circumstances. In Deathing, a blend of both is presented, including utilization of certain mantras, which we'll discuss later.

But first, understand that everyone has the AUM sound, since we live in its vibrating nature like fish in the sea. But like fish, we are usually unaware of our situation. You may hear it first as a sort of ringing sound, especially in your right ear. If you drive a long day's ride in the car, hearing road noise and engine throb, not cushioning yourself overmuch—when you stop the car and turn off the ignition, silence simply roars at you. That is a beginning. Sit for a moment and focus on letting it move through your head and whole body, as you've been "warmed up" to vibrations by listening to the external engine sounds, etc. Also, late at night when all sounds die down and you may be either working late, or just lying sleepless in bed—consciously listen. Often spontaneously, one of the major sounds of the AUM will become startlingly audible, with the sound of silence like a background noise.

Working with Sound

These sounds can roughly be cataloged into ten main states and therefore sounds of AUM, or Nadam, with every state having innumerable subdivisions and varieties. Each can be "ridden" or "surfed" to their source, and to Source itself. There are ten which are frequently heard, as well as being most useful in cleaning out impurities in body and mind—thus giving you an entry to the world past the skin barrier.

The macrocosm and microcosm are passing through the four stages of AUM. These stages are classified according to the letters in AUM. AUM has four phases, three letters, and the fourth is the echo (or original unmodified Sound). The letter A represents the gross food body and the waking state. U represents the subtle bodies (Pranamaya Kosha, Manomaya Kosha and Vijnanamaya Kosha), the sheath of the mind as prana and consciousness, and the sheath of the mind as potential, complete conscious life which includes the dream state. The letter M consists of the sheath of bliss (Anandamaya Kosha), the deep sleep state, which, when embraced by the echo becomes samadhi.

This is the description of the letters in A-U-M, OM, but the original OM (or Nadam) is beyond description and beyond all the states mentioned above. Never has anyone been able to describe Nadam fully. All the scriptures of the world describe it through indications. Therefore a full description of Nadam means to put the infinite into the finite which is obviously not possible.

Note, we mentioned the three stages of OM, such as the waking, dreaming, and sound sleep state, all of which in the purification process are brought up to full conscious awareness. In your normal every day state, you are only partially aware in the waking state, mostly forgetful of the dreaming state, and unaware altogether of the deep sleep state. An enlightened being would be aware and totally conscious of these states. Pure Nadam is beyond these three; therefore, figuratively, it is called Turiya (the fourth in number). It is transcendental consciousness, inexpressible in words, incomprehensible to the material mind, and the greatest of all. Therefore, it is called Brahman, or the greatest, which is known by many other names, according to your culture and religion, all indicating the Supreme, Source, or God. It is beyond consciousness and unconsciousness because in the biological sense these two states of existence have a limited meaning. Actually, the third state, deep sleep, turns into the fourth in such enlightenment.[30]

My first teacher, Paul Twitchell, at a seminar in 1969 in Los Angeles, recommended the following exercise to help people experience the Sound Current. Later my mentor, Ramamurti Mishra (Brahmananda Sarasvati), also recommended it as a means to start listening to the AUM sound. It is a yogamudra technique that goes like this:

1) Close your ears with your thumbs. Close your eyes with your index fingers. Close and press your nostrils with your middle fingers. Close and press together your upper and lower lips with your ring fingers and little fingers, respectively. The mouth should be filled with air, and you should breathe gently through the nose.

By this *mudra* you will see the spectrum of different lights; you will hear the *mantram* from your soul. This is a yogamudra.[31] Through this mudra you will see your soul in the shape of light and you will listen to its music in the form of Anahata Nadam.[32] IF YOU SEE THIS LIGHT WITHOUT OBSTRUCTION FOR EVEN A MOMENT, YOU WILL BE FREE FROM IMPURITIES AND YOU WILL REACH A HIGHER STAGE.

2) When your impurities are removed up to a certain extent, you will begin to listen without placing your fingers on your face. This is called the real state of Nadam.

---

[30]This section was adapted from Mishra, *Fundamentals of Yoga*, chapter 28. Used by permission.

[31]When you practice Yogamudra and both of your nostrils are closed by your middle fingers, you may feel suffocation. To remove this suffocation, allow air through your nostrils slowly and quietly, but don't remove your fingers from your nostrils. Do this daily for a few minutes an you will get the real Anahata Nadam, which will remain with you always and teach you.

[32]Anahata means "without instrument."

There are ten main classifiable Sounds of AUM and you may hear any of the following:

- The hum of honey-intoxicated bees, idling engine vibration, rainfall where there is none, crickets, whistling sounds; or a very high frequency sound (almost a squeal or screech which is sometimes mistaken for the flute call by beginners, Cin Nadam);

- A waterfall, roaring of the ocean (Cincin Nadam);

- The sound of a bell ringing (Ghanta Nadam);

- The sound of a conch shell (Sankh Nadam);

- Nasal sounds, humming that sounds like a wire-stringed instrument (Tanti Vina);

- The sound of a small tight drum coming in a rolling rhythm, then staccato bursts, then rolling rhythm again (Tala Nadam);

- The sound of a flute, melodious and penetrating, finer even than Paul Winter's or Galway's golden flute. Traditionally the sound of the flute is called "Krishna's flute call." You hear it by grace, or after the mindstuff is refined enough to perceive it. It usually pairs with Light of a wondrous gold-white, often with a cobalt blue. This is the mandala some see at death, into which the tunnel between dimensions moves, ring upon ring (Venu Nadam);

- The sound of a big bass drum (Mridamga);

- An echoing sound or an "underwater" sound (Bheri Nadam);

- The roll of distant thunder or a sharp clap (Megha Nadam).

Know that all these sounds are really the vibration of electromagnetic waves and light-play through yourself, manifested as hearing, and/or seeing. These different forces in nature can only be felt when you are totally at rest, which is normally in meditation, or spontaneously when your mind is strongly focused on something, or when you are asleep, or dying. By now you know that the various inner sounds are immensely powerful, cleaning out impurities of the mind and body. You also know that they can be induced by the playing, singing, or chanting of outer sounds, or by the rhythm of breathing. They are *direct* conduits to the Source, which lies all around you and are strong currents to "ride," especially the flute call. If you hear any of these sounds within you, it is like the comfort and safety of being in your mother's arms; *never fear them.* One day, in either meditation or in death's ultimate meditation, you will rest in the Clear Light and Sound of Reality. Learn to recognize and practice for it now and enjoy the benefits.

• • •

As the various "strippings off" of death occur—which is the movement of consciousness through the chakra switchpoints— different levels of these sounds of reality may open up to your inner ear. Many will be quite different from what you may have experienced in your yogamudra practice! Some are stupendous and frightening, the sounds of wrenchings apart and the debonding of the matter of which the physical body and biofield is made; some are cosmic and celestial, utterly lovely.

It is important to first recognize all sounds you hear at death as only the process going on. And then for you to utilize them— ride them—by recognition, as a means to move on to higher processes. Just as I have suggested that you utilize the recognition of the images you see during death and in the afterlife by binding yourself firmly to seeing each image as the Universal, similarly, I recommend that each sound you hear should bind you only the more firmly to Universal Self-Knowing through hearing. You can claim these sounds by going deeply into the deathing exercises and carefully listening past your physical ears, as well as learning to ride these spiritual sounds to their source.

These sounds are starting to spontaneously open up for ordinary people who usually then run to doctors to either explain them, or drive them away with sedatives! Yet they are only the sounds available to an emerging humanity, as well as the means to assist humanity to higher consciousness.

I assure you that you, too, can have the experiences that once and for all utterly reveal you as being more than a phenomenal, finite creature housed in a body of limits—for only the cost of your time, your effort, and your heartfelt SOS—or even desperate "Mayday, Mayday" call—to the universe for grace, as one friend with AIDS put it. He was able to die peacefully, letting go into That which he had already experienced, after he had known a tremendous out-pouring of light through his body, that in turn poured him through creation as he rode the mighty surges of the Sound Current one night in a dream state, to wake "solar dusted."

◇ ◇

MANTRAS

Mantras are mysterious business. In Eastern religious practice, mantras appear to be the product of the organization of existing referents for high consciousness in the form of sounds—like AUM, HUM, SAT, and various other words for the Divine state—as well as "binding" or "entraining" a high level of consciousness onto a series of organized syllables—sounds. When repeated, mantras gain effects in the manifested world, releasing energy in specific desired ways.

Several schools of thought about how, or even if, mantras work can be reconciled and given a framework of modern explanation by observing how sound works. Mantras operate like organizing fields in that they create energy patterns among the infinite criss-crossing vibratory waves, frequencies, levels and octaves operating in the universe. These holograms, or energy patterns, are highly coherent focused energies. They pre-exist the effect they will cause, which they induce by harmonic alignments between fields.

Let's look at the nature of sound for a moment. Any sound has its own unique structure and wave form. This is determined by its fundamental note as well as its overtone or harmonic. The relative intensity or amplitude of the overtone harmonic determines the timbre of the sound. This is what makes the same note different when played on the piano, or violin, or sung by the human voice. The more mathematically pure and coherent the sound is, both in the steadiness of its tone and in the precision of its overtone structures, the more musical and pleasing it is. That's why a musical instrument sounds different than dropping a cement block or banging on a water pipe. And a beautifully trained voice usually sounds better than someone singing in the shower.

Mantras, then, are special intonations designed to set up highly coherent wave patterns which stimulate and purify your chakras and subtle energy fields. Chanted sounds vibrate in the air, the subtle ethers, electricities and electromagnetic fields. Each specific type of sound sets up its own unique geometrical pattern of standing waves. In Eastern philosophies, these geometrical patterns are called yantras, or mandalas. Yantras, created in etheric matter by sound, set up a coherent wave guide for even more subtle astral, mental and spiritual vibrations. In fact, the chakras themselves are highly organized, standing wave nodal patterns which harmonically superimpose and link many wavelengths (frequencies, geometrical modalities, or velocity harmonics of energy) thus enabling the intelligence, love, and power inherent in the higher levels of spiritual energy to imprint the lower harmonics. Eventually, this process works its way all the way to the brain.

Mantras are designed to purify and cohere these chakra standing wave fields so all the bodies are in synchronization with higher forces, providing for evolution. Eventually the kundalini energy will respond, as incoherencies or negativities are removed from the field—the obscurements to a perfect mirroring of higher forces in the lower.

Repetition of mantras also helps focus your attention away from distracting thoughts and emotional disturbances, hence their importance as an aid in dying. The one thing that all yogic and spiritual practices have in common is that they are designed to bring about a steady, sustained focus of attention which *automatically* builds coherency into the subtle bodies and mental waves. Mantras put ordinary mental and emotional distractions and urges to sleep by repetition.

You have read that you can induce hearing the inner sounds of reality by chanting AUM, HUM, doing Yogamudra, etc. Chanting a mantra may start as an external action, practiced without much fervor or belief. But it sets a state of mind and heart going in you that then becomes an internal state, an environment of the "beyond ordinary reality." It may also create a certain configuration of atoms, thereby making a thought form of this state of mind, much as a magnet organizes iron filings into a pattern. The thought form can then be induced simply by chanting that certain word, which in turn induces that level of sound or sound pattern. The outer action leads to the inner experience! Therefore mantras work both through the mind and the heart that experience them, as well as via the symbols that express them, thereby empowering them as well. Remember, the organizing field precedes manifestation.

Once establishing that some kind of encodement process is at work in both mantras and thought forms—as if a cosmic DNA for a future event or physical formation were somehow in the charged words—the distinction needs to be drawn between mantra and merely thought forms on the psychic planes. Both have their place and both work, and both need to be employed in healing. In dying, however, mantra and the name of the Supreme Reality in whatever form or name you most are drawn to is preferred.

By definition, mantra means that which always has referent areas of spiritual inquiry beyond the senses, i.e., the Divine. Words disassociated from Divinity or its form as Sound (or Shabda) cannot be called mantras. This Shabda or Music of the Spheres, uses the mantra as its carrier frequency and gets to and from its function somewhat like a letter gets to its destination through the postal service. Additionally, a mantra has two aspects: Manana, which means that whatever you learned has to be taken into the mind; and second, Traana, which means that whatever has been taken into your mind now has to be firmly preserved there.

Nor can even empowered words such as *svaha* (which means "heaven") be in themselves considered a mantra, although they often finish off a mantric formula. Ordinary words, like rose, or nonsense syllables cannot be a mantra, since they aren't focused beyond the senses, although if the word has literal meaning, like peace, or love, it can draw the mind to reflect on that state through autosuggestion. Thus the mind is drawn to become like that state of peace or love, restructuring the contents of consciousness with corresponding results. It's hard to get a feeling or picture of mere words having divine power; but my experience has convinced me, so I share the idea, and specifically the Gayatri, the catalyst mantra for the extremely serious business you are about—healing and/or deathing yourself!

So you may believe that mantras are magical, and powerful, no matter how they are recited, because they produce certain configurations of vibrations that are activated by saying the mantric formula (much like how a car starts when you turn the ignition). Or you may believe the mantra, affirmation or prayer works because of your spiritual attitude and state of mind and heart, and therefore might not work if you disbelieve in it. Both can be reconciled by quoting one of my teachers, Sathya Sai Baba, who was asked about the Gayatri mantra in particular:

Finally the author inquired, "Swamiji, it is said that if this mantra is not recited correctly, it harms the individual. Is that correct?" He replied, "Yes, it has the opposite effect of enveloping the person in darkness, but if you recite it with Love, God will accept it."[33]

It seems, then, that either intellectual precision, traditional Sanskrit pronunciation to the nth degree, or the open-hearted factor of love will win the day! That would seem the case, confirmed as well by the practice of another of my teachers, Ramamurti Mishra who, among his many accomplishments, is a reknowned Vedic and Sanskrit scholar. He allows the general public and new students outrageous license with the pronunciation and mispronunciation of mantras. Although he is strict with his own students on pronunciation, he is wide open to different styles of chanting. Nor does he ever criticize a heart-felt attempt, even as his own traditional Sanskrit style varies from that of Sathya Sai Baba's in intonation, when chanting the Gayatri,[34] which is perceptible even to an untutored ear. Dr. Mishra suggests through his practice of giving immense freedom to his students, that either just saying a mantra, or a "charged word," especially in the presence and atmosphere of an enlightened being, starts creating the effect it is referent to in the mind and consciousness of the hearer and practitioner, thus drawing the student into the fold of spiritual energy.

Which brings me to the story of Ajamila,[35] as background to why the Gayatri mantra works under any situation, as well

[33]Eruch B. Fanibunda, *Vision of the Divine* (Shri Satya Sai Books, Prashanti Nilayam Post Office, Anatapur District, Andra Pradesh 515134, India). pp. 79–83.

[34]See Resource section for Ananda Ashram and Prashanti Nilayam, respectively.

[35]*Srimad Bhagavatam*, Sixth Canto, Part One, "Prescribed Duties for Mankind," chapters 1 through 5. Translated by A. C. Bhaktivedanta Swami Prabhupada. Published by the Bhaktivedanta Book Trust, 376 Watseka Avenue, Los Angeles, CA 90034.

as the non-mantra, which explains the potency of the Sixth
Technique—the name of God or guru at the moment of death.

The story of Ajamila was literally thrust on me in the London airport in the form of a book forced into my baggage as I
waited for my plane to India. There I was to meet Sathya Sai
Baba in the flesh for the first time, full of questions for this
mysterious miracle man about just the point that the Ajamila
story underscores in vast detail. My question was, "Will the
Sixth Technique work, as described by the *Bhagavad Gita*
(8:5,6,7),[36] and, moreover, will it still work if a person says or
thinks the name of God or that of an enlightened being at the
death moment, without believing, or giving a hoot—except,
being hounded by death, to be tempted to give it a whirl—as
many of the readers of *Deathing* will?" That was the fall of
1985, and I had many explorations and anguishes yet to go
before full proof that Grace was "covering for" even the skeptics
of our time and I was allowed to finish *Deathing*.

The story of Ajamila is in short the tale of a fallen Brahmin
priest who took up with a prostitute, led a rude, crude life,
married her, sired children, lastly, the darling of his old age, little
Narayana. Now, Narayana is one of the most potent names of
God in Hindu tradition and practice, although Ajamila must
have had only a dim memory of that, given his terrific negativity
in every other aspect of life, except love of Narayana, his baby.
It was "Narayana this," and "Won't you have some of Daddy's
food, little Narayana, that?"

His entire mind and attention was focused on the child—
which is one of the points of the story to remember. *For whatever
you put your mind on most during your life, you will most likely*

---

[36]"Anyone who, at the end of life, quits the body remembering Me, attains
immediately to My Nature, and there is no doubt of this. In whatever condition
one quits his present body, in his next life, he will attain to that state of being
without fail."

reflex to at death! Narayana was playing with pots and pans at Ajamila's feet when it came time for Ajamila to die. The Yama lords, or death angels, showed up with a vengeance to carry him away to the just deserts of his negative karma. He was so frightened at his approaching death and the incumbent parting from the beloved child, and so scared of the ominousness of his escort service, that involuntarily at his last breath, he called out, "Narayana!" And died. At which moment the Godsquad arrived at his bedside to escort his soul! These rival angels to the Yama Lords were on a similar, but diametrically opposed mission— since the destination of each was poles apart. The two groups stared at each other, each claiming Ajamila's soul. The Godsquad won out after approaching the highest heaven for judgment which went as follows:

It was declared that Ajamila's saying the name of God, although without his meaning God, i.e., meaning in this case, a small child, still constituted saying the name of God and thus meant Ajamila's freedom. While saying God's name in jest, was, as well, the same, even as while laughing, or in art and music, literature and theater. In all the preceding, the name of God would still have the same efficacy as if conveyed from the heart of the most fervent believer.

A modern analogy can be made about our telephone service, which will work for believer and unbeliever alike, *as long as the correct number is dialed, or the operator contacted.* It operates by physical laws, even as the Sixth Technique operates by cosmic law, a physics of consciousness we will eventually understand. However, by practicing the Sixth Technique enough to learn to reflex to it in crisis, you will begin the turning around of your consciousness, which will engender love—and so there you have it. Try it and see.

In the case of practicing the Sixth Technique you have an example of using both an affirmation and the evocation of a power word, as well as an access code to the Divine focused on a certain being who is already in the Universal state of mind called Enlightenment to which you can resonate. You bypass your own mind's limits. This is a kind of hitchhiking into the Universal Reality that the particular being both evokes and is, by means of calling the name. It works to "dial Central," as Christ, Krishna, or Buddha, even if you don't believe it, because these beings already exist in that enlightened state of Universality. They have access to Divine unconditional Reality which embraces your limited reality as well. That Reality also becomes accessible to you—through them. Essentially, you are only calling on YOURSELF, using them as a focusing device, which a mantra is as well.

Or you might think of a mantra as a magnifying glass able to concentrate and amplify already existing forces—such as the sunlight—due to its shape, thereby producing a flame, although the glass has no particular heat of its own. Whatever the explanation you use for yourself, mantras work, and the Sixth Technique works. The use of an affirmation, mantra and/or power word such as AUM, or SATNAM, Krishna, Christ, etc., is a cleansing and focusing device for body and mind. This results in the restructuring of the contents of your consciousness, allowing healing and spiritual breakthrough—both or either—to occur.

Let's examine a few prayers, affirmations and one mantra which you can use in lieu of making up your own prayer, or affirmation. These should be repeated in practice sessions, could be incorporated into a tape you and your support person might record for use during long, lonely nights, or in programming yourself to reflex to relaxed, comforted, peaceful states of mind. I am conveying only the principle here. Not having conducted research on the world's main prayers, you have to supply your own content of your practice, but this can be the means.

First, a Christian one: "Lord Jesus Christ, have mercy on Me!" This evocation has a tendency to open the heart of the person calling it out from the heart center. Or parts of the Lord's Prayer can be used.

Jewish practitioners might use the age-old "Sh' Ma" (Hear, oh Israel, the Lord our God is One), which would have the feeling of the estranged reuniting with the Whole. While Jews and Christians alike take great comfort from the 23rd Psalm.

Buddhists would likely use the powerful mantram, "Om Mane Padme Hum," which incorporates the primordial OM sound, while Hindus might also use the OM, or the Gayatri Mantra, as well as an invocation of their enlightened teacher, from which the Sixth Technique was taken.

Or you might incorporate various affirmations or mantras with your rate of breathing—the breath providing the basis for meditation and higher consciousness via mediating between body and mind. Out of this healing can result—as well as the state appropriate for death—the non-ordinary reality which is always around you, but which must be tuned into consciously in order to be experienced.

Go to the section on breathing in this manual and skim it quickly. Then establish a gentle normal breathing rhythm for yourself. Often the heartbeat felt through the wrist pulse is used as the pace, with four beats to an inhalation, four for holding, and four exhaling being a nice rhythm.

Establish this and then simply add to it your preferred name for either God, or the Reality process, such as SAT NAM, with Sat" on inhalation and "Nam" on exhalation. You can do the same with the chant, SO-HUM, also a very potent evocation. When done single mindedly, these are very powerful exercises, quickly dissolving you past the "skin barrier" into perceiving yourself as an energy field. Or, conversely, you can do them ab-sent-mindedly, but as a constant background noise to whatever else you are doing, which cleans the energy field, and stills the mindstuff, as well as giving high suggestions to the thought body, replacing negative, destructive thoughts which contribute to disease.

Or say to yourself while breathing, "Experiencing peace, I breathe in, experiencing peace I breathe out." Or choose any quality you need and breathe with it.

Many of my students have found it useful to breathe in the desired quality they are needing, i.e., healing, love, prosperity etc., and then affirm on the exhalation that they are breathing out their infirmity, i.e., drug abuse, alcohol abuse, cancer, etc. I rarely name the infirmity as a specific disease, lest it resonate in the mindstuff of an untrained person and do more damage than help. Infirmity means that anything which is weakening the body or system is expelled with each breath, leaving as it were, firmness, or stability, or firmament and foundation for the person to stand on.

By hooking your healing and the desired state of mind to your breath, you train yourself to positive autosuggestions *millions of times a day*—offsetting negatives in the etheric and subtle bodies that have become rooted in the flesh. That sets the conditions to erase the subtle impressions, which in turn begin to dissolve the gross, physical manifestation in your life and body. Even as everything that is flesh or actual disease was once a thought form which somehow took root, so know you can unroot and dissolve it. *Now.* It is also recommended to always add the affirmation, "Not my will, but thine be done," in partnership with an aggressive program of autosuggestion, mantra and meditation sessions.

Additionally, Sanskrit chanting, or sacred hymns with the charged, mantric forms, or empowered, sacred words can be played at night when the mind is most receptive.[37]

---

[37]A tape is available from the Sathya Sai Baba Book Center of America. See Prasanthi Nilayam in the Resource section for more information.

The Gayatri

The Gayatri, or King Mantra, is often called "Mother of the Vedas," or the "second birth" to those who practice it. It is also a catalyst, which I call the "jump start" mantra, which sets in motion the highest inner forces of the psyche, or Soul, the Consciousness Principle. Focused on the Divine as it is, it can also be aimed at a specific desired effect, such as healing, fertility, artistic creativity, prosperity, etc. Or it can aim even more specifically toward a situation such as a certain healing on a certain person, usually the practitioner. While the word, "Gayatri," itself, means "that which rescues (protects) the chanter is this." The "This" is Shabda Brahman in Vedic thought and language, or Logos in Western metaphysics and spiritual practice.

To gain the full benefits of this mantra, it is useful to know in general how to say AUM to gain the highest benefit. Now that you know what it means, and its potentialities, say it slowly, thinking of all that. Say it as slowly as possible, starting with A (AH) from the navel center through the throat, U rolls over the tongue, and the M ends on the lips. Start slow, rise to a crescendo peak at M and then slowly descend, taking the same amount of time as the ascent. Then let it disappear gradually into the inner Silence—feeling it in your heart—as light, expansion, joy. Go deep into the silence and you will start hearing the cosmic AUM, or the original sound itself, as well as the other ten sounds.

This Pranava is the sound which emanates through prana, or the vital vibration which fills the universe—the etheric "stuff" that connects everything. This prana is a conveyer, a carrier of other vibrations, of thoughts, as we have said before regarding healing. The English translation follows, and after that the Latinized Sanskrit and a guide for your pronounciation.

The *Gayatri* (in English):

THE GREAT RESURRECTION
MANTRAM OF THE LIGHT
—GAYATRI—

In the circulation of Life—coming in, going out, and
    balance,
We fix our attention within that sacred Radiance
of the brilliant, glorious Source of all
which guides in order that it may inspire
our self-revelations.[38]

The *Gayatri* (in Sanskrit):

Latinized Sanskrit:	Phonetic rendering:
AUM;	AUM;
BHUR BHUVAH SVAH;	(Bhoor Bhuvah Suva-ha);
TAT SAVITUR VAREN-IUM:	(Taṭ Ṡavituṛ Varáy-uṅyuṁ):
BHARGO DEVASYA DHEEMAHE;	(Bhargo-O Devasya Dheemahi);
DHIYO YO NAH PRACHODAYAT.	(Dhiyo-Yo Nahf Pracho-dayáat).

Sign (⌒) over, shows that letters have to be joined
        together.
Sign (') over, shows an extra stress on that letter.
Sign (_) under, shows a lesser stress on that letter.
Sign (e´) over, means the letter is to be pronounced as
        the "a" in ancient.
Sign (,) under, means the letter is to be cut short and
        only half-said.
Sign (-) between the letters means a short pause.

---

[38]Translation from the *Rg Veda*, "Tenth Mantra in the Sixtieth Sutra of the
Third Mandala," by Vyasanda.

The *Gayatri* is divided into three sections: the first line contemplates the glory of Original Light, the light that illumines the three lower worlds or regions of experience; the second section and next two lines pictures the glory, the splendor, and the grace flowing from that Original Light. The third section, and last line is a call for final liberation through the awakening of the innate spiritual intelligence that pervades and vibrates the universes as Light—in yourself, as well.

Any mantra, but this one in particular, has immense power to set up a resonance with its referent, in this case Source itself, Unconditional Reality, via the modifications of light and sound. Lesser levels are said to drop away, while benefits stream into all areas of your life. This mantra should be repeated three times at a session, and then said three times more per day, minimally, while visualizing and feeling your desire. Since it tends to harmonize energies and it is de-polluting mentally and physically, it is good to say it before you eat a meal, or during your bathing period, or at sunrise and sunset. Use it *especially* when you have difficulties with your job, or to improve your health, before and after surgery, in pursuit of general wellness, and when you are involved in the dying process. If you memorize it now, you can be sure to know it by heart when you need it. (See Resources for available tapes.)

◇ ◇

PRANA and RE-BIRTH

Let's reflect on the interpenetration of the five sheaths, the chakras and their respective levels and planes of operation in the whole human for a moment. All the levels shade into each other, from denser to finer gradations of energies, registering cosmic vibrations. The material body is built up through nourishment, yet is penetrated and sustained by the vital force of prana. Prana, like electric current which can flow through various mediums of wire, or even without wires, uses the breath, the blood, the nerves, the subtle bodies and chakras as conduits, but at the same time can act independently of these mediums, if focused and coherently directed. For instance, healers can send prana long distance by mind, while the second, etheric body (the Pranamaya Kosha) can, through therapeutic touch, be utilized in healing to charge another person's energy field. It can also operate away from the physical body for a time after the death of the physical body, especially under the conditions of accidental death. The biofield, or lower etheric function, can be a troublemaker in that capacity, which we've mentioned, and which deathing aims to override.

We can't limit or underestimate prana, which has no name yet in modern science. Prana is more than all it modifies into, whether breath, nerve, or blood, the vital forces of semen, or the creative force and faculty of thought, will and intellect, as well as the interpenetrating of the five sheaths. It is prana that is the go-between in the spiritualizing process of body, mind, and spirit in the human theater, the infinitely sacred space of the human body. This vital force exists in all life, like a catalyst or yeast, making things happen.

After the death of the body, when it comes time to prepare for rebirth, the active thought of the Consciousness Principle (influenced by subconscious past experience and associations, the storehouse from which our thought and imagination draws the material to make new scripts), interpenetrates with prana's mysterious function in the in-between life areas. This is how the form of the bodily appearance is determined, as well as its general health, intelligence, or lack of it, *including the healthy or unhealthy state of the etheric and astral bodies, which are crucial to the proper functioning of the physical. These in turn are directly connected to the state of mind experienced at the death moment in the previous life.*[39] That this works—to a terrifying degree, if, for example, at the death moment one is negatively focused when the Light Experience occurs, and records the negative thought—I know firsthand from my own past lives. They graphically demonstrate the awesome power of the death moment—to record and set the stage to reproject the essence of these last thoughts from the previous life into your new "script"—making major repetitions of old leitmotifs, for good or ill.

One negative state of mind that contributes to an impaired body and/or mind in the next life occurs when you have no afterlife construct or expectation at death—for whatever reason.[40] That includes those with mental impairment (which in

---

[39] Rudolf Steiner, *Life Between Death and Rebirth* (Hudson, NY: Anthroposophic Press, 1975).

[40] Steiner, *Life Between Death and Rebirth*. Steiner's research corroborates with mine on this. And I read his after I had done mine!

most cases tends to recycle), as well as people steeped in material-istic, skeptical religions such as communism, and certain kinds of 20th century scientific and mercantile-oriented beliefs that preclude any other reality but the physical body and world. Since our whole society is still permeated by this kind of thinking, in the transition period to a more holistic view of body/mind/and consciousness relationships, *Deathing* makes available certain concepts and reflexes to use at death, which people can resort to, even if their conditioning is such that they don't believe them!

In a way, teaching people how to use death moment karma seems like a quick fix, for many people won't change much this life, but will just use the reflexes, even facetiously. But, even so, the reflexes to positive deaths *will* work, including the fail-safe Sixth Technique. It can be used by believer and unbeliever alike, due to the nature of consciousness and the enlightened teachers awareness of the problems of our time, midwifing a new era of higher consciousness as they are. Therefore, whatever the nature or degree of accumulated negative karma of the individual, a good, positive healthy next life with opportunity for advance-ment of your spiritual understanding is almost guaranteed when you follow deathing's precepts.

When the idea behind deathing is understood and practiced by people in service fields, such as those working with the re-tarded, or in mental institutions, penitentiaries, hospitals, hos-pices and pastoral care areas, they will be better able to assist people to positiveness at the death moment. Such simple assis-tance would usher their charges into a better next life by which to remedy the effects of their this-life situation, by first not repeating them. And that would include criminals and moral derelects, for whom a knowledge of the power of the death moment to transform consciousness would give them a chance, next life. Going by the currents of normal evolutionary flow, these people would tend to temporarily move downward in consciousness in the next life, or have severe retributiory or horrific experiences such as they afflicted upon others in this life, that they would probably repeat being a victim for several lives to come.

A very strange, mysterious business occurs when a criminal, or disbeliever practices the Sixth Technique at death in such deathbed conversions. But every religion and esoteric practice has its stories of whispering the name of Deity into the ears of the dying, especially on a battlefield where anger and mortal concerns have prevailed before death.

Therefore, the situation of accident death is of special concern to my heart. Death by war, murder, prolonged suffering (such as torture and protracted illness), often leaves the individual in such despair that his or her death is helplessly permeated with negative emotions including vengeance, or even righteous anger. Such grim situations, without intervention, and without understanding the role death moment karma plays in the next life, often results in a replay of previous death conditions, or similar ones. *Deathing* can offset this. Such deaths, especially those of young people dying at the height of their youthful energies, as people do from AIDS and cancer, result in the person quite naturally feeling robbed, bitter, and angry. These very justified moods can have the worst results in the immediate next life for that individual. Accident deaths (from war or other mishap) often impair the health in the next life, due to a weak biofield and astral body, resulting in poor immunity to disease. That sets the scene for dying young once again. And again, often by versions of the same ailment . . . and again.

THREE GOALS OF DEATHING

All of deathing's three goals can be achieved by simply *learning to recognize what is happening to you* at death and not fleeing, or recoiling from it as separate from your own consciousness. Accept all as yourself. Then focus and hold an expanded positive consciousness during the death process, at the death moment, and thereafter into the stages of after life.

Goal 1 is to have a good rebirth, which is almost automatic if you keep open and positive, generating calm, having no anger. Since last thoughts at death are immensely powerful, exponentially so, and can fling you anywhere, deathing teaches you to learn to reflex positive mental states, even in the midst of difficult dying, which can, conversely, save your life. I urge your attention to the Sixth Technique to achieve this safeguard, since most ordinary people haven't the mental and emotional stamina, nor training in meditation to monitor all the distractions dying entails for the Consciousness Principle. Please heed this advice.

Goal 2 is to prevent a severely delayed stay in "the Gray Place," also known as Hades or Purgatory, which occurs normally in ordinary death, and is prolonged in a "breech death." I'd also like to see any stay at all prevented, since it only occurs when the Consciousness Principle recoils from the Light, or clenches and contracts (even in awe), creating a bounce-off effect into the lower areas of inner space. This geography of inner space corresponds to the lower etheric body, or biofield, hence our interest in it.

Goal 3 is an open recognition of the Light, which means that your own ray of light both melds and reflects it in Body Five, hence no bounce-off effect occurs and Enlightenment is experienced. This is not the same thing as "meeting with the Light," as all creatures do, and then ricocheting in forgetfulness, shock, fear and awe out into other states. At the moment of death, the lower bodies and sheaths are stripped away, leaving you naked and exposed to What Is—bliss, light, joy, wisdom, pure love and universality as you present to the Source in Body Five. You have enlightenment, if you can only recognize it. The microcosm approaches the macrocosmic Light that comes at death. They are one and the same in kind, but not quantity, the ray of light being of the Whole and yet not the Whole. To recognize this truth is to be it.

In thinking about how to train for enlightenment from an unenlightened point of view, it is wise to get the idea of great Light, like a Sun, or huge all-pervading luminosity, which will come very vividly at the moment of death, so you get used to the idea, and the feeling of openness. It is important to remember what to do at that time. Utterly let go all your assumptions about the world, the light, yourself, God, etc., that are in your head, and feel your heart open. Drop everything and just be there for IT, then in IT. Otherwise you will likely faint at the shock of meeting It. It is called Sunyata, emptiness, void, an absence of anything, a potent presence of all—the Source, beyond even its manifestations. All you can do is recognize and accept the Source of all, unconditionally.

To faint will cause automatic withdrawal although this does not constitute a breech death. Fear and awe will contract you into separation, as the survival etheric centers of yourself erroneously regroup to protect the small egoic self from the Source. This creates the ricochet effect—away from the Clear Light into the

Gray Place, after which you'd wake up three or four days later with no memory of either the Light, or even having died!

Experiences you would have at that time, however, rather quickly would show you that something unusual was going on! You'd view friends and relatives mourning your loss, and dividing up the property. They'd pick out a casket and have a funeral for you. And if you were fortunate, they'd say prayers and evoke the Sixth Technique on your behalf, as well as tell you to let go to the Light as yourself. Likely even then you'd rub your eyes, thinking you surely were dreaming!

What to do? The *opportunity* death offers you is for liberation, first as you meet the Light, and good, *conscious* transference from the physical experience to the afterlife, second. *Both depend on your recognition of what's happening*: 1) to know you are dying, not just dreaming is important, for you may think you're just dreaming your own funeral, etc.; 2) have your support person remind you, if you have one, that you are dead, physically speaking, and yet, as the Consciousness Principle, you are Light, immortal consciousness, Itself—now meeting Unconditional Reality; 3) cling to your spiritual teacher, if you have one; 4) let go both attachment and aversion to *anything*, as well as cease from a sense of territory or false ownership, even of your own mind's wants, *including* any grasping for liberation; 5) *see enlightenment as already having occurred*, not as something outside yourself. Then you will realize it more easily as your own inherent nature. Let the mirror of your own innate spiritual intelligence reflect the Light of unconditionality, which comes in successive multi-exposures after the initial encounter; 6) recognize all lights, sounds and visions as reflections of your own consciousness. Merge into the brilliant lights, not the pale ones; 7) hold tight to your recognition that everything you meet is friendly, no matter what its appearance, for all is ultimately you. *Then* there is freedom.

Otherwise you will tend to slide back into confusion and wake up from the Light, reliving past experiences, such as the much touted life review reported in near-death experiences. That's excellent for near-death, since *then* you have opportunity in the same life to implement the lessons learned. *But at real death it means automatic rebirth to have associations with the memories of the past at that time.* Rebirth simply means a continuation of tendencies, associations, and habits, albeit in re-arrangements like a shifted kaleidoscope, which then, next life are perceived as new patterns, since few people have past life recall at this time in history.

If, at the moment of seeing the Light, you can burn out the force of old habits in their seed form by simply letting go—to what IS—thereby cutting yourself loose—you are *free*. If you do not, and would rather dwell in your past, *for whatever reason*, you will be reborn, as night follows day, unvolitionally. Once enlightened, you are born at your own volition, however. And as we said, there is life after enlightenment.

The dynamic impact of the death moment needs to be harnessed by your recognition and attention to what is happening. You must also *stay* open in recognition to what bursts upon you of unconditional Reality, when all your human, fixed and conditioned realities short-out in the dying process. It may seem like the universe stops, while the tendency of the limited self is to "make it happen again" through thought, because mind likes to cling. Instead, hold to your calm center, and hold to the Sixth Technique at each stage of your departure—cling only to that.

This is the key to utilizing the energy of each chakra switch-point and the biofield itself as a rocket propellant for the Consciousness Principle. It lets go from the body, letting go to itself. Anything short of total acceptance of the Void conditions of the clear Light will result in a ricochet effect into the etheric for about three days, an unnecessary detour. It also makes it harder to pick up on successive exposures to other enlightenment opportunities, on successive days after death, the various other liberating Light experiences the Tibetans talk of, but which are not gone into in this preliminary study. Recognizing and accepting everything as yourself remains constant throughout, on whatever day after death. Enlist your support person's aid.

Many spiritual practitioners through history, and indeed Josip Vidmar in the story, "finish off" their liberation under the dynamic impact of the death experience. At that time, spontaneously, coarse energies dissolve into fine, subtle energies as various experiences arise in your consciousness. These are seen as mental projections by the trained meditator and the situation is very much to a meditator's advantage, since you have mastery over your mind. The whole idea of meditation is that through yogic techniques, you experience before death the stages of "stripping off," the dissolution and disintegration of limits which are experienced dynamically at death's change-of-state. Meditation trains you to maintain control throughout the process so when the dissolving process of death actually occurs, and the various mental projections arise, you can transform them into higher forms of spiritual Reality via your recognition. This is no light task, though the benefits are light, indeed. *For ordinary people, "hitchhiking" on an enlightened teacher's skills, through love, is again urged, and may be the only way for ordinary people to achieve this state.*

In a nutshell, to practice conscious dying, you must be able to spontaneously know what you believe in most. The dying moment is not a time to take on a new teaching! At that time, you can't really say, "Wait a minute—I have to think about it!" What you know has to be spontaneous, and you either have it or you don't.

Through instruction and experience, death can become a liberating and joyful process, not a rude exit. It is a technique, an art acquired through concentrated preparation and practice before the death moment, if at all possible. However, using the breathing technique, or using the affirmation to "Let go to the Light" can be used in emergencies or with strangers unfamiliar with the method, in conjunction with saying out loud, or thinking strongly with heartfelt conviction: "Go to the Light, Be Light." Remember to enlist your own teacher's presence, or choose some enlightened being to help. You are only the equivalent of a paramedic in these matters, so please call the doctor— use the Sixth Technique!

If someone expires in front of you and is declared clinically dead, understand that the Consciousness Principle has yet to depart the body. Do what you can medically as your first duty, otherwise it is not unlike murder. If the person is still "clinically dead," and you are *convinced that there is no possibility that the body is serviceable for that individual, and/or of further medical interventions being available, or useful,* then say, "Go up to the Light, *be* the Light!" and touch the top of the person's head. Meanwhile, think and feel strongly—with all your heart— positive, calm letting-go-*up* sorts of feelings, as if you were the expiring person, exiting out the crown in a long "Ah" sound and with the feeling of letting go. This "Ah" sound corresponds to the "A" in AUM—the gross body and the waking state. Saying or thinking it assists in the letting go process at death, and in letting go emotional tangles during the lifetime. Touch the head once more, for the Consciousness Principle at that stage follows wherever the body is touched and with help will depart at that exit point. Tell the dying person to keep calm; stay calm yourself, slowing your breath, and mentally or vocally direct the Consciousness Principle upward. Tell it to be happy, explain that there is no coming back and that it needs to be open, going up toward the light out the top of the head, and that you'll help with matters here, such as reporting the death, setting in motion the contacting of relatives, etc. *Keep your word to a dying or new dead person.* For they will know.

Even if, in the course of a medical procedure, the "clinically dead" person were touched on the lower parts of the body, you can firmly remind it to let go upward by touching the head, for your touch or a verbal or silent command will re-orient it. Even though you are sure that the body is beyond repair, but especially when you are not—evoke the Sixth Technique as your own fail-safe and safeguard. Ultimately, in this world of organ transplants, trained hospital personnel may one day act as support people to assist dying people. It will be a great service, and avoid much suffering, as people could be assisted in exiting the body with dispatch—not three days later, or ousted by a scalpel or cremation's fire.

The "Switchpoints" in the Dying Process and How to Use them During Departure

Remember that you are a series of force fields with the biofield (or etheric web) as the medium for transmission of the various kinds of ethers (or pranas or forms of modified light), so you can fully understand the mysterious relationship between the various levels and dimensions of existence. You'll have to range further than the boundaries of what is normally the province of religion, or psychology, into metaphysics—quantum reality—which hem we have just barely touched. And you have to suspend your disbelief for a moment.

In humility, then, you note that the lights, various phenomena, and visions that open to the interior view of the dying person result from the stripping off of body-sheaths and the withdrawal of the energies that are housed in the four basic elements identified with the four lower chakras. The Tibetans describe the four elements on which life depends (earth, water, fire and air) as being correspondent with the essences in you (flesh, bodily fluid, bodily heat, and breath), with the fifth being ether—where consciousness resides. Real death is, however, not quite the model near-death would suggest. According to modern day Tibetan teachers there are states to be gone through before you experience the Clear Light of Reality Itself.

You go through these stages, or switchpoints, as I call them, where you are confronted or barraged by all kinds of objective and subjective phenomena. (See figure 3, page 230 to see how these switchpoints work.) However, the switchpoints—and the phenomena they bring to you as they discharge—actually provide valuable opportunities for enlightenment Itself. But, first you have to *recognize the process* and then go with it, become it, accept it. Above all have no fear, or recoil from it, seeing all phenomena as only the features of your own mind, from subconscious to super-conscious—spun out like cotton candy at the carnival. To dissolve the phenomena, touch it with the tongue of your recognition. That gives you pure sweetness, the sugar, from which the cotton froth was spun. Reality is that simple at this time.

Therefore, the switchpoint phenomena is really a series of projections spun from the Self, projected like movies, which then appear as if coming from outside you, both during the dying process and afterward. In the days after true death and the initial exposure to the Light, there are succeedingly subtle engagements with varying colored lights and successive opportunities for enlightenment, IF you can but recognize them.

First, you need to be acquainted with the experiences you may have during the falling away of the four elements in the dying process. They project certain scenarios. Each has different scenery, colors, light and sound phenomena, and physical sensations to go with it, some of which can be discerned by the support person. It is crucial to have positive reflexes to anchor to during this period, perhaps the most difficult period in the process. The power of the Sixth Technique to assist in overriding these sensations and movies should not be underestimated.

In a lengthy, and/or painful death, especially with untrained people, this stripping off process, and the movement of consciousness through the switchpoints can go on quite a while. The dying process often begins before it is apparent to ordinary eyes, although a clairvoyant can see the interfacing fields begin their withdrawals, shifts and transferences of energies, pehaps before the person involved even knows what is happening. In a swift, accidental death, you move quickly through the process, but you still have equally great potential for detouring, especially through shock recoil. It clamps the biofield around the body, the astral body, and the Consciousness Principle, obscuring your perceptions so you cannot see, think, or reason, and you are confined in the etheric body's dullness and animal stupidity for the usual three-day interval. Shock death sets the stage for what I call "breech death," which holds you longer than the three-or four-day stint evoked by not paying attention.

The major trap at any switchpoint is your tendency to become involved in the phenomena you see. You tend to grip onto whatever seems to be real, then begin to react to it, not seeing the projections for what they are—produced, acted, and directed by your own mind. *Wake up.* Recognize what's going on.

The role of a support person can be crucial, especially when the death is caused by accident and the dying person is caught totally unaware. It is then that negative thoughts (as well as shock) can become the cause of a breech death by being impressed in the already constricted biofield. The negative thoughts (or shock) are then projected by the mind, and you fall for the ensuing movie projection as real. Since the biofield's duty is to protect the physical under stimulus of trauma or shock, it closes in and makes itself denser, which is counter-productive to the dying process. It is comforting to know that such a rude, even dangerous, departure can be neutralized by the warm, loving thoughts of survivors, your support person, or your spiritual teacher if you have one.

Prayers on behalf of the new dead should be made, a tradition already available in Christianity, Tibetan Buddhism, Islam, and Hinduism. These prayers need to be used in more than funeral ceremonies. Today, most funerals are still held for the needs of the living rather than the dead, although invocations for assistance of the newly dead individual by all enlightened ones is standard in *Deathing*, before, during and after the funeral. Also, actual instructions are available,[41] aimed as guidance control so the dying and/or newly dead individual can reverse the effects of a negative departure, in order to let go toward the Light. The Clear Light does come, but it comes after the dying body becomes immobile and probably has been declared clinically dead. By that time most of the four elements have dissolved into each other, with attendant phenomena which need crisis management by you and your support person.

The support person should stay by the body for at least an hour after clinical death and use the Sixth Technique. This has a twofold benefit for it finishes off the dissolution of the elements (thus closing the doors to the body for the Consciousness Principle), and you are reminding the departing consciousness to meet the first encounter with the Clear Light. This often takes place in the body at the heart chakra in a non-accident death. Then follow your intuition as to when to touch the top of the head.

In the dying process you are dissolving all that you ever humanly thought was you—psychologically, physically, and spiritually-psychically—you will experience subjective and objective phenomena, scenery, events, images. The following stages are from the Tibetan tradition's descriptions of the dying process derived from workshops led by both Khempo Kather Rinpoche[42] and the Venerable Kalu Rinpoche. The

---

[41]See Ariel Foundation or Secret Forrest Tapes in Resources section. You can also use *Tibetan Book of the Dead* as a guide.

[42]Abbot of KTD Monastery, Woodstock, NY. See Resource section for details.

information in *Bardo Teachings: The Way of Death and Rebirth*, by Lama Lodo,[43] was also consulted, as well as others.

• • •

As the element earth dissolves, it is absorbed by the water element. This switchpoint marks a change in focus from the root chakra (1), to the abdominal center (chakra 2). The attending inner movie has a yellow cast, and the scenario is that everything is falling apart from great floods and earthquakes. The visuals are of water/earth themes. Physically, in this first phase, you feel as if your strength is fast disappearing and you can no longer stand. What to do? Transcend the duality of anything being outside yourself. See all yellow manifestation as having no independent existence. *Call your teacher.*

Stage two occurs if you don't succeed at perceiving all as yourself in stage one. Stage one, successfully melded with, grants a certain level of enlightenment—and stops the movies. (Now is the time to lick the cotton candy with the tongue of recognition. Keep trying. If you don't succeed, keep trying. It's simple. Just melt the illusions with your recognition of what they are— disguised sugar. Reality under cover!)

The attending inner movie of stage two, as the water element (chakra 2) is absorbed into the fire element (chakra 3), has a predominatingly white appearance. The scenario is that the entire universe is flooded with water, while physically the converse is true as you feel your face and lips drying out, and you are very thirsty. What to do? If, when this takes place, you can meditate on all the water and whiteness as products of your mind, with no independent existence, you will attain another level of enlightenment, and be spared further suffering.

---

[43]Lodo, *Bardo Teachings: The Way of Death and Rebirth* (San Francisco: KDK Publications, 1982).

The third switchpoint comes when the third element (fire, chakra 3) dissolves into the air element (chakra 4). The scenario is of everything burning and has a predominately red appearance. You will feel that everything around you is burning, although conversely, during this time you will feel your body heat go away, and sensation draining out of your lower limbs, which by now are numb. What to do? If you can meditate successfully on all this being mind-created, and not having any separate existence whatsoever, you will gain enlightenment. *Deathing* urges you, additionally, to focus on breathing *up*, having your support person assist via voice commands. This will root your mind on breathing, quieting the onslaught of "crazy house" phenomena which have to be gone through. These phenomena can be mild or severe according to how much attention you allot them. Recognize them, then go right on breathing upward in the withdrawal of consciousness. "Chop wood, carry water!" *Carry on with your job of conscious right dying.*

However, failing this, the air element (chakra 4) will dissolve into the ether element (chakra 5), which is consciousness itself. When this occurs, you will have the sensation of the inner appearance of greenness, with the scenario being that all the phenomena in the universe are blown away by great winds. As the biofield breaks up you will hear a grinding roar like ice breaking up on a mighty river like the Inn, Hudson, or the Volga in the springtime. What to do? Meditate that all the sights, sounds, and sensations are mind-created and that nothing exists independently, gain a state of emptiness, and be enlightened. Ride this transition out— this is the beginning of the real letting go and you can catapult yourself out the crown chakra anytime now—*call your teacher!*

• • •

Let's pause for breath, here—and realize that the Tibetans are spiritual practitioners like Olympic stars are athletes or acrobats. Ordinary people cannot come close to such feats of meditation under the duress of cancer, AIDS, Alzheimers, coma, accident death and the like, or even old age. As the safeguard to your not having had any meditation practice until picking up this book, you must seriously consider either working with the teacher ("dead or alive") of your choice, or borrowing the being to whom this work is dedicated. He has promised to protect all who come to this work. I don't want to sound fatalistic here, but I didn't call the Sixth Technique the Failsafe Technique for nothing! The journey of consciousness is just starting its quest after the four elements have been dissolved, each switchpoint offering opportunities for partial enlightenment by recognition of the forces of the psyche involved, which are ultimately of yourself.

• • •

Now the body is totally immobile, and breathing has ceased. You have been declared clinically dead for some time now. How long depends on whether you practiced the Withdrawal of Consciousness (the Fifth Technique) or took "potluck"—which might be as long as three days. The consciousness marathon is just beginning as the Clear Light approaches which is experienced at the heart in the Tibetan system. The switchpoint at your throat is gone through like a lock in a canal, or a rock thrown by a slingshot, or a rocket blast of fiery kundalini energy letting go. . . . or all is void and still. Recognize it. You may have a tendency to faint at one level and open up at another. Your support person needs to address you, as the Consciousness Prin-.ciple, Soul, the eternal. If your name is Helen, you should be addressed as "Soul of Helen," or if your name is Mark, it will be "Soul of Mark," *never just the personality name alone*, for that limit is released and you don't want to re-attach to its limits. This almost fainting state is actually a turning point in your opportunity for enlightenment, and comes after the five elements are dissolved. *You are now really dead, but never more alive.*

Everything turns to velvety darkness. See it and yourself as the Original Reality, formless and perfect, and be free. Light appears—a tunnel between dimensions opens up—joy and peace that pass all understanding are yours to claim and recognize.

Keep to the center of the tunnel and don't bear left or right.[44] It is suggested that you keep to the center because the left or right are both detours into different realities of inner space. You may experience this as a tunnel, or going into a mandala which you may have seen in meditation—gold and space-blue—then white. You likely will hear the flute call, or *Hu*, Krishna's golden flute calling you to recognize your own Divine nature.

As you continue down the center of the tunnel into the light, energies seem to converge in your heart—primordial forces meeting with cosmic forces—and you merge with this experience of utter clarity and perfection which will burst upon you, and be in you as well. It is your own divinity. *If you can accept this union with the native Reality of your being, you become secure from future rebirths unvolitionally. Otherwise you eventually pilgrimage back to Earth.*

All people see the Light upon their deaths, and experience their own nature. But the radiance is such that it can—and most likely will—inspire terror and awe and flight to dimmer radiances, tunnels, and colored lights. But if you are rightly supported, loved, and instructed, and if you can reflex enough positiveness, and/or remember the most preferred beloved Figure of Light, or guru, or personal savior, *it is quite possible to enter enlightenment at that time.* A general rule is to choose the brightest, most awe-inspiring Light of whatever color that presents itself, on successive occasions as well, for these Lights

---

[44]This corresponds to sushumna, a pranic nerve current running through the spine and chakras in which the feminine (negative) electrical force, ida, and the masculine (positive) magnetic force, pingala, are balanced.

are all opportunities for union after the initial meeting with the Clear Light. All the splendid Lights are dimensions of higher consciousness with which you have opportunity to merge, but which you may tend to "bounce" out of. Or else you may flee ignorantly into lesser, detour doors back into manifestation, which can be entries into multidimensional worlds, some not near as savory as others.[45] *So keep your attention focused on great Light*, not on dim cloudy areas, or what appear to be safe, secure, unchallenging hideaways for consciousness. Take the high road, the bold wise high path, not the valley.

• • •

In unprepared death, after the Light Experience, the biofield (or the etheric body) drifts away from the physical body over a period of three or four days or more. The more your energy is dissipated, the less your consciousness is focused, and the more opportunities there are for snags or obstructions to occur.

If you practice the exercises that follow, you can build up conditioned reflexes that will help you at the moment of death. You must stay conditioned and not let these reflexes fade away. Ideally you will have trained with a friend or support person who will be available to coach you through the transition. Your best learning will start with a trusted friend or relative who can be your coach, your support person. Just as a woman in labor has a coach who gives precise commands at each stage to help with the natural birth process, it is easier and safer to choose a friend or relative who agrees to coach you during the transition.

---

[45]There are a series of *lokas*, or planes, corresponding to the evolutionary potential inherent in each chakra—which descend to its lowest range as well. The colors, lights, etc., signal entry points to these areas, whether Hades or angelic realms. There is not time for a road map, so stay to the middle and go for the biggest, brightest Light—and call your teacher.

Your support person keeps you focused on what has to be done—and when.

It is also possible to use the manual by yourself and to experience an eased, conscious transition—whenever and however death occurs. If you must die alone, you will have your insurance and passport to a good deathing, which is your birthright. Keep this little handbook in the glove compartment of your car, or near the first-aid supplies in the cupboard. But above all, read it, study it, and practice it. Even if you don't practice the exercises, you will profit greatly and be relieved at deep inner levels by the information you have read here. It can keep you from harm.

A last reassurance: there is no possibility of accidental death as a result of practicing these exercises, although it's best to choose a practice area where no one will disturb you. Death occurs only when the body is broken down and can no longer support life.

This manual will consistently try to encompass two points of view brought to dying: the outside view of what it seems to be, and the inside view of what it actually is for the dying person. Your support person will always view death from the outside, as witness and spectator or helper, just as a husband or midwife is outside the natural birth process. To some support people, death may seem synonymous with ruin, disintegration, and the pain of impending separation from a loved one. Thus, the support person may be filled with guilt at being healthy when the friend is not, or may be confused or grieving. It is best to lay such ideas aside when helping your friend. For while the preliminaries prior to the actual death moment can be emotionally and physically difficult for both the dying person and the support person, death itself is a highly charged interior experience which needs attending to. The body only needs to be kept comfortable. Nor is a dying person concerned with the physical body that is on view to everyone else. The body has meaning to the dying person only if he or she feels the onlooker's grief, horror, or disgust during the withdrawal of consciousness. These feelings in friends can become yet another distraction that the deathing person has to overcome. Instead, the support person should try to view death as a life process that cannot be compared to anything else except perhaps birth. Who would expect a woman in labor to look cosmetically beautiful? She is beautiful, however, when giving birth, just as the deathing person is busy, beautifully discharging the business of right dying that we call deathing.

The support person and the dying must share their separate perspectives with each other, and then co-assist one another. It will comfort the mother who is tending to her dying child to know that the youngster won't suffer at death, and that she can assist the child's departure in a positive way, her last mother's duty and privilege, despite the farewell. Similarly, a couple about to be separated by death can quiet the pain of loss with the knowledge that they will be able to help one another at the end. Whatever the relationship, the support person will be strengthened by being able to ease the final moments of a dying friend who, of course, will be comforted by the other's presence. Strangers become kinsmen in such deep sharing, as well.

Both perspectives bring a more holistic approach to death by joining the inside view with the outside view; together they put us in tune, at last, with the process of life and death, and death's fantastic function as the final gateway to the transformation of consciousness.

◇ ◇

PREDEATH CONCERNS

The deathing process needs to begin with an understanding of
the nature of death itself—both physically and psychologically.
To practice for a right death requires knowledge and preparation, a mindset, if you will, that allows you to anticipate the
sequence of events happening to you in a wider context than
physical loss. Crisis management of the ongoing experience of
the dying process itself is important. Acceptance and letting go
comes next. But first—

Negativity will arise; expect it, but pay attention to working
it through, as well as superimposing positive thoughts, attitudes,
faith in your religious beliefs and/or teacher's teachings as a way
or quantum door through which to travel at death. In the midst
of pain, of loss of body, of relationships—all that you have spent
a lifetime acquiring and achieving—the cultivation of a good
heart and a mind full of compassion and love will not only help
others, but help yourself, here and hereafter. Negativity of all
kinds will slowly depart from you and your life will improve in
quality as you prepare the "beyond ordinary reality" in your
heart and mind, appropriate for death, out of which healings
may also arise.

If such a sympathetic and cheerful attitude has not been
habitual in your life, it may take a real effort to turn self-centered,
harmful attitudes, now inflamed by anger, loss and grief—and

thus justified (right down to yelling at a nurse who is trying to help you, or at the nurse who has perhaps neglected you)—into positive responses. They will prepare you for a good death. Do it out of self-interest first, in terms of a life insurance policy. As you train yourself to openness, it will spread positively through your subtle body system, for as the physical is waning, the higher parameters of your being must open up to compensate.

Additionally, put yourself to the task of knowing what your spiritual belief is concerning an after-life construct, and reinforce it, supported by deathing. Get your own teaching in a nutshell, before death, for there is no time to find it when you are dying. And if you have a teacher, learn to put that teacher before your heart and mind's eye, constantly. Get a picture and put it at the foot of your bed, or within eye-range, and gaze on it frequently— for "hitchhiking" with an enlightened teacher is the easy way to go through the Door of Death. In fact, the teacher IS the Door! "Now I've told you," said the old Tibetan.

• • •

If you know you are dying, you'll note many changes in yourself as well as demonstrate them to your family and support person. Notably, there are the five stages that Elisabeth Kübler-Ross has identified: denial that your death moment will occur; anger that it is occurring; a tendency to bargain about it; depression that it is going to occur; and finally, some kind of acceptance of your oncoming death. This is what you should aim for—acceptance. Stage One.

If you die an accidental or sudden death, you will still go through the five stages, although they are internal and much more rapid, sometimes cropping up in the immediate afterlife. Sudden death at least gives you no time for building resistance, but necessitates a swift reflexing of the letting go to the Light and/or the Sixth Technique. These assist in keeping your energy fields open, not contracted. This orients you in death to the equivalent of a proper presentation to the birth canal at birth, despite the turbulence, trauma, and shock that accident death usually entails.

Your stage of acceptance may range from rueful fatalism to radiant expectation of a prepared-for death. Acceptance should culminate in total detachment from bodily and social concerns prior to the clinical death of your body. It's helpful to set all your worldly affairs in order so you can cut loose when the time comes, never looking back.

All that said, we know it is not an easy task to keep your attention on the deathing process and away from the myriad impressions that will distract you from what you are doing. Understandably, your disease symptoms may be acute, with attending pain that makes it hard to concentrate. The exercises that follow will grant some pain control by teaching you to relax. But family circumstances, settling wills, and weaning a lifetime of relationships may preoccupy your mind.[46]

It is possible to take responsibility and do something for yourself by directing your fear and anger creatively. Even in sickness and old age, or in the flush of youth, *you can teach yourself to fly, not merely die.* My friend and kinsman, I honor your courage at this difficult moment, but encourage you to reach out for this manual of attitudes, exercises, and techniques that teaches you ahead of time how to die in full knowledge and control, so that you no longer merely die, but reach peak experience when the time comes.

It is most important to train yourself to reach with a new set of responses, rather than give way to the panic (the Sixth

---

[46]For details on how to settle your final paperwork, read the appropriate sections of *Coming Home* by Deborah Duda (Santa Fe, NM: Aurora Press, 1988).

Technique also overrides panic) that may arise from the disintegration of the familiar reality of the body. This manual's exercises use a form of response conditioning to train your reactions and quiet your mental waves.

Ideally you will have begun your exposure to the methods of deathing by the time you have accepted the facts of your impending death. But if you pick up this book and prefer dying with your boots on, that's perfectly fine, too. It's your life—and death. But even so, perhaps this information will help you—in the context of life's ongoingness, to accept your own death and utilize it as a life experience.

Again, to ensure the least amount of physical and psychological resistance at the moment of death, it is best to resolve all unfinished business and conflicts, and discharge all duties before that time. However, if they cannot be resolved, put them out of your mind as if they never existed, guiltlessly. Open your heart, forgive and forget them as inconsequential to the act of dying, or to the attitude of positiveness, peace, and serenity appropriate to conscious dying. *This cannot be stressed enough.*

You must also understand what will happen as death approaches and the feelings and images that arise as you go through the switchpoints. See all as yourself, including the Light that connects with your interior consciousness, as the body and electromagnetic biofield disband, and the Consciousness Principle prepares to depart.

Acceptance, the fifth stage of Kübler-Ross' system of preparation for departure, provides the minimum, but basic setting for an appropriate exit from your physical body. Deathing provides the bridge from stage five—acceptance of death—to stage six, the preparation for and enactment of the death moment as an experience in its own right.

For each of the exercises I have included special notes for the support person. By following these instructions, he or she can help you establish the automatic reactions of letting go that you will need for a successful death.

If these postulates are practiced and repeated often and firmly enough—by both yourself and your support person—they will resurface for you at the moment of death, even in an accident or when senility sets in. Even if you and your support person are separated geographically during the death, your coach can tune in immediately when he or she learns that death has occurred, and can help direct your progress, for you are no longer limited to body constraints. Your support person becomes your backup system and helps create the conditions for conscious and right deathing, keeping you on course.

Pre-death Concerns for the Support Person

It's important to turn inside and confront death within yourself before (or when) you are dealing with a dying friend or patient. Avoid the temptation to manipulate events, or project a version of your own preferred and heroic death on your friend. You may fancy all sorts of nonsense, all of which springs from this idea of a separate self that is engaging in adversarial confrontation with the Divine, or Light, instead of in a recognition process of IT as yourself, and yourself as IT. As you let go your nonsense, so will your friend, and you can be more open in your doings.

The open heart in you—and assisting the heart to open in your friend—is the thing, with love the link and bridge between you, between the form and formless you both are. All these words, all these exercises, are just conveyer belts for the love and beingness. Please, you don't even have to like your friend, or patient! But love is necessary.

One way to get into this love space, this open-heartedness, is to encourage the dying person's spiritual practice, if he or she has one. That is the beauty of the Sixth Technique; it can be adapted and applied to any practice. And you may find you need and use it more than your friend, because you may be more in the body-mind limited consciousness.

Your friend may *not* be in the kind of inner space and beingness that can withstand, transcend or transmute pain, or deal with helplessness. It's difficult not to be able to take care of the family, or to "be the perfect man or woman." Then, by example and practice, you can help them let go.

In pre-death states (days, weeks, or months ahead of time) you can talk to the person about alternatives to "death by hospital" by reading spiritual hero stories, the lives and deaths of saints and great men and women. Try to weave into the stories an application of the Sixth Technique whenever possible, for we are creating our own spiritual heroes thereby. Courage alone is not enough, although it is a requisite for some deaths, including most deaths inside medically oriented establishments.

Hospice is a wonderful organization and is based on relieving physical suffering up to and at the time of death. But even Hospice tends to focus the person constantly on "being the body," the very thing which the dying person is losing. With so much attention focused on the physical aspect of the person's beingness, which is almost useless, there can be a lot of loneliness in Hospice, especially for people who have strong spiritual interests. This includes, at the very end, the futility of even the admirable attempts to bring the family and familiar environments to the person, who, however, may no longer be able to sit up, smell the flowers, or listen to stories about home, or go to the bathroom, or eat without help. The dying person needs to deal with the real issues—the spiritual issues, not the waning body and personality issues. The family tends to play the role of mother, father, son or daughter and needs to wean away from that to unconditional love.

We need to be able to give the necessary support to the failing body while the spiritual parameter—in recognition of other dimensions of being—is opening up as the physical wanes.[47] In order to truly help, we need to both serve the body and reinforce that "place" in the dying person that is not judged by his or her limits.

This inner space in a dying person *can be* inspired, and raised to incredible joy and light and power which simply pours out of a wasted away body when the heart is open. That is the thing. And you will feel it when it happens, like a shift in the air. If it is the first time you are with a dying friend, loved one, or patient—you will notice that other family members, and sometimes medical personnel, may feel embarrassed when this shift occurs in the patient—at first. They may leave the room under the brunt of such intense honesty of presence and beingness. But as love starts to melt into everyone, and if they love the dying person, they will know it and let it be. This then becomes the "high ordinary reality" appropriate for both life or death.

The recitation of a mantra, a favored prayer, or playing sacred music on a tape can be used even for intensive care patients, and has immense power to uplift the dying person into this inner place. Using the Sixth Technique, as well as linking a spiritual teacher to the dying person is very effective to disengage the body and personality ("I am" consciousness) so it can let go physical form and go to formless energy and consciousness.

If the person is able, in pre-death days, encourage him or her to talk about unfinished business. Guide the dying person to know that the business we often think unfinished—someone we haven't made up to after quarrels, or someone we are out of contact with for years in misunderstanding—can be finished simply by letting go of the resentment. For by letting go of the

---

[47]Kübler-Ross stresses the way various quadrants—emotional, intellectual, spiritual—open up in proportion to the body's waning. This is most noticeable in dying children, who have become little wise ones, overnight.

anger you can include that person in the open-hearted sense of kinsmanship with all life that is growing in you. By just dropping the justifications, the anger, the grief, the resentment, the last false self-images in you also fall away. Then there is just the being there.

You may experience negativity in yourself because of your pride in helping your friend, or your powerlessness in not being able to help. Let these thoughts go like bubbles—don't hang on. When pain comes because you cannot help your friend's pain or mental anguish, then let your pain bubble up and out on your own use of the Sixth Technique. This softens the pain. Most often the pain will diminish to bearable levels. You have to separate your fear of the pain from the pain itself. When you do, somehow the pain is transformed into your self—and your friend's sense—of beingness. It is a great mystery—pain—no one even knows what it is. But by experiencing it directly, without letting your fear get in the way, you are not dominated by it. I don't like to use the word "controlled"—but it comes close to control when you deal with it this way.

All these methods are ultimately diversions of the mind so you can bypass the mind to get into an inner space—an open, "high ordinary" state of consciousness appropriate for death, the only state worth considering in your life, as well—love being the link to all.

When the death transitions come, for either or both of you (for there is a distinct telepathic link developed in this kind of sharing), remember, one day you will be the dying one, not the support person. Treat the person like you did the pain—let him or her be, know he or she is Reality, whatever the appearance, here, physically. Therefore there is nothing to fear, although we may fear. Ultimately none of us know anything much about any of this dying business, but love does, and it makes the bridge between form and formless, a high, open space—higher than flying, more even than letting go, although we use those words.

◇ ◇

AT DEATH CONCERNS

Prior to death, whether by moments or months, you may sense that death is coming. It opens up a wisdom or a perspective that reveals areas past the daily concerns in your life. You may become more other-worldly or radiant as you detach from these ordinary concerns. Dreams may warn you of a "change of state" if you are not already forewarned of death by disease or age.

At the moment of death or shortly before, you will feel certain sensations that signal impending departure, much as labor pains signal birth. Some of these sensations will have already been experienced if you practice deep meditation. However, at the approach of death the texture is different because the connection with your body is being severed, which amplifies sensation. You may also feel a heaviness in your lower limbs and body, a sinking sensation; various sounds of the de-bonding process resound, boom, sing and groan, and you feel a coldness turning to fiery heat, or vice versa; a spinning sensation or a floating, a tingling, prickling, or a feeling of dislocation; a sense of pressure, of lightening or softening of your body; shallow, dry breathing; a sense of fast vibrations building up to an explosive level—or, perhaps, a sense of settling into peacefulness, of being absorbed; a sense of pressured heat around your head; and finally, a sense of diffusion and peacefulness. It is all due to dissolving from one switchpoint to another, and you have to monitor this as dispassionately as possible, *without resistance* or any other form of negativity. Just see this stage as a movie, cast upon the screen of your own mind by you, yourself. You are the author and the director and even the cast of players. You are trying to play tricks on yourself. If you really understand this, how then to be afraid?

At this point you may also feel a tingling sensation of expansion and alternating feelings of heat and cold, or dispersion of time and space. Eventually your lower body will go numb. During this phase you may hear more sounds of your changing state and possibly feel an acceleration of speed or feel as if you are floating out of your body. The music of the spheres, the Nadam that you hear, may be electronic beeps, whistles, bells, rushing water, mortar shots, groans, music of various kinds, children's choir voices, flutes, whirring drums, a high-pitched whine, wind, a swarm of hornets, goat bells, a weird-sounding trumpet, or conch shell sounds—almost anything. The harsh wrenching of energy fields in dissolution can create terrifying sounds, while the images of drought, tidal waves, hurricanes or earthquakes, or even shifting landscapes of different colors, must be met knowing that it is all your own mind—the projections of various levels of your psyche. *Accept everything as yourself.*

Remain calm and have no fear. You will feel a numbness starting at your feet as your body turns off, and the energy starts rolling upward toward your heart, then going to your head. This should be familiar to you after you have done the Withdrawal of Consciousness Exercise (page 332). Remember to always feel and aim upward out of your body. Reflex to the Light or to your personal savior and nothing else!

Often, just before death, emissaries (such as angels, your spiritual leader, or a loved one who has gone before) appear to prepare you for the experience of transcendent transition. There are two ways in which the Light Itself may appear—as pure light energy or as a figure-of-Light welcoming you at the moment of death, or both. If you are a Christian, you may see Jesus or a loved saint; if you are a Buddhist, you may see Buddha; or if you have no particular religious affiliation, you may experience the Being to whom *Deathing* is dedicated or pure Light itself. *If you have an enlightened teacher, call on him, visualize him and identify with his state, which you can then attain to.*

As you know by now, the last thought before death has powerful, ongoing effects on the kind of rebirth any of us will take, so you want to take advantage of this phenomenon—not take potluck on the vagaries of fortune. Consciousness transference refers to the practice of influencing your rebirth by positively influencing the mind at the time of death. Some people still balk and claim that meddling with the moment of death, i.e., "death moment karma," isn't playing fair! This attitude reflects a poor knowledge of the many factors that influence the unit of consciousness that each of us is, many of which are variables. And a variable changes the equation.

For instance, some people lead highly virtuous lives, but not having developed control over their minds as part of their deeply felt spiritual practice, they may become overwhelmed by fear, resistance, grief, pain or other torments at the moment of death. This might cause them to present themselves poorly at that definitive moment, and they could, as a result, take a poor rebirth, without say, utilizing the consciousness transference or the Sixth "failsafe" Technique. It can also work the other way, in that people who have led nondescript lives, or even outright negative or evil ones, end up somehow having positive thoughts at the moment of death and thereby gain a positive rebirth.

Of course, this spiritual strategy doesn't bypass or neutralize the good or evil a person creates during a given lifetime. That is still stored in the causal mind as karmic seeds, which, when they find fertile soil, will sprout and must be dealt with. But the short-term of the immediate, next rebirth is assuredly defined by the person's frame-of-mind at the moment of death, which if it can be positively arranged, can gain a rebirth opportunity to further the being's spirituality, thus cleansing the mind of negativities in the practice of the disinterested works (*dharma*). And that is worth training for, even if you are on your death bed! While liberation is also a possibility.

Jesus said, "I am the way; I am the truth and I am life: no one comes to the Father, except by me" (John 14:6). While Krishna said to Arjuna, his disciple-devotee: "Anyone who, at the end of life, quits his body remembering Me, attains immediately to My Nature, and there is no doubt of this. In whatever condition one quits his present body, in his next life he will attain to that state of being without fail!" (Bhagavad Gita 8:5-7). Consider the Source.

The practice of the Sixth Technique, can be used as a shortcut to liberation, if you can truly let go to the pure consciousness reflected in an enlightened being, for that pure Awareness is also *you*. "The Father and I are One," said Jesus, the Christ.

• • •

By this time you will have steadily practiced the Withdrawal of Consciousness Exercise. You will have adjusted your breathing as evenly as possible. If you have a tendency to faint, understand that it is a symptom of the dying process. It signals your passing through the fourth switchpoint, as the etheric, pranic forces dissolve into consciousness itself. There is nowhere to anchor yourself but to beingness itself, letting go all limits, and expanding to meet this increasing potency, the void, the clear light of your own consciousness. Recognize it. By this time, dimly, and with scarcely any interest in the body, you have heard yourself declared dead. But although your breathing has ceased, the Consciousness Principle is not yet gone, which truly signifies death. Mere clinical death is not a complete death, as near-death research has proven recently—and the ancients knew centuries ago.

If you are in coma, and your support person cannot tell in what state you are, the support person can do the Withdrawal of Consciousness Exercise for you, giving voice commands for you to reflex to the Light, be the Light, helping you finish bringing the energy up to the crown chakra, past the fifth switchpoint into the first levels of superconsciousness, the Cosmic I-Am. If you exit at the throat chakra, you will attain that state, as the great sages and saviors assure us, which means rebirth in the heaven worlds, but not enlightenment. So go past that point. Your support person can lightly touch your crown or voice command you to let go from and to the highest Universal Consciousness. Since after you rest in the Clear Light of Universal Consciousness, you get vacation time in the heaven worlds anyhow, why not keep going to the crown chakra, the last switchpoint?

The tendency is to try to get born at any of the lower exit points, just as a laboring mother has the terrible compulsion to expel the baby before it is actually crowning! So crown yourself out the highest door—into the Universal I Am—the original identity of yourself with all that is—the Clear Light beyond all form. *You can have and be God by simply letting go and recognizing all as yourself.* It is so very simple, but it is what we keep coming back again and again to learn in our every incarnation. Every human life is part of the learning process that allows us eventual enlightenment. *Deathing* is our chance to finally understand the riddle of it all, if we haven't achieved it in the lifetime.

And since you already know that you, like anyone over-whelmed by grandeur and unconditionality, may have a ten-dency to faint when you meet the Light, *your support person will be primed to help.* The support person will do the exercise with you, and breathe with you, telling you how to bring the energy up into your head, as energy will automatically follow the voice command. This is the value of having a support person with you at the time of transition.

• • •

The transition can come at any minute. Your consciousness of darkness changes to flickering light. Try to let go. You may blank out for a moment during the transition, but your support person will keep telling you to look for the Light—and merge with it. You may experience a review of your life events at this stage, or it may occur later in the experience. Let it go when it comes. Don't dwell on it now. The Light will flicker, and then blaze splendidly at the last moment. You may cry out in ecstasy. Let it happen.

You will probably also hear your support person calling to you to be one with the Light and calling on your spiritual teacher for assistance. You will rise to meet it at its own level, at its own frequency, joyously, with abandon. All last notions of separateness will be forsaken. Be calm. Allow yourself to disperse, blending and plunging toward the Light through a long tunnel that spins you like a white bullet toward a wave motion of light that is within and without—a seething brilliant clear light of energy, activity, and stillness. Stay in the middle and aim for the white core; don't let yourself go toward the cobalt or yellow circles in the periphery, for they represent different areas of inner space.

Your support person will be telling you to prolong the moment as long as possible, invoking your teacher. IDENTIFY with this enlightened being as the Light Itself. Open to it totally. Put aside all thoughts except letting go. Meet the Light on its own frequency or as close to it as possible in an encounter that boils over you. *Flee from nothing, resist nothing.* Accelerate by simply letting go to what is. No images, thoughts, remorse, emotions, or social notions should mar the forward motion of the deathing person. There is a rhythm and pace to deathing, as there is to birthing. The things of the material existence of earth have no more meaning in the consciousness. They are less than a dream. The whole cast of the deathing experience turns upon your ability to focus attention on the process of withdrawing from your body, as well as your letting go human roles, by looking for either the Light, or a beloved sacred being who will commune telephatically with you and guide you, taking over from your support person. You must blend with all the images that come from the Light, good or ill. Flee from none, whether benign or ferocious, for all experience is created by your own thoughts and deeds through time. Welcome everything. Be all that comes to you. It is yourself. Have a good journey.

◊ ◊

THE SIX TECHNIQUES

The four preliminary exercises or techniques that follow are used to intune both relaxation and movement of energy within you. The Withdrawal of Consciousness Exercise (the Fifth Technique) should be used at the moment of death as well as the Sixth Technique. (To avoid confusion, the Sixth Technique is not an exercise, but the practice of what Easterners call Guru Yoga, which has been discussed elsewhere.) All these exercises are geared to help control distractions; they prepare you for the sense of dissolution of the physical body that occurs at death.

Conditions for practice are optional. You can practice in a pleasant living room, a hospital room, or anywhere you wish. It is important to be comfortable. If you are physically able, you may wish to use the typical Oriental meditation posture. If you are not well enough for that, or if you find that pose unnatural, you can lie flat on your back or sit comfortably in a chair. (See figure 6 on page 316 for example postures.)

At first your outer environment will help you train the inner one, so make your exterior conditions as pleasant and attractive as possible. You can use sacred music to set the mood, as well. I suggest that you get a picture of a natural scene, such as a sunrise, a waterfall, the ocean, or a photograph of your spiritual mentor if you have one. Place this picture in an obvious spot, where your attention will constantly fall on it, for it will trigger

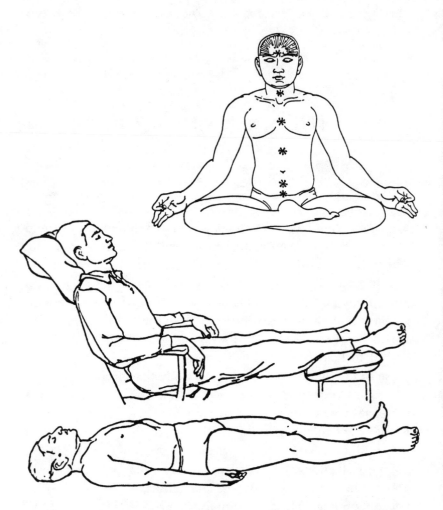

Figure 6. Various postures for meditation and relaxation. The top figure is
the typical pose used in the Orient for meditation. The middle figure shows
you one way to meditate if you have been ill, or feel uncomfortable sitting
with your legs crossed. The "dead body pose" from yoga, shown at the
bottom, is another position you can easily use if you are ill or in a hospital
room. (Adapted from *Fundamentals of Yoga,* by Ramamurti S. Mishra, published by Julian Press, New York, 1969. Used by permission.)

peace, warmth, and acceptance in you. These are the stages you are trying to make habitual, along with letting you be familiar with the movement of energy on the various bodies and fields that composite you. If you are bedridden, it is all the more important to try to rig a screen or frame that will keep your peaceful scene in your range of vision. Buddhists often place a painting or a poster of the Buddha's heaven world at their bedside so they can focus on where they are going, and not on any possible difficult conditions of their passage. Training your attention in this fashion is like buying a ticket for a certain destination. It almost assures your arrival, even before you embark on the journey.

The First Technique: Vibration and Sound

This first exercise sets the stage for higher consciousness. It should be done out loud, at least at first, so you can really learn to feel it. One way is to place your hands in prayer position chest high, resting on the sternum and then chant slowly, feeling the vibration. To preface it, you may want to join with your support person in a short prayer, or repeat the *Gayatri Mantra* (page 274). You can also, simply, firmly, and steadily repeat the sound of OM. Whether or not you believe in it is not the question; the sound *does* have properties to align and quiet discordant vibrations in the body, the subtle bodies, or mind—especially those that are brought on by anxiety or disease of any kind. You can also whisper the word OM mentally, or use earphones to hear tapes of the sound.

Exercise 1: Vibration Exercise

◇   Lie down on your back on a rug, padded surface, or bed and get comfortable. Place your right hand on your stomach with your thumb on your navel area and the other four fingers cupped around the abdomen. Center your left hand on your heart area so you can feel the vibration through your sternum.

Hum a little in preparation for this exercise. Then hum an octave—do, re, me, fa, sol, la, ti, do. Do this a few times starting in different places until you come to a sound that feels comfortable and vibrates strongly. The lower registers work best, but don't limit yourself. It takes some experimentation. At this point start humming *Hm* . . . prolonging the m. You can say "Hmmm" with the "u" sound as in *cup*, or with the vowel sound of *ow*. Make the one that feels best for you, or chant the OM in different octaves. It is best pronounced in its alternative spelling, AUM. ◊   Inhale from your belly by expanding the belly and moving the air up into your chest. Exhale—*Hmmm* or AUM—on the tone that feels most comfortable with your body and which sets up the most noticeable vibration. You will feel it in chest distinctly. Use the externally sensed vibration to build an awareness of internally sensed vibrations (see Exercise 4 on p. 324). The vibrations of energy can be heard as sound, or induced and seen as light. You may see sparks of light, little white or blue stars which may spread over your whole inner eye as you practice. Feel the Hmmmmmmmmm expand out along the tone you choose and move through your whole body.

Pay attention to feeling physical vibration in your body. Pay attention to feeling electrical vibrations past the "skin barrier," and inside various organs and body parts. Listen for the interior ten sounds—the idling of an engine, a high whistle, or a flute call—which are the most usual ones you hear at first (see p. 259). These sounds also spontaneously come during the day and during sleep. Always stay with them when this happens to you. Drop everything you are doing and go deeply into the sounds, for they will penetrate all the different levels of yourself. Do the same if and when the light comes. Usually gaze obliquely at it in order to "hold" it—very relaxed.

• • •

This exercise should be practiced for half an hour a day. You should do it before you do your other exercises, reciting twenty *Aums,* or *Hu(m)s* at a time out loud. Then go into the silence, feeling the after vibration for a few moments. The real sound is past the outer vocal induction, as is its counterpart—light. Then whisper *Aum (Hum)* mentally, moving your lips silently to keep your mind focused on the sound. See what happens— you won't perceive anything at first. But eventually the subtle energy of the body that flows through and exists around the physical will stir, and you will feel it in your head, especially, and in your heart and belly. During the time when you are whispering silently, with your eyes closed, keep an eye out for the Light, too. You may see a few flickers without having to use the heels of your hands as starters. As the nervous system tones and tunes up with the exercises, nerves will process the increased flow of energy.

The Second Technique: Breathing and Relaxation

Next you need to get acquainted with your breath. Breathing connects you with both the most physical seat of yourself and the most subtle forces that sustain you. You can do without food and even water for a time, but not breath. Breathing is the conduit for the life force. It enters through the breath into the lungs and blood, and then goes back out again through the breath. In yoga, this force is called prana. The biofield body of its expression is called Pranamaya Kosha, which is the energy field that interpenetrates and surrounds the body.

Your rate of breath influences your heartbeat and mind: a slow breath induces a quiet mind, calms anxiety, and dispels fear; a swift rapid breath reflects emotional and mental distractions that can be redirected by slowing your breath. Remember always to inhale from your diaphragm and exhale out the head area.

During practice sessions, the support person should be attentive to the style and rate of breathing you are practicing. When either shallow breathing, rapid breathing, or deep, torn breathing occurs prior to death, the support person should breathe with you to stabilize you. It is important to maintain the style of breath being used, however. This will help the dying person focus on the withdrawal of consciousness. The support person may have to improvise according to the situation, practice, and cooperation of the dying person. If you are deathing alone, watch your breath and try to keep it as even as possible. Use it to focus on withdrawing your consciousness upward from your body.

It is also important that you memorize a list of positive affirmations so you can use them to train your attention *before* death so that at death you can override distractions of any kind. (See page 345.) Knowing the affirmations by heart will help you reflex to these higher thoughts during the dying process. Your support person can help a great deal in reminding you of these, or by playing a tape of them that the two of you may have recorded before you need them. You can also tape your affirmation of yourself as "God," or assume the identity of your spiritual teacher, i.e., "I Am Buddha," "I Am God," "I and Christ are One," etc.

Exercise 2: Breathing

◊   Lie down on a firm but padded surface, or sit crosslegged with your head and spine straight. If you sit on a chair, gently cross your ankles and place your hands in your lap folded into one another with the palms up. Watch your breathing with your mind's eye until you aren't self-conscious about it and it resumes its natural movement. Put your attention in your belly area as you draw in air and with a closed mouth, exhale out the nostrils, thinking high thoughts or use your own prayer, or mantra, or the *Gayatri Mantra*. (See page 274.) Then inhale through your nostrils while gently thinking deep, centering thoughts. Keep this up for twenty breaths at a time. With each breath, visualize that you are inhaling energy from subtle forces and exhaling negativity and anxiety. Often you may drift off to sleep or drift into a reverie. This exercise can be done in a hospital, at home, outdoors, or anywhere you feel safe.

An alternate breath and mantram exercise that is very powerful is to inhale on either the word SAT, or SO, and exhale on NAM or HUM. SAT-NAM—GOD. SO-HUM—Universal reality as focused on and expressed by the breath. Get into a rhythm with these charged words and your breathing.

• • •

When we first attempt to get in touch with other levels and energies in ourselves, our normal way of thinking of ourselves as solid material objects usually intrudes. The body is really an energy pattern and process, and it reflects the major and minor stresses of our lives by distorting its normal functioning—which eventually results in death. Our bodies hold the locked in patterns of our mental set. Therefore, when we want to connect with other than usual patterns and processes in ourselves, we break the cycle of the body-mind's habitual ways by quieting it in various ways—in a kind of "body-work." Higher consciousness and healing go hand in hand with a new perspective on what we are as humans. Relieving ourselves of the notion of our materiality, and seeing ourselves as life process—whether in or outside the body—has an astonishing effect upon the life and death process often resulting in healing, whether of body or mind.

Exercise 3: Relaxation

◊   Lie down on your back in loose clothing, or loosen your belt and neck areas. Get comfortable, keeping your arms held loosely at your sides with your legs apart. Once you are in position, you won't move until the exercise is complete or your support person has taken you through the relaxation of all major systems and muscle groups. Give up the responsibility for your body; let your body go. (A comforting note: If you become troubled by an irritation or itch that steals too much of your attention, there is no need to prove your discipline by refusing to move; scratch the itch and return immediately to the exercise.)

◇   Relax as much of your body as you can reach mentally. Relax all of your major muscle groups—calves, thighs, buttocks, belly, arms, shoulders, heart area, neck, face, scalp. You may want to consult an anatomy book to help you imagine your body parts. If you have a specific disease, be sure and address the afflicted areas specifically. Always draw in positive energy with each breath, and breathe out disease.

◇   Now feel where stiffness or tightness still exists. Starting with your toes and working upward, say mentally, "I relax my toes, inner and outer." The idea here is that you send a postulate to the subconscious and autonomic nervous systems, as well as to the conscious mind, which commands them to relax. Once in the natural state of relaxation with no tension, other sensations are perceptible. Go through your entire body with at least twenty injunctions to "let tension go in the _____," or "relax your _____." Each person carries different areas of tension which are jammed energy pockets. Talk to your support person about these areas. (A touch of the support person's fingers can help trigger relaxation in each body part at first. Later, just give the command to that part of the body.)

By the third week you should be able to count down the body into a relaxed state, moving from outer muscles to interior areas of organs as well. When relaxing the heart, for instance, give the postulate, "I relax my heart," and then wait in silence for it to take effect, deepening the whole relaxation level expanding out. Numbness or tingling will start to take hold—heaviness, yet elevation and spinning sensations—think no thoughts—just let it happen. Nothing can happen that is not you.

◇ Continue breathing evenly from the midsection, in and out, slowly. You can use AUM, HUM, SAT-NAM, SO-HUM—inhaling, exhaling. Let the breathing just happen on the same waves as the relaxation. Go deeply into the relaxation state and you'll begin to sense pure energy, to feel an expansion, a throbbing, as the body becomes a circle of energy focused in the body outline. Wait and feel.

The Third Technique: Learning to Sense Energy Fields

Now that you have learned how to relax, you need to learn how to sense energy fields. This is not easy for Westerners, for we have been taught to think, not to sense, so this is a process you must relearn. You used to be able to do it when you were a child. The sensing exercises can only begin after you have learned to relax. You'll no longer be able to define your body, but you'll perceive sensations around it, such as, "I am floating . . . heat energy is in my head . . . electrical flows are moving around."

Many people want to know what the difference is between deep sleep and meditation. In deep sleep, psychological or psychosomatic consciousness, the body and the mind are all sleeping. When you engage in meditation, your ego-state, separate-self I-am, or psychological consciousness, is transformed into a universal I-am, and your mind and body stay in deep sleep. So if you want to meditate deeply, imitate the body and mind as they would be if you were in a deep sleep. Death is only the greatest imitation, after all. Your consciousness should remain perfectly awake. If you learn to do this, you can experience healing on the one hand, and also experience the operation of cosmic forces in your body and mind. Most certainly this is the best preparation for death and demonstrates that you are not the body!

When you experience the flow of energy, you will have the sensation of vibration all over your body, you may feel that your body is weightless, you may feel extremely happy, you may hear humming or buzzing, the sound of church bells, etc., you may sense that you have lost body consciousness in its physical form. Tingles, chills, thrilling sensations, or feeling electrical impulses in your body may take place. You may experience various forms of inner Light, or you may feel that you are a clear sky, pure awareness, or pure consciousness. When you return to your physical body after such meditations, you may find that you are partaking in a divine healing process. And the happiness you feel may be beyond expression—you may not be able to communicate your feelings or bliss to anyone, even to your support person.

You may wish to work only with the following Sensing Exercise. However, I have included two other exercises that may help you. "The Dynamic Meditation" and "The Meditation on your Electrical Body" are from Shri Brahmananda Sarasvati (Ramamurti Mishra). They continue where the preliminary sensing exercise leaves off. In the healing process, matter, thought, and energy interchange by restructuring consciousness. "The Dynamic Meditation" and "Sensing Exercise" bring subtle energies to bear on the physical body. "Meditation on your Electrical Body" brings even more refined Light (in both its aspects) to bear on your biofield, which holds the thought-forms that produce the physical body. These two meditations will be very useful practice for both living and dying. You may find yourself feeling healed when you use them, while the healing energy can also bring great relief from pain.

Exercise 4: Sensing

◇   Examine where your energy flows are, and let them be. Watch what gentle breathing does to shake loose the pattern of energy that is you. Deepen your relaxation by watching the energy in your lower limbs. Then, using your attention, draw the energy to another higher spot in your body.

◇ Focus on your hips and belly. Feel the tip of the tailbone emit energy and take it in. Pay attention.

◇ Feel the heart area; feel it vibrate. Feel the head and throat area; feel them vibrate.

◇ Breathe in from your midsection gently and feel your whole body expand, then exhale. Repeat this breathing ten times. Each time you'll grow larger as energy—reaching out—being reached out to. Try focusing on your heart area, seeing it as light and love—to get a huge expansion—to all loved ones, first, then to enemies, then to the World.

◇ Now do the opposite ten times. Try breathing in your expanded energy and boiling it down to a smaller size, a bead of light. Make it smaller, yet. Be able to shrink and expand your energy field by using the breath as a focusing mechanism. This also is practice for movement in the out-of-body state, which utilizes instant expansion/contraction.

◇ Rest in either the expanded state or the contracted state. Learn to know the difference between the two—which is crucial, especially in an accident death. Just as the La Maze mother must learn to let go at the end of a contraction and relax, so must you learn to let go tension first, and then actively expand, *at will* or voice command, *overiding all tendencies to contract.*

Exercise 5: Dynamic Meditation

◇ Close your eyes. Lie down or sit in a comfortable position. Do not think of anything. Watch your body and mind as a witness. Do not take part in any thinking. Neither control your thinking nor encourage it. If thinking comes, watch it as if it were a dream. Watch your body and mind in the same way a mother would watch her baby.

◇ For one minute, watch attentively and feel that your entire body is breathing. You will find your breathing goes from shallow to deep; your entire body will breathe—even your hair and nails and bones. Don't try to correct your breathing, just allow your body to breathe naturally.

◇   Feel the pulsation of blood from your fingers and palms in both your hands—feel it move to your heart. You can feel this more easily if you close your hands so they form a fist. Now feel the pulsation.

◇   Next feel the pulsation of blood in both your arms, including your bones, muscles and skin. Feel the pulsation from your arms, palms and fingers to your heart, and back again. Go back and forth from the heart.

◇   Now feel the pulsation of blood from your heart to your entire chest, including both lungs and the heart muscles. Feel the pulsation of blood from your chest to your heart.

◇   Feel the pulsation of blood moving from your heart to your neck, face, eyes, nose, ears, entire head, all up to the brain—the upper, middle and lower brain. Feel the blood pulsing from the brain back through your head and to your heart—back and forth—to and from the heart.

◇   Visualize a blue and white Light in the center of your brain. Feel that Light vibrating through your entire body. Your brain controls your entire body, every tissue and every organ. Understand that your brain carries commands from your mind (or psyche) when you are in this plane of energy. Let your brain send Light from its nerve current to every part of your body.

◇   Feel the pulsing of blood from your brain to your upper abdomen, to the middle and lower abdomen. Feel the blood pulsing through the liver, spleen, pancreas, kidneys, suprarenal glands, intestines, your reproductive organs and your bladder. Then feel the pulsation of blood from your heart to your lower legs, and all the joints, bones, and muscles of both your legs and your feet. Feel this pulsation vibrating from the brain to the legs, feet, and toes—and from them to the brain. Back and forth, to and from the brain.

◇ Feel that your entire body is connected to your brain, including the palms of your hands, the soles of your feet, and even your hair and nails.

◇ Feel electricity throughout your entire body. You can feel every tissue and cell vibrating with this electricity. You have more than 300,000 cells in your body and each is a powerhouse of electricity. This you will know directly as you meditate.

◇ Feel your own subtle body.[48] It is behind this physical body. Your subtle body is cosmic and it communicates with the entire internal and external atmosphere, subconscious, superconscious Mind and all the five bodies by means of your nervous system and your skin.

◇ Feel and hear cosmic music, the music of the spheres, Nadam.[49] This inner music within your head is often a ringing sound, a humming or buzzing which shifts to other sounds as well. This inner cosmic music is the mother of the subjective radio waves that make up your program. When you feel this, you will experience the highest bliss, happiness, and natural healing. Some students may want to work with a tape entitled *Dynamic Meditation* available from Ananda Ashram.

Exercise 6: Meditation on Your Electrical Body

◇ Close your eyes. Behind your physical and physiological body is an electrical body (body #2). Your physiological body consists of chemical, biochemical, and biological force. Relax your body as much as you can and let us work with the electrical force.

---

[48]Pranamaya Kosha.
[49]See Exercise 1, page 317.

◇   Follow the flow of electricity from your heart to your entire chest, through the shoulders, upper arms, lower arms, palms, fingers. Go back and forth from them to your heart, from your heart to your fingers.

◇   Follow the flow of electricity from your heart to your neck, face, head, up to the brain. Include the special sensory organs—eyes, nose, ears, tongue and skin—and from them back to the heart. Go back and forth to and from the heart.

◇   Follow the circle of electricity from your heart to your entire back, and then from your back again to your heart.

◇   Follow the flow of electricity from your heart to your abdomen—from upper to middle to lower, including the liver, kidneys, and all the abdominal organs. Go from the abdomen back to the heart, and back and forth, back and forth.

◇   Follow the flow of electricity from your heart to your upper legs, to your lower legs, to your feet and toes, and from them back to your heart. Go back and forth a few times, back and forth to the heart.

◇   Follow the flow of electricity from your heart to your skeleton, your muscles, to every joint in your body, to every bone, your skin, and from them back to your heart.

◇   Follow the flow of electricity from your heart to your entire body, and from your entire body to your heart, simultaneously.

◇   Follow the flow of electricity from your entire body to the atmosphere around your body, and from the entire atmosphere to your body simultaneously.

◇   Follow the radio waves, like remote control, from your body to the sun, the moon, and all the planets, to all the stars and all the galaxies, and come back to your body of electricity.

◇   Follow the radio waves and radar waves from your inner space to your outer space and from the outer space to your inner space. When you have developed the flow of energy (kundalini), you will feel the tingling, the buzzing, hear the flute and see the Clear Light.

The Fourth Technique: Introduction to Visualization

In order to see the Light, which is really only letting go to that unconditional state that is here all the time, you must establish an idea of immense light. Look at pictures of the sun, or use any means you can devise. A simulation of the inner light must be achieved by outer means, to train you to hold your concentration on the Light when it does come, either during practice sessions or at the death moment itself. By now we've explored alternate ways to do this, including mantram, sacred uplifting music, and breathing—as the inner Light and inner Sound are aspects of each other, and can be induced by outer catalysts.

Exercise 7: Visualization

◇   Remove your glasses or contacts. Press your eyeballs with the heels of your hand. On first practice, the pressure should be very gentle until, through experience, you know how much pressure will be effective for you. Watch inwardly as darkness turns to various colors and streaks and into a hot core of light for a moment. When you release your hands it rapidly returns to reds and then back to darkness again. But there will be a moment when it is spreading out across your inner vision in live fashion, which gives a beginning sensation of the kind of light energy you will encounter.

Do this twice a day, and try to remember and reconstruct the moment of hot core light. Do this while your support person says in a low, warm, firm voice: "Watch for the Light." When you start pressing your eyeballs with the heel of your hands, do so firmly but not to the point of pain. Start with 15 seconds of pressure;

experiment to find the point at which you seem to see a flash of core light before it alters into geometric shapes. Hold the image. Reconstruct it. When your support person says, "Watch for the Light," practice reconstructing the image on command.

◊ Next, take a 60-watt light bulb in a globe (preferably a small upright lamp, not a ceiling light or lamp with a white shade). If a 60-watt bulb is too bright, use a lower wattage bulb or a candle until your eyes adjust themselves. Stare at it with your eyes wide open but unfocused; try to see a smear of light at first. Keep looking at the light but now close your eyes and see the same image. Hold it for a time, fading to light shining through the lids. Practice to get the feel of the light. Then practice to prolong and hold the open-eye image with the eyes closed. Next, reconstruct the lamp (or candle flame), detail by detail (choose a simple shape with few details). Learn it perfectly.

By the end of eight weeks you should be able to reconstruct it at will without gazing at it first. This ability will carry over into other areas. It will help you memorize and reconstruct the face of your revered spiritual teacher, should you desire to imprint that face in your memory.

A variation of this exercise is to practice visualizing a figure of Light. If you have your own spiritual mentor, he or she will be your "take-away" person that you'll see at the moment of death. Ideally, it should be an enlightened being—Christ, Buddha, Krishna, or a modern teacher. For when you train yourself to "dial" that form and name as a reflex during the death process, you tune into that being's state of consciousness. You wouldn't want to dial your favorite dog, therefore, at this crucial time— nor would you want to dial an old friend unless that friend is enlightened and you're sure of it.

◊ Obtain a picture of your chosen person—a large picture. Stare at it as you did the bulb (or candle) and then close your eyes and see the image on the inner eye. Repeat, each time attempting to prolong the inner image. For the first two weeks, study the photograph or picture carefully, feature by feature, mentally, and then do the exercise. By four weeks you will be able to hold the image for ten minutes and reconstruct it at will. This is one way to get started using the Sixth Technique we have talked about.

The Fifth Technique: Withdrawal of Consciousness

Preceding the Withdrawal of Consciousness Technique you will do a composite of the preceding exercises you have learned through daily exercise sessions. At the moment of death, breathing will be monitored by your support person or yourself, bearing in mind that any alteration in breathing is connected with a shift in emotional or mental images. Thus to modify fear, calm the breath. Slow, deep, diaphragm breathing also slows the rate of images and distractions that flood the mind, allowing the letting go process to proceed better at the moment of death. When the time arrives for the final passage, the Fifth Technique, performed with your support person, will ensure an orderly, conscious celebration.

If you are aware that death is imminent, practice this exercise daily. If you are a normal, healthy person, practice this exercise and the others preceding this daily for at least six weeks, and then once a week to ensure that the proper responses will be triggered within your consciousness in the event of your untimely demise. Anyone who practices these techniques will find many beneficial effects, regardless of their state of health. Be sure to at least practice Exercise 1, the Vibration Exercise on page 317, or Exercise 6, the Meditation for Your Electrical Body on page 327, for fifteen minutes a day—especially in the case of terminal illness.

All of the various exercises should be practiced by both the dying person and the support person whenever possible. If the support person is unable to practice daily with you, you should practice alone. The value of the support person doing the exercises is two-fold: (1) He or she will recognize the various changes of consciousness that may occur and can use this knowledge to know when to be verbally supportive and when to be silent, simply feeling and thinking positive loving thoughts which is a therapeutic presence the dying person senses; and (2) As with any meditative practice, personal benefit will be obvious for the support person as well.

Practice Exercises 1–7 until you feel comfortable with them. Then add the Fifth Technique, the Withdrawal of Consciousness (Exercise 8) to your practice schedule.

Exercise 8: Withdrawal of Consciousness

◊   Lie down on your right side, or have your support friend arrange your body so. Or, if you lie on your back, have your head and neck supported by a thin pillow so your neck is slightly bent. Stabilize your breathing by breathing gently in and out from the midsection of your body. If your breathing is shallow and/or gasping, try to concentrate on it and modify it to slower wave motions, less jerky, less panicky—getting into a rhythm with your inner energies. Have your support person encourage this; he or she needs to breathe with you. The sympathetic nervous system is breaking down and erratic signals to your body are discharging to the various organs, including the muscles and lungs. So, calm the breath. This will help your body's electromagnetic field in its discharging of energies through the various switchpoints more swiftly and easily.

◊   Now start with your feet and lower trunk and imagine drawing up energy with your inhalation breath. (Use SAT-NAM) Continue this practice. Make a circuit of it by pulling the energy from your toes and blowing it out the top of your head, then going down in a circle and pulling it up again in a loop. Do this until you start feeling your energy pull up toward your heart. Then just suck yourself upward as through a straw—exiting in your imagination through the top of your head with each exhalation—as you will in your final take-off. Energy will gather behind your eyes, but pull it on up to the highest switchpoint— the top of the head (the crown chakra). You will feel the energy spinning inside the expanded circle of your Self. Let yourself expand as large as you wish—into the universe.

Deep inside yourself you will feel a vast contentedness and joyousness as the process draws you higher and higher into focusing the energy that is You, the real you, the one who will leave this body, the one who always was and is "You."

Gradually you will feel your feet and lower body go numb. By now your energy will be in your heart. Your heart will be expanded and pulsing with electrical energy. There may be a sense of pressure. All the audio and visual symptoms described before may also be going on. Continue breathing from the heart to the head and making the circuit, from heart to head, from head to heart, each time drawing upward a bit more.

If you faint or your consciousness drifts, your prompter will tell you to keep awake and to breathe out the top of your head, or can breathe for you with his or her attention—starting telepathic communication, which you can receive, even though comatose or in a faint.

Draw the energy upward from wherever it seems located in you, nudging it upward, blowing it out in your mind's eye, through the top of the head steadily. During practice sessions this exercise will likely have gotten you out-of-body, so the experience will not be strange, but if it is your first time out, don't falter. Just keep at it. Know your spiritual teacher is with you, or call on the being to whom this book is dedicated. Being out-of-body at this or any other time doesn't mean you are dead!

All the subtle bodies are still connected, even though you are "out" of your body.

The conditions during the actual deathing are different from the practice sessions because at death the bioforcefield body is breaking up, like ice on a river. Don't be afraid of the sound effects that may accompany this—some of the sounds can be stupendous, even hideous. But by not resisting or fearing them, they die down to below your sensing of them, as the Light sensation starts to dominate. If you resist them, the freed energy discharge will create wilder sound effects.

◊   Continue breathing yourself up your entire body, from your heart now, into your throat. Your supporter can gently lay his or her hand on your throat and massage upward along the voice box which helps draw the energy upward while it directs your (possibly) fading attention. If you are alone, you can place your own hand on your throat to remind yourself to go upward in your attention.

Suddenly the energy will be in your head, all of your "you-ness" will be there, and your body may feel as if it's utterly gone, or you may feel suspended in space. The energy will be pushing behind the sinus bones and in the eyes, expanding outward, turning into light, and will stream rapidly upward as if it is rushing out. Or, it may disperse in wide swirlings. You will have the sensation of this Light Energy flowing at incredible speed up a long tunnel.

Keep your attention on top of your head or above. Start visualizing light pouring out of your head like a waterfall upward. You are at once the Light and you are now rushing to meet the Light. The discharging upward now becomes a sucking motion like a cosmic vacuum cleaner. It is the attraction of Light for Light. The rocket boost of the discharging bioforcefield body is at the fourth switchpoint, as the etheric-pranic energy turns to superconsciousness. The sucking motion of Light's attraction for Light takes over, tugging you irresistibly up and out. You may see waves of Light, but even if you see nothing, *you will feel It.* Don't falter, continue focusing your breath and energy at a point above the body with every exhaled breath—letting go with each one, letting it happen.

There will come a point in your upward stroking with your breath and attention that the energy breaks lose from the weakening magnetic biofield which releases its hold on the body and switches bondings. The effect can be likened to being slung like a rock from a slingshot by the sudden outpouring of rushing energy from the discharging fields, or it can be more mellow. *You may have the tendency to faint. Stay awake and have your support person assist by telling you to recognize the pure Light as yourself.* The support person can help you keep alert and aware—so you can let go all else. You have learned to reflex to the name of the Supreme Reality as either Light, or by the name of your spiritual teacher. Your support person will also evoke this name on your behalf. But don't count on anyone but your own efforts to say the name of God or guru as the energy pours out the sutures of the head like a waterfall traveling uphill, streaming upward in a jet spray at an incredible rate; or it may boil itself down into a bead of pure Light riding upon a sea of Light, bearing your energy up and out on its silent waters. The sense is of radiant wonder, utter silence, and awe. You will laugh with joy as easily as a child or a bird on the wing at liberation.

Have no fear or apprehension though you may feel you are moving faster than a jet plane, which contradicts your human sense of yourself. Let it, let go—the body dream is fading and the reality is approaching.

Allow nothing whatsoever to deter you from departing into the great Light which will welcome you. Keep your attention on the upward movement which will turn into the semblance of a tunnel through which you will surge and spin. At the end of it is the Light toward which the Light in you joyously rushes and moves to merge with it, and it with you—as a child recognizes its mother, it is said.

The principle to remember, that must be drilled into you while training, is: "Don't stop accelerating or letting go—which is the same thing!" Stop for nothing, no one, no idea, or image, save that of speed and light and expansion and freedom. You will meet the Light with the Light of yourself, as close to its own frequency as possible and with as much non-resistance as you can manage and *mirror it, as two become one—part and whole.* It is best to train for a fast departure. If you have time to take the Clear Light experience leisurely while consciousness is still in the heart center, it is more easily monitored by your support person. Try to prolong the Clear Light by recognizing what it is.

You may, in a fast take-off, have a moment of blackout. This is normal, but the ideal is to have continued consciousness across the gap. Your support person can help you here and needs to "tune in" at least three times a day to remind you to invoke your spiritual teacher's aid as well as to let go to Light, be Light and see all as yourself. Time is not clock time for the dead, so this black-out may last as long as several days, or take just a moment. Prior to this time, clinical death will have occurred.

A cessation of the apparent activity of all body systems is not the real death for people who haven't practiced conscious dying. Only when the five bodies are released does the Consciousness Principle depart its former dwelling place permanently, shifting to the astral body as a base of operation. Medical science doesn't know yet that clinical death precedes real death as long as three to four days in most cases. Oddly, some advanced meditation practitioners deliberately delay as they finish all the levels of enlightenment before final severance, even as breech deaths at the other end of the consciousness spectrum are also delayed departures. *Ordinary people are in between.* The process we call deathing attempts to move us through the four switchpoints less hazardously, and to gain the Clear Light volitionally—in a relatively short time—which is extremely important in an era where organ donorship and mortuary practices usually intrude on the timing of "real," not just "clinical" death. As hospital personnel learn of the deathing process, they can give mental and voice commands for the consciousness principle to depart, as part of a growing humanity's awareness.

The Final Exercise

Once the preliminary exercises included in the five basic techniques become familiar, this final exercise should also be practiced daily. *No harm can come from it.* If you think you are dying, begin implementing the technique. If you don't die, you will have had one more valuable practice session. You can practice with or without your support person being physically present. It would be wise to experiment occasionally by practicing Withdrawal of Consciousness while your prompter is in a different place. This helps establish the telepathic link that may be necessary if your death occurs at a time or place when your support person is not available. If he or she is present, he/she will observe your progress, giving verbal injunctions as necessary. Your supporter's own practice of the exercises, with and without you, will aid in knowing the states of consciousness that you are going through.

Exercise 9: The Trial Run

◊ Begin by invoking Exercise 1, the Vibration Exercise. This will prepare your inner senses for all that is to come. You will hear the voice of your support person throughout the exercise uttering an insistent *"Hmmm,"* or the Aum, or saying the name of your teacher.

◊ Move on to Exercise 3, the Relaxation Exercise. By habit and practice, all parts of the body are quieted or relaxed. The support person checks for tension, possibly gently touching known troublesome areas, and through habit and practice, that area relaxes. It is for this that you have practiced so long, for this moment.

◇ Invoke Exercise 4, Sensing. Expand yourself into energy all around your body, letting the body disappear. The electrical pulsings will be much stronger than usual if the etheric is indeed dissipating.

◇ Your support friend will whisper to you to start the inhalation breath through your whole body from toes to head. Then blow it out like a whale would—through the blow-hole in the top of your head which is your crown chakra. Imagine it jetting out. Continue this practice, matching it with the breath. Time a "name of God" or your own teacher's name with your breath. Or use *SAT NAM*.

◇ Imagine a hoop slung around your body, with one side down the front and one down the back. Breathe up from your feet, exhaling through the top of your head. Start inhaling slowly as your attention moves down the other side of the hoop toward your feet. Then continue inhaling up through the heart and exhale through the top of your head.

The support person will watch the vital signs and watch the breath, urging you to match it with your concentrated withdrawing of the energy of the body. You are setting up a circuit through which the energy will exit eventually, via your attention and focus. Continue your breathing cycle, preparing the circuit for the final exiting.

◇ When the support person gives the word, start withdrawing your hoop up to hip level—your legs will feel numb by now—they will feel pure energy—if you can feel at all.

Your energy will be focused in your heart now. It will be expanded and pulsing with electrical energy. Audiovisuals commence. The support person stands by, giving appropriate commands of watching for the Light and being calm.

◇   "Remain calm," says the supporter in a low, firm, warm tone (See the check list of affirmations on page 345 for suggestions.) The support person may begin the transition mantram, interspersed with injunctions to watch for the Light. You will be hearing sounds and experiencing erratic stimuli in the brain and nervous system as well as in the psyche beyond the brain terminal. "Remain calm. It is only the sounds of a discharging field." This injunction will be given at any time the prompter sees or senses signs of apprehension within the dying person.

◇   Try to keep awake. The support person will whisper the circuit to you so it goes on, even if you slip away or move in and out of this plane of consciousness. Your supporter's attention keeps yours going in your inner self. Telepathic communication is beginning, if necessary, with the light-body or secondary body, into which you will transfer. If you are in coma, you are already established there. Your energy will begin to surge toward the throat as the bioforcefield nears dissipation level.

◇   Focus your attention on keeping your energy *up*. Touch your throat with your mental attention or have the support person stroke your throat to remind you to keep energy upward—steadily moving upward—vacating the towns of the lower body. You will think *Hmmm,* or the support person will chant *Hum, AUM,* or your teacher's name.

◇   Begin Exercise 7, the Visualization Exercise (page 329). Invoke either the Light or figure of Light, according to your preference. Suddenly all the energy will be in your head. Keep it there. The body has gone away—you are expanding outward— upward—your eyes, the bones of your head will feel pressured.

◇   Look for the Light; it's all right. See Light pouring out of the top of your head. Visualize it flowing like a waterfall heading upward. Waves of light will be behind your eyes now. BE LIGHT. BE GOD. Know your spiritual teacher as yourself. Let be.

◇ ◇

INSTRUCTIONS FOR THE SUPPORT PERSON

Deathing is a technique, an art, a practice that is acquired through concentrated preparation and review before the death moment. While only half of the world's population may experience childbirth (prepared or unprepared), all humanity must experience biological death. We can no more practice the actual experience of dying than we can have trial runs when giving birth, but this short manual can help us all prepare for this exciting celebrative moment and opportunity. An intelligent grasp of how to die inevitably produces an expanded psychology and philosophy of how to live. We fear death as a final termination, misidentifying ourselves with the body. Death is actually a transition from one state of consciousness to another, closer to our real identity. Death can be seen simply as a rearrangement of our focus of attention in an extended out-of-body experience, as well as a direct encounter with the Supreme Reality, Itself, in the Light Experience. How this is met is the whole cast of deathing. If you are reading this book, you may have already consented to be a support person to a friend or relative, or you are considering the idea. Essentially, you will be leading another human being on an exploratory trip, with some access to maps and destination. Just as you would if you were a midwife at a birth, you don't experience the birth, but you are there to guide it, and this is a very special privilege. It also may bring up some fear and doubt on your part about your qualifications, and you may experience a number of different things, which we will discuss. But for you, as well as your friend, the Sixth Technique is of inestimable service and security in the face of the unknown.

Ancient texts map out forty-nine days which can be representative of different presentations and projections of the psyche which emerge at death. Keep in mind that a day could be months or years, or a blink of an eye, subjectively. These stages can be helped by a support person. Using the methods outlined in this manual, and in recognition of a changing modern-day consciousness, we can focus on the critical first four days of transition, which correspond to the traditional first stage. It is suggested to "tune in" three times a day for the whole period, or make a tape ahead of time which you play every day. Do this for a minimum of ten days after the death. First, you will be working with your friend in the following four areas:

1) You will learn the Withdrawal of Consciousness Exercise, so you can use it at the moment of death. This is also known as an out-of-body technique, and is a modification of the Tibetan consciousness transference called *pho-wa*.

2) You will assist your friend in expectation of the Clear Light, via recognition of the death process, thus keeping your friend on course to letting go to the Light. You'll also be discussing this with your friend.

3) Since the conditions of departure foreshadow the conditions of survival and arrival in afterlife and rebirth states, extraneous thoughts and images of the person's old life need to be left behind, so attention can be focused on the pure Clear Light at the tunnel's end. Generate positive, peaceful thoughts by means of mantra prayer, music and evocation of your teacher. You need to understand this concept so you can help your friend in

the preliminaries of letting go to the Light, and then to let go, to being it.

4) You need to talk with your friend about establishing a spiritual guide, the Sixth Technique, firmly in his or her attention, visualizing this spiritual guide, and calling the guide's name in practice sessions, so at the last your friend will be ready for reception service on the other side. Guides, a master, or friends will take over from you on the other side, but they often make contact by being called from this side. This should be a comfortable idea for you, for you won't be working alone.

Being a support person is difficult, for it is not easy to watch another person die, especially if you love this person a great deal. If your friend is an unknown kinsman who has asked your assistance either early on or at the last moment, the techniques and concepts can be adapted to the situation. Or, if you have been summoned to the scene of an accident involving total strangers, these methods can assuredly be utilized, especially breathing with the person, being loving, and telling him or her to let go and to look for the Light.

In most instances of your assistance, however, you will be on close terms with your friend. It is hoped that you will both have time to spend going through the exercises and states of mind, as well as to make the attitudinal shifts necessary to convey this teaching I've adapted from ancient practices for our modern age.

It is important that you clear yourself of your own guilts and sorrows so that you can be attentive in heart and mind to the situation at hand. If you are full of yourself and your own feelings, you won't be able to help your friend in your function as support person and coach. Additionally, your own mental waves can influence the mental and emotional environment your friend is transiting from. But, in emptying yourself, be honest about your feelings. And if it is appropriate, share them with your friend as part of the workshops you devise as practice time for the methods of this manual. Admit you are overwhelmed sometimes, as well as feeling guilty that you are in good health while your friend is dying. Remember that loving thoughts are always welcome; undue grief and anger are not. Although we are assured that death itself is a celebrative act, it is getting to it that is hard—especially in terminal illness. Your friend should know that you understand. You may also be afraid of how you will handle the ugly details of the dying process as you watch a system break down as surely as the ice on a river breaks up. You may wonder, as well, if all this is really going to work. Or how will you ever know, once your friend is dead? I can only assure you that you'll know. You will sense with the subtle senses that the victory was complete for your friend, partly due to your efforts and loving attention. You can live with that.

So, despite the distractions, despite the temptation to skip sessions of practice of the methods in this manual, despite your knowing that your friend is really not up to this detailed program—which is really meant to be looked at before you need it—you must be determined to work with the basic points of this method and unabashedly turn to the Sixth Technique which embraces all others.

Your practice sessions should run an hour, depending, of course, on the condition of the patient. If the person is bedridden, concentrate on the breathing exercises. You may have to do the exercises for the person. You can still elicit a response from the person, however, even if he or she is comatose. The body will relax according to your instructions. If the person is in a coma, the verbal affirmations will be enormously useful, and you will use them as well if your friend is conscious. Sample affirmations and an overview of their use follow. Say them slowly and clearly.

Affirmations

1) *"HUM"* or *"AUM"*—to be used throughout as a focusing and stabilizing device.

2) *"Relax. Relax your arm, relax your legs, etc.,"*—to be used during the Relaxation Exercise and early stages.

3) *"Remain calm"*—to be used at any time when fear or apprehension is sensed in the dying person, or even after death. It is not simply your words that will calm the person; the conditioned response he or she has built up during the practice sessions also will serve as a calming influence.

4) *"Watch for the light. You are the light. Go for the light, Be Light"*—to be used during the Withdrawal of Consciousness exercise. The last phrase, *"Go for the Light, it's all right,"* is especially soothing and effective and can act as white noise to cover distractions. Bend close to the person's ear and whisper it. Also whisper the name of that person's enlightened teacher. You should discuss this beforehand.

5) "Christ and I are One; God and I are One; I am Soul; Buddha and I are one; Allah and I are One; Sathya Sai Baba and I are one. Krishna and I are one," etc., are all phrases you can use.

6) Address the dying person as "Soul of _____." Avoid using only the personality name. If you do not know the person, "Dear Soul" is fine.

7) Before and after the last breath you could say as often as you like (aloud or silently) "Soul of _____, in the name of _____ (if you know their teacher's name) listen carefully. You are now experiencing the radiance of the Clear Light of Pure Reality. Recognize the Light as your own pure consciousness. Abide in this state of recognition and union of no birth or death, enlightenment Itself."

It is important as the support person that you use these affirmations repeatedly. Use a slow, firm, gentle voice. Utter your suggestions while you breathe with the dying person. Your chief function is to guide the person to the Light, helping him or her focus attention upward toward the Light, never down into the body. Encourage, guide, and support. These are your roles.

It is also important for you to understand the reasoning behind some of the exercises. The role of relaxation is great in the ultimate letting go process called death, and its milder counterpart, sleep. To achieve that end, we teach each body part to relax at the support person's instruction. Breathing becomes a means of controlling tension and fear. It is also a means of tuning in to the life energies of body and mind at many levels.

The techniques of yoga practice, from which some of these exercises are adapted, stress the role of suggestion. The dying person enters a state of closing down that he or she may attain only by training when still well. This state produces a relaxed condition in which the mind is wide open to suggestion. Since the person is so open, you, the support person, must be very sure to make each word or phrase a positive one. Phrase all instructions in such a manner that affirmation is conveyed. For example, instead of saying, "Do not be afraid," restate it as, "Remain calm and secure." The last word tends to linger in the subconscious mind and resonate there, and you wouldn't want the word "afraid" to create effects that are counter to the role you play or that the affirmations serve.

Breathing is a major tool which both calms and stabilizes the dying person and helps discharge the electromagnetic body. It also distributes energy while living. For both you as the support person and for the dying person, synchronization of the breath in a co-meditation experience creates an intimacy of sharing when practiced ahead of time, as well as being the means to guide erratic, distracting malfunctions of the body during the dying process.[50] Having shared in this manner before death, your grief and loss become transfigured by the gift of sharing. You don't experience the helpless impotence of simply watching a loved one die, because you can empower your friend in this experience.

The breathing patterns of your friend convey the stage the person is at. Fast, rapid breathing creates a state of mind that is flighty, whereas slow, widely spaced breaths create a calmer state of mind. Since the mind tends to follow the breathing, you can help your friend adjust his or her breathing. As your friend edges toward the death moment, if he or she is conscious the breathing will tend to become irregularly spaced. In many instances there will be longer intervals between each breath. You should make sure that you are repeating the Vibration Exercise during this period, as well as reminding the dying person to remain in the light of pure consciousness. Religious verses or statements from your friend's religious background may also serve you well. Never repudiate the spiritual heritage of a patient; always work with it to deepen, not erode, faith. Repetition of a religious or lyrical phrase or using the Sixth Technique helps keep the dying person from being distracted and focuses him or her on the business at hand.

By using the breathing process as a means of directing the energies upward through the body toward the head, one is prepared to sail out of the body in a stately fashion, assured of a conscious, accomplished act of freedom. This is deathing—not merely dying.

Death is a mystery, but it can be solved. The secret is both in letting go—in elegant submission to the inevitable—and in

---

[50]See Richard Boerstler, *Letting Go* (S. Yarmouth, MA: Associates in Thanatology, 1982).

consciously directing the expiring energies otherwise locked in a failing physical body. If, at the end your friend is dozing or fainting, try to bring him or her back to focus on what is about to happen—that he or she will soon be face to face with the Clear Light, the divine Universal Nature, which their own nature will both be and mirror, as one.

In ancient times, and still in Indian and Tibetan esoteric practice today, it is often the best loved friend that takes one through the death transition. The ancients called these people "dharma brothers." Or the student's beloved Master took him through deathing, or it was a Master's most beloved student who guarded and kept watch through the passage. The guardian's job was done by loved ones, not by strangers who didn't understand or who didn't care. In addition, there used to be specially trained beings who keep telepathic contact with their charges after the moment of clinical death. They navigated the departed and helped them finish off the last de-programming from the earth life, as well as keeping them on course in the seas of eternity.

By becoming a support person, you are simply returning to an old tradition and becoming a very valued and special friend, which also makes you responsible for keeping the journey smooth, at least from your end. Most people grieve when a friend dies, but in this instance, you must do your grieving before, and a long time after. For during death, you need to channel positive energy for your friend and for yourself, by acting in a support position during the dying process, and immediately after death as well. By sending loving positive thoughts, you will help your friend, even if there was negativity at the end. You can re-route him or her, as we have discussed previously. If you think angry, hard thoughts, or feel guilty, or are very sad and anguished, you will be hindering the death process, and creating distractions hard to resist. The departed, having successfully exited the body, is now established in a secondary light-body, which is totally telepathic, and very sensitive to the thoughts you send, especially from our plane. If the person is not quite sure he or she is really dead, it becomes crucial that the support person monitor properly, continuing to tell the person to accept all that comes as himself, perhaps addressing the dead as the Tibetans do, i.e., "nobly born," or "Son or Daughter of God," which is more appropriate to the Christian tradition. You can either tack on the given name (Soul-of-so and so) or simply think of the person as you address him or her.

You could discuss the arrangements to be made at death with your friend while you are practicing these exercises. The Tibetans, who are experienced at working the multi-dimensional level of bodies we have, suggest that cremation take place after four days, to be on the safe side. They also suggest that one not allow embalming or an autopsy, if you want to best assist the soul on its way. You cannot make anyone do anything he or she doesn't want to do, but understanding the process here will help both you and your friend. In other words, your friend may be fighting with other family members about how the body will be handled, and your friend needs you to support whatever choice he or she makes. Remember, positive thoughts are necessary at the end. Keep the dying person content, whatever is going on.

As I said, the corpse remains a resonating device for the energies of the other bodies—the light-body, the soul (or essence self, the Consciousness Principle) until the connective field of the etheric is totally discharged. The length of time required for this depends on whether the person *died* or *deathed*. Normally, a human takes a minimum of three or four days to die, to discharge the connection to the physical body via the various elements and the etheric biofield. With *deathing*, it can be discharged in the Withdrawal of Consciousness process, however. But even until the body is cremated, or totally decomposed, it in turn can act as a transformer, receiving impulses from the environment, as well as the biofield, which slowly wears out, returning to Universal Prana, unless it has been converted as "propellant" via deathing, or a similar departure procedure.

As you probably know, many autopsies are performed today right after clinical death. I think this practice is barbaric, especially in the light of what we have been discussing in this book. Ideally, the body should be left alone in a morgue cooler, which is not unlike a waiting room in the bus station, for four days before it is touched. (Actually, it wasn't so many years ago that we left the body in the parlor for three or four days before burial without any help from morticians.) During the time the body lies there, the Essence and Consciousness Principle is busy extricating itself (in normal dying), and even after it's out, the biofield persists, muffling the Consciousness Principle's perceptions, especially in shock death. The support person can speed the release process in such cases with firm voice commands.

During this period, the consciousness is very sensitive to impressions. The body actually acts as a radio receiver/sender set, which is in contact with the probably bewildered, newly dead person. It is extremely sensitive to casual chatter, and callous comments, jests, grief, an autopsy, for any unnecessary disturbance can be experienced by the newly dead.

The dead have ears. Although a person is not supposed to look back, once in the light-body after the Clear Light experience, when he or she "wakes up dead," there is confusion and the person is usually drawn back to earth life for a while, especially if he or she is ignorant of conscious dying. In conscious dying, the Consciousness Principle must keep on the way, for the new opportunities for enlightenment rigorously demand full attention. Yet the coarse call of the physical can override even his or her intent. So the support person *must* continue with prayers and loving reminders of the new dead's spiritual "sonship." And to let go to the Light of being, always recalling the new dead to his or her spiritual teacher. After this stage, people can go "visiting," if they want.

This all begins to happen when the initial blackout period is over, after the initial contact with the Light has occurred. Most people don't stay in the Light for four days while this process is going on. They usually ricochet into the etheric Hades area for three days and then "wake-up" on the fourth day and start having the other experiences. At that point it's crucial to divert them back to their task of self-recognition in succeeding Light Experiences and opportunities for liberation—*not* earth life. And this is hard to do. A constantly playing tape of instructions is suggested as a means to neutralize all the earth life impressions.

The newly dead may be besieged by rudeness at the mortuary, or at the funeral. The newly-dead will hear others speaking about him or her, as old acquaintances and family members speak aloud, telepathically, or totally unknowingly of the effect of rude gossip and extraneous matters. The burden rests on the quick learning that the dead have ears, even as the new dead should not be distracted and annoyed by their relative's ignorance, and most usually, neglect. *The support person needs to stand by.* Knowing this in advance will help you to help your friend through this period. Don't be shy about reading out loud or just talking to the new-dead. The newly dead will need all the loving thoughts you can give as a guidance control system, even if your friend has an enlightened teacher, and especially if your friend has not.

If it's possible that you won't be with your friend at the moment of death, you can tape instructions at your practice sessions so your friend can use them in your absence, or in the long, perhaps painful nights when the mind races in fear of the oncoming event. Even if you and your friend are separated geographically during the death, you can tune in immediately when you find death has occurred and help to direct your friend's progress.

You are your friend's coach and support system, like a midwife to a laboring woman in the birth process. Being a support person helps channel positive energy for your friend and for yourself by allowing you to participate in the dying process. It is a great privilege.

◇ ◇

A CHECKLIST OF NECESSITIES FOR DEATHING

1) The necessity of an after-life construct, as opposed to no after-life expectation! You may use conventional religious expectation, the tunnel and the joining with the Light itself, or the name and form of an enlightened teacher—the Sixth Technique.

2) The necessity to let go of limited self-concepts of age, sex, form, relationship with support-person, type of disease you are dying from, planet you are on, offspring you leave behind, any unfinished business such as feuds, business or artistic projects, or the *notion* of an unfinished life, or any sense of tragi-comedy or irony of life and death.

3) The necessity to always look up during the deathing process, toward your head. Never put your attention *down* into the body.

4) The necessity to direct your attention to the Light. Have no thought save "I am LIGHT,—or I am GOD," or think only of your spiritual teacher, or assume his or her identity, i.e., "I am Christ, I am Buddha, Krishna, Sathya Sai Baba, etc."

5) The necessity to know LIGHT only in the form of pure energy, to see it visually or in the form of a revered enlightened being.

6) The necessity to know you will not drown in the LIGHT which you are! You will not disperse beyond recognition, but are initiated, baptized, reborn into the LIGHT of pure consciousness. You do not lose yourself, but find yourself.

7) The necessity to get above electronic sounds, beeps, bleats, past the huge motor sound, past the whizzing hum of hornets or bees, and into the high, clear flute sound which will pull you in with the LIGHT which will blend with a pulsing throbbing— the AUM sound itself.

8) The necessity to listen for the sounds that are equivalent to the CLEAR LIGHT: high flute calls; bagpipes skrrying; winds rushing, fugues and choir sounds, trumpet or conch shell calls— which may go totally silent as well.

9) The necessity to know you can do it!

10) The joy factor is love—the link between form and formless, and heart and heart.

◇ ◇

REFLEXES TO TRAIN BEFORE DEATH

You want to train yourself so that you can reflex after death when you need these basic concepts. You can either remember to reflex yourself, or you can respond to a command suggestion of your support person. Your family can help as well, if family members have been made aware of this, helping you in this critical change-of-state.

1) See even the aggravation of physical body breakdown, frustrating as it is, as *positively* as possible. If you never have exerted self-control, exert it now, for the last thoughts during the last weeks and days have a great capacity to either uplift, or trivialize, or downgrade the kind of afterlife experience you will have— and the kind of rebirth. Even if you don't believe in reincarnation, like the adolescent may not believe in birth control—be careful. Play safe. Use the Sixth Technique whether you believe it or not. Remember old Ajamila!

2) In the event of major earth changes and natural disaster, buddy systems of total strangers must be effected so people can assist each other in deathing—in dying well no matter what the circumstances. Remember, the newly dead can be re-routed even after a bad death by loving thoughts, affirmations, and by handling the situation.

3) Know yourself to be the son or daughter of God, a ray of Light, the Consciousness Principle, Atma, a sound of AUM. You are nobly born of spirit and are only returning to spirit via death's transition. To know yourself as God—as Light, as all that is, both positive and negative—is to have your true nature revealed.

4) Find an easy image, such as Light, to identify with. And keep identifying with it in your last weeks and hours. For instance, when you eat your food, or urinate, think, "I am pure light energy emitting pure light energy." It may sound foolish, but it's not.

5) An alternative to this is for those who have found and been found by an enlightened teacher. You may use the being to whom this book is dedicated for this purpose—he will cover for you. Link your name with the teacher's. For example, "Sathya Sai Baba and I are one." Or, "Christ and I are one." Or "Buddha and I are one." Or "Brahmananda Sarasvati and I are one." If you want to be bolder, call yourself by your enlightened teacher's name. "I am God." Or, "I am Sathya Sai Baba." *But know you are identifying, not with your personal self, not theirs, but with the universal self you share with all.* An enlightened being is totally conscious of this.

6) Train to the light via the Visualization Exercise (p. 329) so you command it at will inside your mind's eye or to your teacher's face. Verbally affirm your true nature as light, for this will reflex in an accidental death, or in difficult delayed deaths. When you are lying helpless in those last days, remember you are only pure light energy going into transformations of itself, de-incarnating from the solid form, incarnating into subtle forms, like melting ice. Don't identify with the breaking down, but with the wonderful freedom of the break UP of the ice on your River of Life—so your current can go swiftly, fleetingly, and wonderfully Home.

7) Say, "I am not me! I am God, I never change. I am perfect. Fear and grief can never touch me, for I am eternal." And know this throughout the dying process, turning it into *deathing*.

8) Sing or say inspirational songs, or mantras, such as Bajhans, *Beautiful Savior*, the 23rd Psalm, the Gayatri; play devotional music.

9) Know you are immortal consciousness, unborn, undying, although you wear bodies like the body wears clothes! Knowing this of yourself, or of your patient, creates the atmosphere of right dying—*Deathing*.

10) Say the Word—the Word is love.

MAHA MRTYUNJAYA-MANTRA

OM Tryambakam Yajamahe
Sugandhim Pustivardhanam,
Urvarukam Iva Bandhanan
Mrtyor Muksiya Mamrtat
SVAHA

THE GREAT DEATH-DEFYING MANTRA

I look within to the pure, tranquil light
of inner vision, sweet and nourishing
with the fragrance of life.
May I be freed painlessly
from the bonds of death,
like a ripe fruit falling from the vine.
May I never again forget my immortal nature.[51]

---

[51]Original Sanskrit translation from the *Rg Veda*, Section 7-59-12, by Ramamurti S. Mishra. English translation by Vyasananda.

◇ ◇

RESOURCES

This section aims to provide suggestions for further help and information for the dying person, the support person, and family members. The lists are suggestive, not definitive, and they aim for immediacy and relevance. Although the focus is holistic, it does not exclude current religious beliefs. Included are books, organizations, and periodicals that may be of help.

Reading List

It is impossible to list all the books that have been published recently about death and dying. The following list includes many types of references that relate directly to the deathing experience. There was not enough space to list all the related subjects that might be of interest for your changing consciousness. Try your local metaphysical bookstore—you'll find it opens a whole new world for you.

Aries, Philippe. *The Hour of Our Death*. New York: Knopf, 1981.
An enormously interesting book on the styles of death and dying in Western culture. It shows how individuals assimilate and act out the cultural attitudes of their times.

Arya, Usharbudh Pandit. *Meditation and the Art of Dying*. Honesdale, PA: Himalayan Publishers, 1979.
Offers instruction in meditation designed to overcome the fear of dying. A discussion of some of the finest yogic teachings on the nature and relationship of death and enlightenment.

Assagioli, Roberto, M.D. *The Act of Will*. New York: Penguin Books, 1985.

One of the masters of modern psychology in the line that runs from Sigmund Freud through C. G. Jung and Abraham Maslow, Assagioli developed a comprehensive psychology known as psychosynthesis. Psychosynthesis sees the human race as tending naturally toward harmony within and with the world. The concept of the will is an especially key part of that vision. To train the will is a major aspect of success in anything—living or dying. Too often people have a false fear in spiritual matters of exerting will, or controlled desire from the personal to the transpersonal into the realm whereby the individual will merges with the universal. It is important to have a will that doesn't melt like ice cream.

Balsekar, Ramesh S. *Pointers from Nisargadatta Maharaj*. Bombay: Chetana, 1982.

Maharaj points to the Eternal Truth that IS—before time ever was. This is a dissection job on one's self-assumptions, especially valuable in the event of on-coming death, which democratically we will all experience. If one can "get it," dying becomes superfluous, as does rebirth.

Bentov, Itzhak. *Stalking the Wild Pendulum: On the Mechanics of Creation*. Rochester, VT: Inner Traditions Destiny, 1988.

Please read chapter 4, "An Experiment in Time," in which you can prove to yourself your own ability to move time's constraints. Read the tiny mighty introduction as the crux of the situation we are in, happily. Don't beat the dead horse of "where do I go, IF I go," after death without checking first with Bentov's model. No organized energy is ever lost, including you and me, what we've been and who we will be. With or without a body. See also Monroe's *Far Journeys* and Twitchell's *Key to Secret Worlds*.

Bentov, Itzhak and Mirtala. *A Cosmic Book: On the Mechanics of Creation*. Rochester, VT: Inner Traditions Destiny, 1988.

If you haven't read it, or marked it to read by the time you get this far, what's to say?

Boerstler, Richard. *Letting Go: A Holistic and Meditative Approach to Living and Dying*. South Yarmouth, MA: Associates in Thanatology, 1982.

Describes an ancient practice—co-meditation—by which the dying can be assisted to reduce pain and stress, moving toward clear mind and a peaceful heart. (If you cannot get this book in bookstores, write the association at 115 Blue Rock Road, S. Yarmouth, MA 02664.)

Brunton, Paul. *The Ego/From Birth to Rebirth*, Notebooks of Paul Brunton, Vol. 6. Burdett, NY: Larson Publications, 1987.

This is a deeply moving, profoundly inspiring book by a thoroughly modern man. This man has loved deeply, suffered deeply, thought deeply, and wrestled mightily with the existential dilemma presented each of us by simply being born—that is, we die. The wry, tender, ruthlessly authentic and honest commentaries on the human condition are unique in the history of self-realization. He straddles both worlds and so can we. *From Birth to Rebirth* has unusual insights that are more accessible than most sages, or those of Rudolf Steiner who covers the same territory. You cannot fail to reach for more courage in the face of PB's unflinching integrity.

Camath, M. V. *Philosophy of Death and Dying*. Honesdale, PA: Himalayan Publishers, 1978.

Inspiring, heroic stories of great men and women from diverse cultures and the way they died.

Capra, Fritjof. *The Tao of Physics*. New York: Bantam, 1977.

Capra shows the relationship and relevance of the new physics to ancient and modern mystical insights.

———. *The Turning Point: Science, Society and the Rising Culture*. New York: Simon & Schuster, 1982.

This was the turning point in my thinking. Getting a handle on the Newtonian/bio-medical model of Man, that our society employs as its common sense reality, and seeing its permeation of the fabric of our thought in every major field, with the contrasts drawn—this is invaluable.

Cavanaugh, Robert E. *Facing Death*. New York: Penguin Books, 1974.

Chaney, Earlyne. *The Mystery of Death and Dying: Initiation at the Moment of Death*. York Beach, ME: Samuel Weiser, 1988.
A mystic and a Christian looks at the final moments of life, and discusses the soul, the purpose of life, and life after death. An uplifting presentation. Give it to your relatives and pastor. Adds another dimension to the understanding of basic tenets such as grace, the Holy Spirit. It also puts kundalini into the Christian framework in a non-threatening way.

Colgrove, Melba, Harold H. Bloomfield, and Peter McWilliams. *How to Survive the Loss of a Love*. New York: Bantam, 1977.

Dowman, Keith. *Sky Dancer: The Secret Life and Songs of the Lady Yeshe Tsogyel*. London & Boston: Routledge & Kegan Paul, 1984.
Read in conjunction with *Sky Cleaver*, available from Ariel.

Duda, Deborah. *Coming Home: A Guide to Dying at Home with Dignity*. Santa Fe, NM: Aurora Press, revised edition, 1987.
This wonderful, helpful book is so honest. Practical instructions plus how and what to do with a body after death.

Ebon, Martin (ed.). *Reincarnation in the Twentieth Century*. New York: Signet, 1970.
Short and to the point. Chapter 4 shows examples of death moment trauma.

Evans-Wentz, W. Y. *The Tibetan Book of the Dead*. London: Oxford Press, 1960; New York: Oxford University Press, 1960.
Carl Jung's commentary and Lama Govinda's foreword opened my eyes when I was still being a smug behaviorist.

Fiefel, Herman. *The Meaning of Death*. New York: McGraw-Hill, 1959.

―――. *New Meanings of Death*. New York: McGraw-Hill, 1977.

Flach, Frederic. *Coping Creatively with Personal Change*. Philadelphia: Lippincott, 1977.

Foos-Graber, Anya. *Skycleaver*. North Haven CT: Thadian Publications, 1975. Available through Ariel; see Resources.
    A modern *Pilgrim's Progress* and space odyssey through inner dimensions, told with passion and a disarming irreverence in poetry-to-be-read-as-a-novel.

———. *One Soul Rising: Four Past-Life Recalls*. North Haven, CT: Thadian Publications, 1976. Available through Ariel; see Resources.
    Four tales: a sunflower, sea turtle, a humanoid female child and a male strippling, respectively, express individual and species consciousness. The two humanoid tales evidence wider-than-species or tribal consciousness.

Frankel, Viktor E. *The Doctor and the Soul*, New York: Bantam, 1967.

———. *Man's Search for Meaning: An Introduction to Logo Therapy*. New York: Washington Square Press, 1963.

Free John, Da. *Easy Death: Talks and Essays on the Inherent and Ultimate Transcendence of Death and Everything Else*. San Raphael, CA: Dawn Horse, 1983.
    Just glancing through this banquet will change how a person chooses to live life. This enlightened man talks about what goes on at death and after death, transcending fear, and loosing the knots of self-possession as one ceases a contractive, adversarial relationship with life. See Part V, "How to Serve the Dying," as well.

Garfield, Patricia, Ph.D. *Creative Dreaming*. New York: Ballantine, 1974.
    A very useful book. Pay attention to chapters 1, 2, and 7.

Gerber, Richard, M.D. *Vibrational Medicine: New Choices for Healing Ourselves*. Santa Fe, NM: Bear & Co., 1988.
    The book provides a plausible explanation of how and why so-called occult or "snake-oil" methods of healing work. It shows

the logical, scientific connection between different methods and surely is a door to a medicine of the future—beyond our mechanistic approaches which treat symptoms, and not the cause.

Golas, Thadeus. *The Lazy Man's Guide to Enlightenment*. Palo Alta, CA: The Seed Center, 1972.
A brief, witty, and wise discussion of what enlightenment means in psychological and behavioral terms and just plain fun! Accept everything as a modification of yourself, i.e. God. Resist nothing—especially in your dying.

Gold, E. J. *New American Book of the Dead*. Nevada City, CA: Gateways, 1987.
"Unlike the earlier American variation on the Tibetan model by Leary, Alpert, and Metzner, this book stresses the application of formulas to all experiences, rather than psychedelic experience or the experiences of formal meditation only."—Claudio Naranjo. And there is a text intended to be read from day 1 to day 49 to the newly dead. See Mullin, for script from Tibetan model, and Secret Forrest Productions (under Resources) for deathing tape.

Gould, Roger L. *Transformations*. New York: Simon & Schuster, 1978.

Govinda, Lama Anagarika. *Foundations of Tibetan Mysticism*. York Beach, ME: Samuel Weiser, 1969; and London: Rider & Co., 1960.
A handbook to refer to as you get deeper into the psycho-therapies and metaphysics of yoga's multi-dimensional nature.

Greenhouse, Herbert B. *The Astral Journey*. New York: Avon, 1974.
This book explains the enormous creative potential of astral travel and other states of consciousness that have been known in earlier cultures.

Grof, Stanislav and Christina. *Beyond Death: The Gates of Consciousness*. London: Thames and Hudson, Ltd., 1980.
These authors show how various cultures' concepts of the afterlife bear striking similarities: heaven, hell, the afterlife journey of the soul, and the life review.

————. *The Human Encounter with Death*. New York: E. P. Dutton, 1978.

All descriptions of psychedelic reality are useful in that they show aspects of the psyche that are not normally encountered, except in dreams and at death.

Head, Joseph, & S. L. Cranston. *Reincarnation: The Phoenix Fire Mystery*. New York: Julian Press, 1979.

This East/West dialogue on death and rebirth from the worlds of religion, science, psychology, philosophy, art, literature, and from great thinkers of the past and present should be in every library and every home for this next generation to read. For hard-core Catholics and Protestants, for whom reincarnation is "against their religion," read pages 156–160. References to the *Catholic Encyclopedia* permit the conclusion, "on at least technical grounds, that there is no barrier to belief in reincarnation for Catholic Christians."

Hislop, John. *My Baba and I*. San Diego, CA: Birth Day Publishing Co., 1985.

This book provides a rare opportunity to get "up close" to the enigmatic Sathya Sai Baba through the eyes and experience of a long time follower and author of *Conversations with Bhagavan Sri Sathya Sai Baba*. Both are highly recommended if you want to see some of Sai's policies, practices, and teaching drawn through the very able mind and heart of this wise man.

Humphrey, Derek. *Let Me Die Before I Wake*. Hemlock Society. Write to them at P.O. Box 11830, Eugene, OR 97440-3900.

A guide to self-deliverance (voluntary euthanasia or suicide) for the terminally ill. Tells how to obtain potentially lethal drugs and the amounts needed. Be careful! I know you don't want to hear this—I didn't either. Your life—and your death—is part of the "enlightenment project." Keep it light, by not intruding the lower desire factors, such as recoiling from pain, suffering, or putting someone out of misery. Instead, like a woman in childbirth, give way to the labor, the work in the dying process, which transmutes pain into process. You alter the state of your self-identification thereby. And if you die, you die high. And if you turn around—

into remission—then you have protected the investment of cosmic forces in your life from premature withdrawal. There is an exception to every rule. Do everything in the name of God, especially your mistakes!

Huxley, Aldous. *Doors of Perception*. New York: Harper & Row/ Perennial Library, 1970.

Jacobson, Nils O., M. D. *Life Without Death*. New York: Dell, 1971.
A fine overview of the paranormal for the beginner or someone who has to put their life together quickly—as did Selma.

Jackson, Edgar N. *Telling A Child About Death*. New York: Channel Press, 1965.

Joy, W. Brugh, M.D. *Joy's Way: A Map for the Transformational Journey*. Los Angeles: Jeremy Tarcher, 1979.
This man rediscovered the body fields and body energies that have been mapped by the ancients, up-dating and making accessible much that is otherwise clouded in mystery. His own availability as teacher and seminar director should not be overlooked. This book should be read in conjunction with LeShan's *You Can Fight for Your Life*, and Bernie Siegel's *Love, Medicine and Miracles*, as well as the Simonton's *Getting Well Again*.

Jung, C. G. *Memories, Dreams, Reflections,* Revised edition. Aniela Jaffe, (ed.) New York: Vintage Books, 1965.
Be sure to read chapters 10 and 11.

Gopi Krishna. *Kundalini: The Evolutionary Energy in Man*. Boston: Shambhala, 1971.
A personal account of one man's awakening of kundalini and its significance for human evolution. His was a "hard birth" into higher consciousness and could have been eased if he had an already awakened being as "transducer" and "breaker switch" for opening up the nervous system to higher consciousness.

Kübler-Ross, Elisabeth. *Death, The Final Stage of Growth*. Englewood Cliffs, NJ: Prentice-Hall, 1979.

These essays describe different cultural contexts from which to view death. It is must reading.

———. *Working It Through: An Elisabeth Kübler-Ross Workshop on Life, Death and Transition.* New York: Macmillan, 1982.
This book is the next best thing to attending one of the workshops. Page 23 describes EKR's famous OOBE.

Lakhovsky, Georges. *The Secret of Life.* Mokelumne Hill, CA: Health Research Press.
Lakhovsky says that disease is the outcome of oscillatory disequilibrium resulting from certain modifications in the human field by cosmic waves, solar and lunar emissions, etc. He has evolved a new therapy and offers provocative avenues for research, while enterprising people can adapt the concepts for themselves.

Leadbeater, C. W. *The Astral Plane.* Wheaton, IL: Theosophical Publishing House, 1941, 1984.
This is a classic first published in 1895. Describes our living conditions after we die, detailing the astral plane inhabitants.

LeBoyer, Frederick. *Birth Without Violence.* New York; Knopf, 1975.
So, too, death without violence. The pictures of smiling, not scowling babies right after birth are eloquent statements.

LeShan, Eda. *Learning to Say Goodbye: When a Patient Dies.* New York: Macmillan, 1976.

LeShan, Lawrence. *How to Meditate: A Guide to Self-Discovery.* Boston: Little, Brown & Co., 1974.
Pretty sage advice that cuts through the weeds about styles of meditation.

———. *You Can Fight for Your Life.* New York: M. Evans, 1977.
Character profiles of people with life-threatening diseases who used psychotherapy to turn around the internal situations that caused their cancer.

Levine, Steven. *Who Dies: An Investigation of Conscious Living and Conscious Dying*. New York: Doubleday, 1982.
> This is an intimate and very caring book. Profoundly moving.

Lewis, C.S. *A Grief Observed*. New York: Bantam. 1963.

Lilly, John C. *Simulations of God: The Science of Belief*. New York: Simon and Schuster, 1975.
> Anyone who is trying to get a "fix" on what's real has to take a long look at his or her meta-belief system—your beliefs about beliefs. Most people trade the various levels of experiencing being for a belief, or a religion about being. Finding out what your system of belief is based on frees you to accept those of others, tolerantly, at the very least. At best, you may transcend your own programs to a closer approximation of things as they are.

Lindemann, Erich. *Beyond Grief*. Northfield, NJ: Jason Aronson, 1979.

Lodo, Lama. *Bardo Teachings: The Way of Death and Rebirth*. San Francisco: KDK Publications, 1982.
> These are oral transmissions from the Ven. Kalu Rinpoche, who has released heretofore secret information to the West about the death process and the "in-between" stages. It is best to have a background of dharma practice, for the mind will otherwise not recognize what is happening at the time of death, which is the whole key to gaining enlightenment.

MacLaine, Shirley. *Out on a Limb*. New York: Bantam, 1983.
> She talks about her controversial OOBE on page 333.

Mishra, Ramamurti S. *Fundamentals of Yoga: A Handbook of Theory, Practice and Application*. New York: Julian Press, 1986.
> Read it, study it, put it into practice. Especially if you have had an NDE. Or, if you wish you had—without having to "nearly die" to gain the experience! If you are dying—remember that mental suggestions are in every process of life, whether they are unacknowledged, or acknowledged. By identifying yourself with the highest cosmic principles, you turn around the energy express-

ing through you. Remission is such a turnaround, so is enlightenment! See chapters 16, 20, and 23 on healing. See Resources for
the Ananda Ashram location of this great sage.

———. *The Textbook of Yoga Psychology: The Definitive Translation
and Interpretation of Patanjali's Yoga Sutras.* New York: Julian Press,
1986.

It is a rare pleasure and privilege to have a sage discourse and give
the explication and new translation of a sage, especially if it is
himself at both ends of the enlightenment "stick." Additionally,
there are four new aphorisms.

Monroe, Robert A. *Far Journeys.* New York: Dolphin/Doubleday,
1985.

I can't say enough about the value of this book, as well as Monroe's
training programs. (See Resources.) This book is liable to give
quite a few jolts, however. Other than Dante's inferno and purga-
torio descriptions, some Theosophical literature, E. J. Gold's
American Book of the Dead, along with some near-death experiences—which are usually, but not always—light, I have found this
to be the only formal presentation of what I call "the Grey Place,"
other than my own work. But there is much more in this fascinating book about the native province of souls, which Monroe calls
"curls" and their propensities. Simply refreshing, mind-blowing
and fair warning to try on your OOBE skills before you need them
permanently! At least read this book—especially if you are dying.
Read it for flying!

———. *Journeys Out of the Body.* New York: Doubleday, 1977.
A classic in the field, but out-dated by *Far Journeys.*

Moody, Raymond A., Jr., M.D. *Life After Life: The Investigation of
a Phenomenon—Survival of Bodily Death.* New York: Bantam, 1977.
This book started quite an avalanche. It is still important reading
for those unfamiliar with near-death experience.

Morgan, Ernest. *A Manual of Death Education and Simple Burial.*
Brunswick, NC: Celo Press, 1980.

An excellent overview of death and dying from the standpoint of preparing for it legally, financially, and humanely.

Mullin, Glenn H. *Death and Dying: The Tibetan Tradition.* London & Boston: Routledge & Kegan Paul/Arkana, 1986.
Especially read chapter 2, "Tibetan Traditions of Death Meditation," and chapter 7, "The Yoga of Consciousness Transference." The book completely shifts one's priorities to the eternal verities, less to the short-term, feel good philosophies so prevalent today. Chapter 8 has a ritual for caring for the dead that you can use as a script for yourself, or adapt for your own afterlife instructions. Although operating within the Buddhist camp, this can be especially helpful in deepening an understanding of deathing as a practice.

Murphet, Howard. *Sai Baba: Man of Miracles.* York Beach, ME: Samuel Weiser, 1973; London: Rider & Co., 1973.
One of the best documented books to date on Sathya Sai Baba, avatar, reputed to be the "world teacher," transcendent exemplar of the new man, *homo noeticus,* and Josip Vidmar's psi human . . . but more.

Odier, Daniel. *Nirvana Tao: The Secret Meditation Techniques of the Taoist and Buddhist Masters.* Rochester, VT: Inner Traditions, 1986.
Another student of Kalu Rinpoche has prepared a very important book of fundamentals and foundations of Buddhism, special techniques, and little known stories.

Ohsawa, Georges. *Cancer and the Philosophy of the Far East: Enemy or Benefactor of Man?* Binghampton, NY: Swan House, 1971.
The father of macrobiotics makes for fascinating reading in this frontal attack, flanking action and cure-from-within on dis-ease, whether of body or mind, health being the same as freedom.

Parrish-Harra, Carol. *A New Age Handbook of Death and Dying.* Marina del Rey, CA: DeVorss, 1982.
A very fine overview of death and dying, with guidance for helping the dying and the bereaved.

Pearce, Joseph Chilton. *The Crack in the Cosmic Egg: Challenging Constructs of Mind and Reality*. New York: Pocket Books, 1973.

This is a handbook for our time by a brilliant, playful, integrative mind whose work has assisted many of us in our self-deliveries.

Pelletier, Kenneth R. *Toward a Science of Consciousness*. New York: Dell, 1978.

This book reassures me that the new science and the conventional are branching out to meet each other.

Portwood, Doris. *Commonsense Suicide—the Final Right*. New York: Dodd, Mead, 1978.

Just as there is a short-term thinking process about pleasure, and the gratifying of pleasure, there is a short-term thinking about pain and suffering, and the relief of suffering. First, who suffers, why and how? Where did it come from? Will it follow you in your mind later? What of the implications of having to return to re-experience what you evaded by taking your life wilfully? These are the questions you must answer.

Powell, Arthur E. *The Etheric Double and Allied Phenomena*. Wheaton, IL: Theosophical Publishing House, 1969.

Useful information which supports the need for a method to deal with any trouble in the biofield at death.

Rampa, Lobsang. *You—Forever*. York Beach, ME: Samuel Weiser, 1990.

Some good material on astral travel and survival. Rampa's books are always good reading.

Rawlings, Maurice, M.D. *Beyond Death's Door*. New York: Bantam, 1978.

He suggests that life after death may not be all good.

Rigo, Scott D. *Leaving the Body*. Englewood Cliffs, NJ: Prentice-Hall, 1983.

Eight different systems to enable one to astral project.

Ring, Kenneth. *Heading Toward Omega: In Search of the Meaning of Near-Death Experience*. New York: William Morrow, 1984.

Undeniably the NDE floods its experiencers with exposure to aspects of unconditional reality, according to angle of entry and depth of probe. The NDE seems both a progression toward a state of being and a stripping process by which a state of being is revealed. NDEers may well be the largest practicing religion in the world, part of the secret smile of the universe into which an emergent form of human being is coming in myriad ways, NDE included.

————. *Life at Death: A Scientific Investigation of the Near-Death Experience*. New York: Coward, McCann, & Goghegan, 1980.

Ring documents the stages of a typical near-death experience and the impact of an NDE on later life.

Rinpoche, Kalu. *The Dharma that Illuminates All Beings Impartially Like the Light of the Sun and the Moon*. State University of New York Press, 1986.

For the scholar and lay person, this is a fascinating account of human and non-human affairs and conditions.

Roberts, Jane. *Adventure in Consciousness: An Introduction to Aspect Psychology*. Englewood Cliffs, NJ: Prentice-Hall, 1975.

This is a very informative, exciting book in the other universes, other selves game. It is a great help in finding a modern language for the styles of influence that impact a human being—who is, by nature, a conglomerate.

Sandweiss, Samuel. *Spirit and Mind*. San Diego, CA: Birth Day Publishing Co.

The author of *The Holy Man and the Psychiatrist*, concerning his early contact with Sathya Sai Baba, now takes on a monumental task, that of referencing the enigmatic Baba and his teachings into our 20th century trials—the burden and quest of our mortality and immortality. Dr. Sandweiss is unfailingly honest in his self-revealings as he struggles to integrate Baba's presence and teachings with his function as a therapist. Includes a reader's guide to certain important spiritual precepts, hidden, oddly, in the appendix of the book. Appendix III, "Psychology and Spirituality," is a rundown on the evolution of psychology, which is very useful, especially his précis of Ken Wilber's work.

Sannella, Lee. *The Kundalini Experience: Psychosis or Transcendence?* Lower Lake, CA: Integral Publishing, 1987.
Anyone with an NDE should read this. There are many symptoms that likely are kundalini manifestations cropping up in our culture. The more we know of this mechanism in humanity for "higher birth" as well as the vagaries of its expression, the better.

Schulman, Arnold. *Baba*. New York: Pocket Books, 1972.
A short personal memoir of a successful playwright and script writer who was moved to find out about the reality of the mystic, Baba, who could cure the incurable, manifest objects out of thin air and command life and death. Considered by many to be the best kept secret in the world, Sai Baba is available to whoever dials his name.

Siegel, Bernie S., M.D. *Love, Medicine and Miracles*. New York: Harper & Row, 1986.
This physician is trying to put himself out of business as a cancer surgeon by using alternative therapies of love and visualization of the cancer as gone from the human body, in conjunction with conventional therapies. See Resources under ECAP.

Simonton, Carl, M.D. and Stephanie. *Getting Well Again*. New York: Bantam, 1978.
The sicker you are, the more important it is that you read this terrific book. Their method uses visualization and shows that you can change the rules of life and death.

Smith, Houston. *Forgotten Truth*. New York: Harper and Row, 1976.
An excellent commentary on the transcendent unity of all religions, esoteriscism and the perennial philosophy.

Steiger, Brad. *The Mind Travelers*. New York: Award Books, 1968.
Just exposure to the idea that you are not only a physical body can help your wings grow.

Stoddard, Sandol. *The Hospice Movement: A Better Way of Caring for the Dying*. New York: Vintage Books, 1978.
> Hospitals and hospices are not equally hospitable. They reflect different views of the meaning and value of human life and the significance of death.

Tansley, V. David. *Radionics Interface with the Etheric Fields*. North Devon, England: Health Science Press, 1975.
> If astral travel opens up a hidden chapter in man's former history, the etheric body also opens up a plethora of possibilities, especially in the healing arts and communication.

Tart, Charles T., *Waking Up*. Boston: Shambhala, 1986.
> A textbook on the psychologies associated with various sacred traditions and consciousness-expanding systems.

Trungpa, Chogyam and Fremantle, Francesco. *The Tibetan Book of the Dead: The Great Liberation Through Hearing in the Bardo*. Boston: Shambhala, 1975.
> This version is more readable than the Evans-Wenz edition, but the commentary by Jung and Govinda in the Evans-Wenz edition still provides the best frame for any version.

Twitchell, Paul. *Eckankar: The Key to Secret Worlds*. Minneapolis, MN: Eckankar, 1987.
> It was the point of view of this book, as well as the OOBE exercises which opened me to an entirely different way of being human, a state this age is just now beginning to consider possible.

Wambach, Helen. *Life Before Life*. New York: Bantam, 1981.
> Valuable reading which tallies in most part with esoteric lore and Tibetan Buddhism.

White, John (ed.) *The Highest State of Consciousness*. New York: Doubleday, 1972.
> A study of cosmic consciousness and its many names throughout history.

————. *A Practical Guide to Death and Dying: How to Conquer your Fear and Anxiety through a Program of Personal Action.* Wheaton, IL: Theosophical Publishing House, 1980.
This is a rather dull subtitle for a most comprehensive book. I'd like it to be read as a companion piece to my book.

————. *What is Enlightenment? Exploring the Goal of the Spiritual Path.* Los Angeles: J. P. Tarcher, 1984.

————. *What is Meditation?* New York: Anchor Books, 1974.
A survey of meditative traditions by experienced meditators of those traditions.

————. *Kundalini, Evolution and Enlightenment.* New York: Anchor, 1979.
These are fascinating exerpts from true life stories.

Wilber, Ken. *The Atman Project.* Wheaton, IL: Theosophical Publishing House, 1980.
A transpersonal view of human development that brilliantly maps the stages of growth from birth to enlightenment, and extends modern psychology through a synthesis of Eastern and Western insights. Good stuff! Strong medicine for behaviorists.

————. *Eye to Eye.* New York: Doubleday, 1983.
A collection of closely focused essays on the quest for a new paradigm of humanity's relation to the cosmos. The first two chapters alone are a milestone in science and intellectual history, writes John White.

————. ed. *The Holographic Paradigm.* Boston: Shambhala, 1983.
The results of extra-ordinary dialogue/debate on the relationship between science and mysticism previewed in *Re Vision Journal,* as the quantum revolution of fifty years ago comes of age.

————. *No Boundary.* Boston: Shambhala, 1981.
The best introduction to Wilber's work and to consciousness research in general. This man's work is astonishing in itself for our time. With good reason, some are calling him the "Einstein

of consciousness research." It's a witty book, the next best thing
to being there! Had Wilber been available in the 1960's, it would
have changed the course of history, I dare say, for he takes the
conspiracy out of Aquarian and mainstreams the paradigm shift,
inevitably.

————. *Up From Eden.* New York: Doubleday, 1982.
A transpersonal view of human evolution that reveals the divine
within history in a way that is wholly compatible with modern
science and spiritual traditions, and that demonstrates the evolution of consciousness as the driving force of humanity.

Yogananda, Paramahansa. *Autobiography of a Yogi.* Los Angeles:
Self-Realization Fellowship, 1946.
The memoirs of a yogi sage who introduced Westerners to the
realities of the yogic life of self-mastery. And it is charming as
well.

Yukteswar, Swami Sri. *The Holy Science.* Los Angeles, CA: Self-Realization Fellowship, 1977.
The perennial wisdom inherent in both the Christian tradition and
the Sankya philosophy of Patanjali is revealed in this little book.

Zelazny, Roger. *Lord of Light.* New York: Avon, 1969.
A science fiction novel about a future Buddha. Chapter 3—mark
it. It could be you.

Organizations

Ananda Ashram
R.D.#3
Box 141
Monroe, NY 10950
Telephone (914) 782-5575

Also known as the University of East-West Unity, this one hundred
acre retreat in the Catskill Mountains offers year-round courses on all
aspects of yoga, Sanskrit, natural healing, music, dance, visual arts and
drama. A summer festival highlights the year. Ramamurti S. Mishra,
M. D. (Brahmananda Sarasvati) is in residence most of the year, and

is available publicly at morning and evening meditation and satsang. To be in the presence of an enlightened being is healing at all levels of mind, body and spirit.

Ariel
P.O. Box 386
Middlefield, CT 06455

Founded by Anya Foos-Graber. Coordinating Director, Mary Ellen Maybury. Books are available, including *Deathing, Skycleaver, One Soul Rising,* and others. Write for details and price list.

Association for Death Education and Counseling
2211 Arthur Avenue
Lakewood, OH 44107

ADEC was created in 1978 as a forum for Death Education and Counseling. The membership is made up of educators, nurses, physicians, mental health professionals, social workers, and many others who are involved in health and well-being. Membership benefits provide a newsletter, an annual international conference, opportunities to present aspects of work in this field to other members at regional meetings, an annual membership directory, and an opportunity to become certified as a Death Educator and/or Grief Counselor, plus providing a book service. Write for full membership details.

Associates in Thanatology
115 Blue Rock Road
S. Yarmouth, MA 02664
Telephone (508) 394-6520

Richard Boerstler, Ph.D. is a practicing thanatologist and psychotherapist. He conducts seminars and workshops on transpersonal counseling, death education, and assistance in grief, loss, and pain, using co-meditation and breathing techniques. He is the founder of Associates in Thanatology, which is a collective of health professionals, educators and psychotherapists working with people having life-threatening disease. The organization sells a videotape made from a 30-minute interview on ABCTV called *Letting Go: New Heaven New Earth.* Boerstler is the author of *Letting Go.* He will also arrange to make special tapes for you and your special needs based on several interviews and therapy sessions with you. Write or phone for more information and details about workshops, etc.

Compassionate Friends, Inc.
P. O. Box 3696
Oak Brook, IL 60522-3696
Telephone (312) 990-0010

Compassionate Friends is a self-help support group that offers friendship and understanding to bereaved parents and families who have lost children. They have a Resource Guide and publish a quarterly newsletter for members. Write or call for more information.

Concern for Dying
250 W. 57th St.
Room 831
New York, NY 10107
Telephone (212) 246-6962

This organization developed the first modern "living will." They advise people of their rights regarding being ill, and help you learn how to refuse further treatment if that is what you wish to do. They also publish a quarterly newsletter providing you with the latest information in the field. If you send $10.00 they will send you the newsletter and provide you with three copies of a living will, along with instructions as to how to set it up.

ECAP Exceptional Cancer Patients
1302 Chapel St.
New Haven, CT 06519
Telephone (203) 865-8392

ECAP is a tax-exempt non-profit organization founded to offer services for exceptional cancer patients and for those dealing with catastrophic illness, irrespective of their financial condition. They offer support groups and therapy to patients, using visualization and meditation in a therapeutic setting. Most groups run for ten weeks. You have to live in the area. However, ECAP also offers internships to other therapists who wish to return home and run similar groups in their home towns.

If you don't live in the Connecticut area, you can call or write to see if there is a support group near you.

Dr. Siegel is the author of *Love Medicine and Miracles,* a book that details his experiences with ECAP, published by Harper & Row. He is the founder of the group and offers workshops all over the country. He is a surgeon in private practice, and assistant clinical professor of surgery at the Yale University School of Medicine. In 1978, he originated the "Exceptional Cancer Patient" group therapy. His publications and articles have appeared in *New York Times Magazine, Connecticut State Medical Journal, New Age Magazine, Science Digest, New Woman, Psychology Today, Town and Country,* and *American Therapist.* He has appeared on the Phil Donahue show, People are Talking, and Good Morning America.

Hanuman Foundation
Taos, NM

Some of you may have heard of this organization and that's why we have listed it here without an address. The organization was founded by Stephen and Ondrea Levine (see the booklist), who now want to take a vacation after ten long years of counseling people who were dying. They will continue to do occasional workshops throughout the country, and they have established Warm Rock Tapes, which is a tape library of the guided meditations and lectures that have been inspired by their work. You can send two postage stamps to Warm Rock Tapes, P. O. Box 100, Chamisal, NM 87521 to get notification of available tapes. You can probably learn about any Levine workshops scheduled by writing the same address and asking for the information. Include a stamped self-addressed envelope.

Hartley Film Foundation
59 Cat Rock Road
Cos Cob, CT 06807
Telephone: (203) 869-1818

Films and videos on meditation, the major religions, mind/body relationship, holistic health, psychic research. Featuring such experts as Alan Watts; Huston Smith, Ph.D.; Dr. Jerry Jampolsky and Dr. Bernie Siegel; Ram Dass, Elmer Green, Ph.D.; Ken Ring, Ph.D.; and Joseph Campbell. A recent video, *Deathing: An Introduction to Conscious*

Dying, features Anya Foos-Graber, John White and Gay Luce. Write
for information and price list.

Hemlock Society
P. O. Box 11830
Eugene, OR 97440-3900

You can write for information about death. They will provide information about self-deliverance (voluntary euthanasia or suicide) for the
terminally ill. Tells how to obtain potentially lethal drugs and the
amounts needed.

Himalayan International Institute
of Yoga Science and Philosophy of the U.S.A.
R.R. #1
Box 400
Honesdale, PA 18431
Telephone (717) 253-5551

The Himalayan Institute was founded by Swami Rama, and is a re-
spected resource for programs and publications concerning the philosophy and tradition on which yoga and meditation are based. Located
three hours from New York City, the Institute offers weekend workshops fifty-two weeks a year, plus five- and ten-day sessions for special
problems. Seriously ill people can also ask to be treated there. They
have space for 70–110 people, there are doctors on staff; and they
promote a lacto/vegetarian diet along with proper breathing techniques, yoga, meditation, in a program that combines with holistic
concepts. They sell books and tapes. Interested readers should write or
phone for more information. Also note they have other centers around
the United States and the world, and you may want to contact the main
office in Honesdale to learn of the center nearest your area.

Hippocrates Health Institute
1443 Palmdale Court
W. Palm Beach, FL 33411
Telephone (407) 471-8876

Where there's life there's hope! This is a place that teaches you how to
change your diet. If you are very sick, you may be so because your

body needs to detoxify itself. Along with medical supervision, you can come here and stay. You will work with living food—wheat grass, juices, etc. They recommend that you stay for at least three weeks to clean out your system. You learn to cook differently, prepare interesting meals for yourself, and to exercise. Books and tapes are available to help you change your eating habits. We were told that families go together to stay there, and often when one person is trying to overcome an illness, the partner goes along and also detoxifies. Call or write for details.

IANDS: International Association for Near-Death Studies
P.O. Box 7767
Philadelphia, PA 19101

For professional and lay person alike, IANDS serves as a clearing house for information that ultimately affects everyone—the relationship of human consciousness to the life process and the possibility that some aspect of consciousness may continue beyond physical death. The association publishes *Anabiosis,* a semi-annual scholarly journal, and *Vital Signs,* a quarterly magazine of general interest. Workshops and research conferences are sponsored to both professional audiences and the lay public. The association also offers supportive services to near-death experiencers, their families and professionals working with them. Write them for information about how to become a member, or for information about "Friends of IANDS" chapters in other areas of the United States and Canada. Or call for support help.

KTD: Karma Triyana Dharmachakra Monastery
Khempo Kathar Rinpoche, Abbot
352 Mead Mountain Road
Woodstock, NY 12498
Telephone (914) 679-5906

This center has in residence several enlightened beings, serving in the Kagyu lineage. They conduct on-going programs, introducing Buddhism, the Tibetan language, and other traditional resources, as well as exploring the connections between Buddhism and western culture in the cross-fertilization and grafting process that has been happening since Tibetan Buddhism dispersed from East to West. KTD is a center for such break-through work. Located in the mountains, with facilities for short and prolonged stays, and with steady contact with the abbot, Khempo Kathar Rinpoche, KTD provides a special service.

Elisabeth Kübler-Ross
Shanti Nilaya
South Route 616
Head Waters, VA 24442
Telephone (703) 396-3441

This is a non-profit organization founded by Elisabeth Kübler-Ross. It is dedicated to the promotion of the concept that unconditional love is an attainable ideal. They feel that we can live free, happy and loving lives, at peace with ourselves and others if we can accept full responsibility for all our feelings, thoughts, actions and choices, as we, in a safe environment, release negative emotions that were repressed in the past. They sponsor weekend and three-day workshops all over the United States, Europe and Australia. These workshops train dying care specialists, as well as people dealing with impending death or who are coping with crisis. They also work with families and loved ones at a support level. They offer books and tapes at the center. They are presently building a center in Virginia where workshops will be held on a regular basis—and hope to start teaching there sometime in 1990. Write or call for information.

The Learning Center for Supportive Care
14 Orchard Lane
Lincoln, MA 01773
Telephone (617) 259-8936

Director Hulen Kornfeld, R.N.M.A. combines experience in chronic care and hospice visiting nursing. She specializes in counseling and symptom management. She has lectured widely on the interweaving of holistic and traditional medical concepts, transitions, and the dying process. The center offers private consultation services to evaluate your specific situation, they make recommendations, teach nursing care and collaborate with your physician to complement any pre-existing treatment plan. Hulen would be happy to talk to you about your situation, she can provide family counseling, nursing assessment, a care plan, and she also does private counseling if your situation requires that. She can also develop continuing education programs for hospices, nursing homes, hospitals, etc.

The Monroe Institute of Applied Science
Route 1 Box 175
Faber, VA 22938
Telephone: (804) 361-1500

Founded by Robert Monroe, the institute is a non-profit educational and research organization devoted to the premise that focused consciousness contains all solutions to the questions of human existence. Greater understanding of such consciousness can be achieved only through interdisciplinary approaches and coordinated research efforts.

The tools and technology of the Institute have been used to alleviate pain, erase its memory, to relieve personal or interpersonal stress associated with life-threatening illness, death or dying, by helping patients establish a "beachhead" beyond physical matter reality. The organization is devoted to bringing peace, comfort and harmony to dying people and their families. They provide a system to be used via audiotapes. They will be happy to send you a brochure describing their products, services, and on-going programs. Programs and seminars are offered to patients as well as people involved in the helping professions and in education.

National Hospice Organization
1901 North Moore St.
Suite 901
Arlington, VA 22209
Telephone (703) 243-5900

Most Americans are now familiar with the hospice organization, and the help they provide for the terminally ill. From only a few hundred chapters in the United States ten years ago, they now have over 1,700. If you don't know how to contact your local hospice for help, call or write this office Monday through Friday 9–5. They will send you information about your local groups and what hospice service really can do for you. They also help interested groups get started, so if you want to form a hospice group in your neighborhood, write or call.

Optimum Health Institute of San Diego
6970 Central Avenue
Lemon Grove, CA 92045
Telephone (619) 464-3346

Directed by Raychel Solomon, Optimum Health features an educational program geared to help you understand the whole body. The program offers to teach you how to detoxify your system and rebuild your body by working with nutrition in a supportive environment. A diet of wheat grass, juice, sprouts, fruits, and other fresh foods, avoiding dairy and animal products, can be used for handling stress, weight loss or serious illness. The Institute can accommodate 70–110 people for varying lengths of time. Call or write for more information.

The Phenix Society
Box 351
Cheshire, CT 06410

A reading/discussion group for people who want to develop a personal life-philosophy. The members are people who have been through a wide variety of life's shocks, who are aware that they can't live the second half of their lives according to the values and standards of the first. There are now about twenty such discussion groups across the country. There are no dues. There is a newsletter, the Mind-Expander, published four times a year for a modest fee. Books are also available. Write for more information.

Prasanthi Nilayam
P. O. Anantapur District
A. P. 515134
India

This is the main residence of Sathya Sai Baba. Prasanthi Nilayam is a large ashram in the small town of Puttaparthi, in south India, 127 miles north of Bangalore. Normally, you would fly to Bombay, stay overnight there, and then go on with a local flight to Bangalore. There are buses and taxis at the airport which will get you to Puttaparthi. Sometimes, however, he resides at Brindavan in Whitefield near Bangalore, so it is wise to ask the locals where he is. The accommodations at Whitefield are poor, while Prasanthi Nilayam is rapidly expanding to handle the increased flow of pilgrims, seekers, the desperate, the curious, a few holy men and women, saddhus, sanyasin, some representatives from foreign government and churches, thousands of Indians per day, and more and more groups of Westerners. Morning and evening darshan with Sai Baba, plus bhajan or devotional singing, is standard each day. Cost is minimal, while accommodations range from dormitory barracks to private rooms.

Sathya Sai Baba Book Center
P. O. Box 278
Tustin, CA 92681-0278

This is a general address for any Sathya Sai Baba materials. Write and ask for information and a price list.

Shanti Project
525 Howard Street
San Francisco, CA 94105
Telephone (415) 777-2273

This project was once a general hospice service that is now devoted exclusively to AIDS care. They provide information and support and a referral service to AIDS patients, their families, friends and loved ones. Although they are only able to help residents of San Francisco County in their program, they can offer assistance to people who need information from other parts of the country. You can call and get information on a national and an international level regarding AIDS services. They will refer you to groups in your area. They also sponsor a training program for other health care professionals who are interested in using the Shanti program elsewhere in the country. This is a very well-known organization. They have sponsored programs throughout the country, and have been on national television talking about their various services.

Periodicals

The following list is only some of the periodicals available in this field. Write for information about subscription rates.

Anabiosis: The Journal for Near Death Studies
International Association for Near Death Studies
Box U-20/Psychology #258
406 Cross Campus Road
Storrs, CT 06268
U.S.A.
(You can also write to them for subscription rates to **Vital Signs,** which
is geared to lay readers.)

Forum for Death & Counseling Newsletter
International Forum for Death Education and Counseling
P. O. Box 1226
Arlington, VA 22210

The Laughing Man: On the Principles of and Secret of Religion,
  Spirituality and Human Culture
Dawn Horse Press
750 Adrian Way
San Rafael, CA 94903

Revision: A Journal of Consciousness and Change
c/o Heldref Publications
4000 Albermarle St. NW
Washington, D.C. 20016

Sanathana Sarathi (the English Edition)
Sathya Sai Books and Publications
Prasanthi Nilayam
P. O. Anantapur District
A.P. 515134, India
(Your new subscription will commence about two months after receipt
of the subscription fee. Write for details.)

Shanti Nilaya Newsletter
South Route 616
Head Waters, VA 24442

Thanatos*
Florida Consumer Information Bureau
P. O. Box 6009
Tallahassee, FL 32301

Wildfire
The Bear Tribe Medicine Society
P. O. Box 9167
Spokane, WA 99209

Tapes

Some readers may want to hear tapes because reading is difficult. Some may want to hear guided meditations or musical tapes geared to help you meditate. Most of you are probably familiar with new age music— and these musical tapes are available in most metaphysical bookstores. The tapes listed below are audio tapes or special tapes that may be of interest. The list is by no means exhaustive. You will find the organizations who sell tapes listed below for your convenience.

Ananda Ashram (see listing under Organizations)
Several tapes are available, including *Dynamic Meditation* and *Meditation on Your Electrical Body*. Write for information about tapes and a pricelist.

Ariel (see listing under Organizations)
The Harley Film Foundation video is available. Also available is a *Deathing* script audio tape, with voice over music on one side, music alone on the other side, recorded by Anya Foos-Graber. Write for information and pricelist.

Associates In Thanatology (see listing under Organizations)
Video tape available—a 30 minute program shown on television. Personal tapes can also be made by this organization after you have met

---

*Try to get Volume 7, No. 4, Winter 1982, and check the bibliography by Darell Crase.

with a therapist and determined what you need to hear. Write for more information and for an up-to-date pricelist.

ECAP tapes (see listing under Organizations)
Some of the tapes available from ECAP are as follows:

Dr. Bernie Siegal: The Exceptional Cancer Patient & the Process of
            Healing
Dr. Bernie Siegal: Guided Imagery and Meditation
Dr. Bernie Siegel: Visual Imagery Meditation
Marcia Eager/Robert McGrath: Gift of Inner Peace through Deep
            Relaxation
Marcia Eager/Robert McGrath: Progressive Relaxation and Guided
            Imagery

Write to ECAP for information about tapes and an up-to-date pricelist.

Hartley Film Foundation (see listing under Organizations)
Films and videos available. For up to date information about what's available, call or write for prices and details.

Himalayan Institute (see listing under Organizations)
They supply books and tapes to people involved in their programs. Write for information and a pricelist.

Elisabeth Kübler-Ross Center (see listing under Organizations)
They supply books and tapes. Write for information and a pricelist.

Monroe Institute (see listing under Organizations)
Supplies an audio guidance system. Write for information and a pricelist.

Secret Forrest Productions
P. O. Box 1011
Trumbull, CT 06611
Will supply Anya Foos-Graber's tape on *Deathing*. This includes Anya speaking on one side of the tape, with music on the other side. Write to them for pricelist and information.

Warm Rock Tapes (see Hanuman Foundation)
They supply the Levine tapes. Write for information and pricelist.

◇ ◇

NATIONAL HOTLINES

AIDS
1-800-342-AIDS
Spanish hotline:
1-800-344-FIDA
Hotline for the deaf:
1-800-243-7889
A four-minute recorded message provides information about this syndrome 24 hours a day. Stay on the line and an operator will come on to answer further questions you might have.

ALCOHOLISM
301-468-2600
Not a counseling line, but a good number to call for information.

HOSPICE EDUCATION INSTITUTE
1-800-331-1620
Referral information to hospices throughout the country.
Provides informal support services about hospice care.

CHILDREN'S HOSPICE INTERNATIONAL
703-684-0330
For support of children with life-threatening conditions and their families.

CANCER

AMC CANCER RESEARCH CENTER
1-800-525-3777
This organization will refer you to resources in your area. A 24-hour hotline, they will also provide brief counseling and advice for those in need.

NATIONAL CANCER INSTITUTE
1-800-4-CANCER
A 24-hour hotline, this number automatically connects you to the cancer information service in your area.

CANDLELIGHTER'S CHILDHOOD CANCER FOUNDATION
202-659-5136
This is a network of over 155 self-help groups of parents of children with cancer and of the medical and psychological professionals who serve them. Call between 9 A.M. and 5 P.M. EST.

RONALD McDONALD HOUSE
212-876-1590
A home away from home for children with cancer and other serious illnesses.

LOSS

PREGNANCY & INFANT LOSS CENTER
612-473-9372
For bereaved families who have experienced miscarriage, stillbirth and infant death.

PARENTS OF MURDERED CHILDREN
513-721-LOVE
A resource and referral center. Call between 9 A.M. and 1 P.M. EST.

COMPASSIONATE FRIENDS
312-990-0010
For bereaved parents and siblings. Call between 10 A.M. and 3 P.M. Central.

LUNG DISEASE

NATIONAL JEWISH LUNG LINE
1-800-222-LUNG
Referral and information.

KIDNEY DISEASE

NATIONAL KIDNEY FOUNDATION
1-800-622-9010
Referral and information service.

NATIONAL CYSTIC FIBROSIS FOUNDATION
301-951-4422
A referral and information service.

NATIONAL DOWNE'S SYNDROME ORGANIZATION
1-800-221-4602
A public awareness group that will send you information and refer you to resources in your area.

SECOND SURGICAL OPINION
1-800-638-6833
This organization will refer you to someone in your area so you can get a second opinion.

INDEX

affirmations, 320, 345
air, 287, 292
Ajamila, 267, 268, 269
aleph, 214
anahata nadam, 258
Ananda, 228
anandamaya kosha, 228, 257
annamaya kosha, 226
Arjuna, 310
astral, 11
astral body, 143, 223, 249, 289
astral plane, 10
astral travel, 11
at-death psychology, 22
Atlantis, 253
atma, 227, 235
atman/brahman, 219, 228
AUM, 251–259, 263, 265, 270,
    273, 318, 323
autosuggestion, 272
avatars, 80, 82

Bailey, Alice, 240
bang, bang theory, 254
bardo, 206, 223
Bardo Thodol, 208
Bentov, Itzhak, 12, 79, 205, 218,
    241–243, 247, 254, 255
bheri nadam, 259

biofield, 206, 212, 226, 227, 235,
    251, 260, 277, 282, 287, 289,
    292, 295, 302, 319, 335, 350
Blavatsky, Madame, 240
bodily fluid, 287
bodily heat, 287
body of inspiration and bliss, 228
body of truth, 223
brahman, 214, 257
brahman-atman, 199, 228
breath, 147, 183, 287
breath body, 226
breathing, 147, 209, 250, 271, 319,
    320, 329, 332, 338, 346, 347
breech death, 10, 214, 281, 289,
    336

candle flame, 330
chakras, 88, 89, 200, 207, 228–233,
    243, 244, 251, 264, 277, 287,
    290–292, 295, 333
chakra switchpoints, see
    switchpoints
chanting, 272
ch'i, 241, 247
cincin nadam, 259
cin nadam, 259
clear light, 153, 183, 235, 236, 260,
    282, 287, 290, 293, 295, 311,
    336, 342, 348, 350

clinical death, 203, 235, 286, 290,
    293, 310, 336, 337
coma, 311
co-meditation, 347
conscious dying, 200
consciousness principle, 10, 77, 185,
    192, 201, 203, 207, 212, 213,
    220, 225, 228, 233, 234, 249,
    250, 273, 278, 281, 283, 284,
    286, 289, 290, 293, 302, 310,
    336, 349, 350
consciousness transference, 309
consciousness transformation, 87
cosmic egg, 89

death angels, 269
death moment karma, 213, 214,
    218, 220–222, 279, 280, 309
deep sleep, 323
dervish orders, 11
dharma, 91, 310
dharma brothers, 348
dharmakaya, 214, 223
divine fire, 240
divine light, 240
dying daily, 11
dynamic meditation, 325

earth, 233, 287
electrical body, 327
electromagnetic biofield, 10; energy,
    226; field, 264; waves, 242
emptiness, 282
empty-mind, 136
energy field, 271, 323
energy transference, 209
enlightenment, 200, 203, 213, 220,
    221, 242, 269, 282
ether, 233, 234, 287, 292
etheric biofield, 349; body, 10, 226,
    227, 277; energy, 235; plane, 212
exercise
    breathing, 320
    final, 337

relaxation, 321
sensing, 324
vibration, 317, 347

figure of light, 330
fire, 233, 287, 292
five bodies, 336
five- body model, 223
five-body system, 240
five elements, 234
five sheaths, 226, 277, 278
flesh, 287
flute call, 294
forty-nine days, 144, 164, 342

gas, 234
Gayatri Mantram, 138, 181, 183,
    186, 266, 267, 271, 273, 274,
    275, 317, 321
ghanta nadam, 259
Gopi Krishna, 245
gray place, 11, 149, 235, 281, 283
Great Death Defying Mantra, 181
guru yoga, 22, 156, 315

hades, 11, 144, 235, 295, 351
Hafiz, 70
harmonic wave frequencies, 207
holograms, 263
holy spirit, 241, 251, 252
homo noeticus, 78, 80, 84, 85, 245
homo sapiens, 81
homo spiritus, 77, 80
hospice, 304
Hu, 294
HUM, 255, 263, 265, 323
hundredth monkey, 86

ida, 234, 242, 251
imaging, 209
incarnation, 225

jivan mukti, 200
jivatma, 228

ka, 10
kabbalah, 11
karma, 217, 219, 220
Khempo Kather Rinpoche, 290
ki, 241
king mantra, 273
koshas, 226
Krishna, 310
Kübler-Ross, Dr. Elisabeth, 19, 20, 300, 302
kundalini, 21, 22, 81, 83, 86, 98, 220, 229, 235, 239–245, 249, 250, 264, 293

liberation, 200, 220, 351
light, 8, 56, 64, 83, 131, 158, 182, 192, 199, 203, 206–214, 221, 223, 225, 234, 236, 250, 253, 281–284, 288, 290, 294, 295, 300, 302, 308–313, 319, 323, 329, 334–336, 340–343, 346, 351
light body, 10
light experience, 19, 70, 199, 278, 295, 341, 351
liquid, 234
logos, 214, 252, 254, 273
lokas, 206, 223, 295

Madame Blavatsky, 240
manana, 266
mandala, 148, 253, 264, 294
manomaya kosha, 227, 257
mantra, 165, 209, 231, 233, 263–266, 270–275, 305, 320
mantram, 258, 321, 329
meditation, 83, 209, 251, 260, 272, 285, 323
megha nadam, 259
mental illness, 243
Mishra, Ramamurti S., 244, 245, 254, 258, 267
Monroe, Robert, 11, 12

Moody, Dr. Raymond, 8, 20
Motoyama, Hiroshi, 241
mridamga, 259
mudra, 258
music of the spheres, 265
mystery schools, 11, 252

nadam, 250–252, 256–259, 308
Narayana, 268
near-death experience (NDE), 6–13, 20–22, 83–87, 142, 240–245, 284
neurohormonal mechanism, 244
nirmanakaya, 223
nirvana, 200

OM, 317, 318
one without a second, 244
out-of- body experience (OOBE), 11–12, 19–20, 208
out-of-body state, 8
out-of-body technique, 342
overself, 199

panic, 302
pho-wa, 12, 342
physical body, 226
pingala, 234, 242, 251
planes, 223
point of consciousness, 227
prakiti, 147
prana, 69, 147, 226, 235, 241, 242, 249, 273, 277, 287, 319, 350
pranamaya kosha, 10, 226, 257, 277, 319
pranava, 273
prayer, 209, 231, 320
prevesa, 82
PSI human, 77, 80, 81, 82, 86, 87, 98
purusha, 214
Pythagoras, 252

quantum theory, 204

real death, 83, 203
rebirth, 219, 284
reincarnation, 71, 207, 217, 218, 219, 222
relaxation, 319
Ring, Dr. Kenneth, 20, 241
Rinpoche, Khempo Kather, 290
Rinpoche, Venerable Kalu, 290
Rumi, 70

sacred music, 304
samadhi, 242, 244, 257
sambhogakaya, 223, 228
samkhya system, 223
samkhya yoga, 223, 253, 254
Sandweiss, Samuel, 244
sankh nadam, 259
Sannella, Lee, 242, 243, 250
SAT, 263, 321
Sathya Sai Baba, 81, 89, 94, 105, 138, 254, 266–268
satnam, 214, 270, 271, 321, 323, 332, 338
satori, 200
satsang effect, 21
schizophrenia, 243
secondary body, 10, 223, 228, 249
self, 288
self-creations, 205
self-realization, 200, 212
sense, 323
sensing, 324
shabda, 245, 247, 252, 265
shabda brahman, 273
shabda yoga, 250
sheath of bliss and reality, 228
sheath of revelation, 227
Sheldrake, Rupert, 21, 22
shift point, 209
Sh'Ma, 271
siddhis, 91

silver cord, 249
six techniques, 28
SO-HUM, 271, 321, 323
solid, 234
soul, 77, 186, 201, 204, 225, 227, 235, 249, 250, 273, 293, 349
sound, 64, 206, 211, 250, 257, 265, 317, 329
sound current, 89, 245, 247, 250–255, 258, 261
source, 260, 275, 282
spiritual guide, 343
subtle bodies, 231, 247
sugmad, 214
suicide, 170
sunyata, 282
support person, 28, 201, 303, 311–313, 320–339, 343, 346, 351
supreme reality, 214
sushumna, 234, 242, 249–251
svaha, 266
switchpoints, 206, 234, 244, 260, 288–293, 289, 291, 292, 293, 307, 311, 332, 334

tala nadam, 259
tanmatras, 234
tanti vina, 259
technique, fifth, 214, 215, 293, 315, 331; first, 317; fourth, 329; second, 319; sixth, 142, 150, 153, 156, 163, 165, 186, 201, 213–215, 221, 231, 233, 251, 268–271, 279–293, 301–310, 315, 331, 342–344, 347; third, 323
Tesla, Nikola, 241
thought-body, 227
thought power, 231
thoughts at the death moment, 208
three-body system, 223
Tibetan Book of the Dead, 130, 132, 133, 179, 208
traana, 266

trikaya, 223, 228
tuning fork, 215
tunnel, 8, 20, 48, 131, 158, 294, 334, 340
turiya, 257
23rd Psalm, 181, 271
Twitchell, Paul, 12, 22, 24, 250–255, 258

unconditional reality, 207, 275, 283
unio mystica, 200
universal sound, 255

Venerable Kalu Rinpoche, 290
venu nadam, 259
vibrating field, 251
vibration, 251, 317, 323
vibratory waves, 263
vibuthi, 156
vijnanamaya kosha, 227
visualization, 329
visualization techniques, 250

void, 136, 236, 282, 284
voidness, 255

waiting rooms, 159
water, 233, 287
wave frequency, 225
wave patterns, 264
White, John, 245
white crows, 80, 81, 82
wind, 233
withdrawal of consciousness, 147, 215, 233, 293, 308–311, 315, 331, 332, 337, 342, 349

yama lords, 269
yantras, 264
yoga, 21, 27, 225
yogamudra technique, 258, 260, 265
yogic fire, 240

zeitgeist, 87

About the Author

Anya Foos-Graber is a lecturer, linguist and survivor of near-death experience. She received degrees from Peabody College and Vanderbilt University, studied art in Yugoslavia, taught in high schools and colleges, and has been a yoga instructor in Connecticut. Her work with the deathing process has attracted attention in the media and health professions since 1984, when she published an earlier, unexpanded version of *Deathing*. Her work has also been the inspiration for a film by the same name, made by the Hartley Film Foundation. She has published two other books, *Skycleaver* and *One Soul Rising*. She is currently at work on a new novel.

DEATHING
An Introduction to Conscious Dying

A video from
THE HARTLEY FILM FOUNDATION

Most of us dread the thought of death, partly because it is unknown and partly because our culture teaches us to fear it. This video dispels that fear. Doctors Gay Luce and Roger Woolger, John White and Anya Foos-Graber prepare us — through near-death experiences, actual exercises, customs in other cultures — to experience a peaceful and even pleasant exit.

Conscious dying is to death what natural childbirth is to the birth process. Deathing, like birthing, requires preparation. By practicing deathing, you will be able to face your own demise with equanimity. This video, both informative and inspirational, is excellent for hospitals and hospices, and for anyone who wants a more enlightened view of the transformation called death.

"Deathing, through a beautiful blending of image, music, and timeless wisdom, is a major contribution to the conscious dying movement."
Kenneth Ring, Ph.D.
Professor of Psychology, University of Connecticut

"Beautiful photography . . . well done . . . This tape should be available to every hospice."
Richard W. Boerstler, Ph.D., Hulen S. Kornfeld, R.N., M.A.
Associates in Thanatology

"My students in death and dying had never seen the subject approached in a practical way . . . most impressive . . . I highly recommend it for courses in adult development as well as death and dying."
Frances O'Neil, Ph.D.
Professor of Psychology, Tunxis Community College

This video and others are available from:

THE HARTLEY FILM FOUNDATION, INC.
CAT ROCK ROAD COS COB, CONNECTICUT 06807 (203) 869-1818

Please write for up-to-date listing and prices for either renting or purchasing.